Sociological Practices

M. Reza Nakhaie

NELSON EDUCATION

NELSON / EDUCATION

Table of Contents

Preface

The main purpose of this book is to introduce students to important sociological concepts, theories, and research and to use examples of how sociologists do research. The introduction sets the context by describing what sociology is, how it studies society and social relations, and what kind of general explanations are used by sociologists. Chapters 2 and 3 focus on sociological tools of theory and research. These two chapters help to establish the foundation of sociology. Chapter 2 describes and explains the work of the principal founders of sociology—Karl Marx, Emile Durkheim, and Max Weber—in some detail, and Chapter 3 provides an overview of the variety of social research tools that are used by sociologists to test theories and discover a new understanding of human social relations and society. The next six chapters use the core tools of the sociologist's toolbox (theory and research) and apply them to six subjects that are often included in introductory sociology courses. These subjects include culture, socialization, crime and deviance, gender relations, social inequality, and race and ethnic relations. In each of these chapters, examples related to evidence and original quotations from sociologists are used to ensure a better understanding of *sociological practices.* These six chapters are each supplemented by an example of how a sociologist does research. In each of these supplementary chapters, the subject matter is presented through a series of basic steps that are standard to sociological research. In each chapter and in relation to each subject, key research questions are asked, theoretical models developed, hypotheses proposed, data collection discussed, findings described, conclusions reached, and policies suggested. The goals of the supplementary examples are to help students understand that even though subjects may differ, the process of sociological research for each is the same. That is, sociologists use a toolbox that includes theory and research in order to solve social problems, identify potential solutions, and suggest policies. Finally, at the end of each core and supplementary chapters, students are encouraged to contemplate what they have learned and how they can put their learning into practice by answering specific critical thinking questions. In using such a range of topics and examples, students are introduced to sociology, sociological theory, and research from the perspective of a sociologist at work.

Acknowledgments

In preparing this manuscript, I was fortunate to benefit tremendous support from Maya Castle, Lindsay Shipman, Stefanie Bradley, Erin Moore and Susan Calvert, all from Nelson Education. Aaron Doey, Stephanie Keyes, and Patrick Lalonde at the Department of Sociology, University of Windsor, were helpful in summarizing the supplementary articles. Farrah Nakhaie read through the book several times and suggested constructive comments.

Chapter 1

Introduction to Sociology

Introduction

You may have pondered questions about sociology in the past, such as what sociology it? Why should I take a sociology course? Should I pursue sociology as my major? How do I use it in my everyday life? What is it good for? You may have also asked other kinds of questions, such as how do infants learn ways of life of their society? Why are some people poor while others are rich? How distinct is Canada from the United States or other countries? Why is there crime? Why do some people commit suicide and others do not? If you have asked questions such as these, then sociology can help you answer them, or at least help you critically evaluate potential answers.

Essentially, **sociology** will help you refine your thought processes in a critical, systematic, and orderly way. However, sociology is not about all aspects of your thoughts; it is about only those that focus on group-based relations. That is to say, sociologists are interested in studying individual characteristics within groups, institutions, and structures. When we say that we are interested in group-based relations, we mean that we like to study individuals in group settings. For example, we may want to know how university education shapes students' knowledge, values, beliefs, consciousness, as well as their future access to scarce resources (e.g., occupation, income). In order to do this, we study the impact of education on student attitudes and achievement. We can *observe* students in a class setting in order to see how they interact with each other and with the instructor. We may *experiment* on them in order to see if students taught in, say, a lecture hall, learn, think, and behave differently than those who are taught via new electronic technology (e.g., email, online courses, etc.). We may *compare* different groups of students (e.g., males and females, upper and lower classes, immigrants and those born in Canada) in order to see if there are differences in their values, beliefs, and ideas as they move through the education system or at different times. Similarly, we may study students by following them through life in order to see where they end up in the socioeconomic hierarchy and why (i.e., by paying attention to their life history).

Once we have learned more about student life, we can use this information to *predict* the future. For example, if we find out that students who go to university have higher occupations and earn more income than those who go to college, we can predict that this difference will emerge again and again with different data and perhaps at different times and places. Therefore, we can recommend that students attend university rather than college as a means of upward mobility.

In these examples, we used scientific methods of observation, experimentation, comparison, and prediction, as commonly used in the natural sciences, but we also included the historical method, which applies more to human society. We used these methods in order to understand students' values, behaviours, and opportunities, which took place in group and/or institutional settings. We would then use our research in order to provide a tentative explanation (i.e., theory) of students' values, behaviours, and so on. Therefore, we may say that sociology is a science that intends to construct **theories** about the *social relationships* making up society. Sociology is a science similar to chemistry, biology, or other natural sciences, because it, too, aims at systematically constructing and validating tentative explanations (i.e., theories) about the real world. It develops and uses a scientific approach for understanding individuals' relationships in and to society. In this regard, sociology is indebted to the principal founder of sociology, Auguste Comte (1798–1857), who coined the term "sociology." He believed that the role of sociology is to understand the world based on methods of science. This method, known as **positivism,** adheres to the idea that there are "natural laws" which govern society and asserts that the role of sociologists is to discover these laws and use them to improve the human condition.

Distinctiveness of Sociology

If sociology is a science, then how is it different from other sciences? First, the science of sociology is different from that of the natural sciences. This is because the subjects of sociology are humans, which are unlike the inanimate objects and animals as studied by the natural sciences. Humans have feelings, emotions, values, and beliefs that are structured in a social setting and that influence human understanding and behaviours. These human characteristics influence what subject is studied, how the results of the study are interpreted, and what conclusions are made. In fact, as your sociological knowledge grows, you will be exposed to other sociological theories (e.g., feminism) that challenge our notion of sociology or present science itself as a social construction (e.g., postmodernism). They argue that impartiality and objectivity, the cores of scientific inquiry, are difficult because people react to the research process in a conscious manner. Social values profoundly affect what theory or method is chosen, what questions are asked, and how the results are interpreted. Nevertheless, despite different theories and empirical findings, as sociologists, we aim to further improve our understanding of the social world by accumulating knowledge and evaluating our theories.

Second, sociology is different from other disciplines in humanities and other social sciences. It differs from economics because we look at the society as a whole, not just its economic aspect. We pay attention to the economic, political, cultural, and social forces that influence human thought, ideas, and behaviours. Sociology is also different from social work because we give primacy to intellectual and knowledge development. Social work is primarily interested in the practical application of knowledge. We differ from philosophy because we rely on data and evidence in order to substantiate our theories. We differ from psychology because the focus of our inquiry is more social than individual. Finally, we differ from journalists, too, in that we aim to build theories that explain the society and human relationships. Journalists report events and rarely explain them (see Westhues, 1982).

Social Relations and Social Structures

Theories are developed about social relationships. **Social relations** are binding relationships that connect individuals to groups or society, such as friendship, family, motherhood, university culture, criminal culture, and community. In the *Rules of Sociological Methods,* Durkheim referred to such social relationships as **"social facts"** (see Box 1.1). Social facts have distinctive characteristics. They are external to individuals, endure over time, and have coercive power independent of the individual will. As such, individuals are born into an ongoing society that already has a definite organization and structure and that thusly conditions their personality and exercises constraints upon them. For example, when you are born, you would be exposed to values, beliefs, and ideas of the society you are born into, and these cultural elements exert power over you. If you are born in a middle class family, you would be exposed to the middle class culture, in a middle class neighbourhood with middle class friends. If you are born into a religious family, you will be exposed to it and might become religious yourself. If you are born into an ethnic group, you would be exposed to its culture. Once you enter university, you are exposed to another culture that is external to you and constrains your behaviour: you must respect the class environment, you must not cheat, and so on. Similarly, individuals become fathers, mothers, friends, and employees, among other roles, all of which are subject to external social constraints that are identified with these roles. Fathers and mothers provide for and rear children, friends do not betray each other, and employees express corporate loyalty. Sociologists

Box 1.1

A social fact is any way of acting . . . capable of exerting over the individual an external constraint; or: which is general over the whole of a given society whilst having an existence of its own, independent of its individual manifestations.

(Durkheim, 1982, p. 59)

study these social facts the same way that natural scientists study an object or a thing. They are treated similarly to atoms or organisms in natural sciences, as objects of research. In sum, sociologists are concerned with the study of large scale structures, shared moral beliefs, institutionalized laws—and their impact upon individuals.

What is a social structure? **Social structures** are stable patterns of social relationships which bring the society into the individual. These structures can be a) **macrostructures** such as capitalism, class relations, and political or economic systems, or b) **microstructures** such as family, friendship circles, or club associations. Macrostructures such as capitalism can be detrimental to development of wealth and cause poverty. Microstructures such as friendship circles can be important in helping with finding a job or can lead to becoming a gang member and committing crime.

Sociological Imagination

By now you may have realized that being a sociologist requires having what C. Wright Mills (1916–1962) called a **sociological imagination.** Such an imagination allows for creative thinking that enables an individual's awareness in relationship to the wider society. It enables us to comprehend the links between our immediate personal social setting and a more remote impersonal social world. A key element of this imagination is to view one's society as if an outsider (see Box 1.2).

Anthony Giddens (1987) breaks up the sociological imagination into a threefold exercise of sensitivity: *historical, anthropological,* and *critical.* As you sit in class in your comfortable clothing, enjoying your laptop, audio, and PowerPoint presentations and feeling free to challenge your instructor or those outside the university, you may ask yourself whether such comfort and freedom would be possible without the industrial revolution of the latter part of the 18th century, primarily in England, and the political revolution of the same period, primarily in France. These "two great revolutions" brought the world into your home via radio, TV, Internet, and satellites, and gave you the rights of democratic citizenship within a nation state and globally. They enabled Chinese citizens to watch *Gossip Girl*, *House,* or *American Idol* in Peking, while North Americans consume Chinese-made products or watch *Three Kingdoms* in Canada, the United States, and elsewhere. They enabled a Canadian Aboriginal woman to take her government to the International Court and win her Aboriginal title right. These are changes that can be attributed to the last 200 to 300 years. We can go even further and understand that without the East Indians discovering and Muslims providing the Greeks and Europeans with the number zero (0), we may have not developed the binary code so important in computer technology. There are many other examples that illustrate how our present comfort and knowledge is the result of our past. Suffice to say here that our knowledge of past history is an important type of sensitivity necessary for understanding our present world.

The second type of sociological imagination refers to anthropological sensitivity. This requires us to break away from the notion that our way of life, and particularly the Western way of life, is superior to other cultures and ways of living and away from the idea that all societies must undergo a similar process of evolution and development as that of the Western world. This tendency is referred to as ethnocentrism or Eurocentrism and should be challenged through our anthropological imagination. A cursory knowledge of different cultures and societies will inform us that many such cultures existed far before us and had far fewer social problems (e.g., crime and violence) than us. They seem to have developed institutions that were necessary and sufficient for peaceful coexistence. The tendency to use Western culture to judge others is rooted in the history of colonization and capitalist expansion aiming to exploit cheap labour and raw materials of other societies and to make these societies consumer havens for capitalist commodities. In order to colonize and exploit, Western capitalist powers viewed First Nations peoples and Africans as godless savages who needed to be brought into step with the civilized world. For example, in Canada, such ideas justified forcing the First Nations peoples onto reserves and their children into white Christian residential schools away from their parents. Similar justifications were used for the enslavement of Africans and other groups in the U.S. and elsewhere. Anthropological imagination allows us to comprehend and appreciate the diversity of human life. Such an appreciation also helps us to understand ourselves—the human race—better.

Finally, by combining historical and anthropological imagination we will arrive at critical imagination, allowing us to break away from thinking only in terms of the society we are part of here and now. This enables us to see alternative societies, futures, and forms of development. It also helps us critique existing societies. You will note that such critique is based on analysis and evidence.

A discussion of types of sensitivity helps us understand that, despite the fact that we use the methods of the natural sciences, our discipline is different from theirs. Human beings and human societies are not like inanimate objects, which are similar in kind and governed by some natural laws. Human society is diverse, and its history shows alternative paths.

The preceding descriptions suggest that sociology allows us to question or critically evaluate what we take for granted in everyday life. It allows us to evaluate our choices and opportunities, considering constraints and limitations imposed on us since we were born. Moreover, it teaches us that we can become active citizens and influence the direction of the world. We can learn to transform personal problems into political issues. We can test whether the proverbial "fat cats" are really fat or whether birds of a feather really do flock together. Instead of saying that there is something wrong with my neighbour because he or she is unable to find or keep a job, we may be able to say that there is something wrong with the economy because my neighbour and many like him or her have searched everywhere and there is little opportunity for finding a job. These examples suggest that sociology enables us to consider and understand the interplay between the individual and society. It makes us aware of the relationship between elements of society and their influence on individual opportunities and life chances. This quality of mind that enables us to understand that personal troubles are public issues is what C.W. Mills called sociological imagination.

Sociological Theories

Theorizing involves summarizing, connecting, condensing, and organizing ideas or a great deal of information about the social world. Theories are logical and consistent statements. They guide our research and are themselves modified by it. That is, theories are consistent with known facts and thus are testable in the real world. They are also general statements applying to a large group of people but may exclude some people. For example, when we say that male students are more likely to be violent than female students, we do not mean that each and every male student is violent and each and every female student is nonviolent. We are merely pointing to the violent tendency, probability, and likelihood of male and female students. Therefore, because sociology studies social relations, there is a good probability that a sociologist can approximately predict your future if asked. For example, based on the knowledge of your social class background, gender, and/or ethnicity, the sociologist would be able to estimate the chance of you getting a good job, the age you will marry, number of children you will have, how much housework you will do, the age at which you may get divorced, or even the age at which you will die. The sociologist does this by looking at previous research and then identifying the general patterns for any specific individual.

Humans have always been involved in the development of some form of explanation about their social world. However, the history of modern sociological theories in the West started with the Age of Reason or **Enlightenment** and the changes that took place during the 17th and 18th centuries. Zeitlin (2001) identified six social conditions that helped the emergence of the Enlightenment:

1. *Political Revolutions* (e.g., the French Revolution): These revolutions resulted in breakdown of traditions and replacement of new social order. Such titanic social changes challenged scholars to explain the order and disorder, stability, and change that resulted from these revolutions. Marx wrote about the progressive role of revolutions, while Emile Durkheim lamented the breakdown of old social orders.

2. *Industrial Revolution:* This revolution was associated with technological advancements and the development of large industries and bureaucracies. These changes were the impetus for the migration of people from farms to urban centres for the purpose of finding employment in large industries. Scholars became concerned with the disruption of traditional social relations as well as the conditions of the working class in the urban centres. Marx and Engels wrote extensively

about the situation of the working class in these new industrial complexes. Weber wrote extensively about the iron cage of the bureaucracies.

3. ***Rise of Socialism:*** People working in harsh urban and industrial environments and experiencing poverty and exploitation searched for an alternative way of life. Similarly, scholars sought to envision a social system with more equality in ownership of the means of production (e.g., machineries, tools, and factories) and less misery for working people. Marx and Engels wrote about positive aspects of socialism, while Weber emphasized the bureaucratic nature of the new social system.

4. ***Urbanization:*** People were uprooted from their village communities and entered big cities, which had problems such as overcrowding, pollution, noise, traffic, and crime, among others. These issues became part of the new research agenda and discussion among scholars such Ferdinand Tonnies about the advantages or disadvantages of *Gemeinschaft* (community) and *Gesellschaft* (society).

5. ***Religious Transformations:*** The various changes, as stated previously, affected people's views on life and the afterworld. One such fundamental transformation was the emergence of Protestantism, which entailed a distinctive worldview as compared to Catholicism. Karl Marx, Max Weber, and Emile Durkheim all wrote about the role of religion in relation to social stability and change.

6. ***Growth of Science:*** New scientific methods emerged for analyzing and explaining the world and its elements. The natural sciences, such as chemistry, physics, and biology, enjoyed substantial status. Sociology also adopted the methods of the natural sciences. Auguste Comte, Durkheim, Weber, and Marx all wrote extensively on how to scientifically study and understand human conditions and their views became incorporated into grand sociological theories.

Functionalism

The Durkheimian task of explaining social order and stability became known as **functionalist** theory, also known as structural functionalist theory. This theory was first systematized and presented by the American sociologist Talcott Parsons (1902–1979). Functionalists are interested in explaining a particular social institution by its function and how it helps meet the needs of the system and/or helps the survival of larger society. They are interested in identifying the basic functions of any institution or social system and then explaining how it is held together. As an example, in his book *Suicide* (1951 [1938]), Durkheim theorized that suicide varies with the degree of integration of individuals in society (see Box 1.3). The reason that those who are married or have many friends or are involved in political groups are less likely to commit suicide than their counterparts, he argued, is due to an understanding that they are attached and integrated into society. In this sense, marriage, political participation, and friendship networks are functional to individual survival.

Box 1.3

We have thus successively set up three propositions:

Suicide varies inversely with the degree of integration of religious society
Suicide varies inversely with the degree of integration of domestic society
Suicide varies inversely with the degree of integration of political society

This grouping shows that whereas these different societies have a moderating influence upon suicide, this is due not to special characteristics of each but to a characteristic common to all.

(Durkheim, 1951, p. 208)

In other words, functionalists tend to view human society in a form analogous to an organism that has many interrelated parts and in which each part performs a specific function that meets the organism's needs and helps its survival. In human society, these parts constitute institutions such as family and education that help with the socialization of individuals into predetermined roles and behaviours. The function of family is to reproduce the next generation both physically and socially. The function of education is to help students learn the necessary skills for the employment market. This does not mean that all functions are **manifest** or obvious. Some functions are **latent** (Merton, 1967). For example, one can say that the function of education is to provide jobs for your teachers or to act as babysitters keeping the children and youth off the street who otherwise may potentially commit deviant and criminal acts. These functions are not manifest or the stated goals of an educational institution. They are not articulated goals. They are latent. There is also potential for *dysfunction,* such as crime, which can threaten the stability of the social order. Similarly, a latent function of education could be to produce student radicals who do not help with the stability of social order but instead may question and transform the social system (e.g., the student movements of the 60s).

Functionalists also believe that the social structure is based on shared values among individuals, which in turn help produce stability of the social system. For them, we have common values, beliefs, and ideas (e.g., religion), which act as a glue for the maintenance of institutions such as family, education, and government. These shared institutions are responsible for a state of **equilibrium** or orderly self-regulation where if one part fails to act, the other part fills the void and thus ensures the stability of the society. In sum, functionalists believe that every social structure fulfills certain needs and this fulfillment explains the stability of the structure. Therefore, They tend to explain the existence and stability of a social structure by its consequences. As such, the functionalist theory is tautological—based on circular reasoning. They argue that a social system is stable because it meets certain needs, and if you ask why those needs are functional to the stability of the society, they respond that the proof is in the stability of the society. However, they have not provided a society without certain functions that did not survive and one with different functions that survived. The theory does not provide an avenue of falsifying it. After all, everything has some function. For example, crime, which could threaten the stability of the society, is also functional because it ensures employment for police, judges, probation officers, and lawyers, in addition to security tasks such as locksmithing and/or surveillance monitoring.

Conflict Theory

The views of Marx became incorporated in what is now known as **conflict theory.** Conflict theorists see inequality as a social evil that helps produce oppositional organization, social movement, and revolution. They point to the strong relationship between large businesses, media corporations, and the class background of the politicians and the consequent government policies that tend to favour business interests. They note that the prevalent views on private property, the judicial system, and religion tend to promote and protect the interests of the capitalist class and dominant groups in modern societies.

Contrary to the functionalists, conflict theorists see values and ideas as organized relations of power that determine access to scarce resources and thus justify inequality. This does not mean that there is no consensus of values and beliefs. They suggest that such consensus, if it exists, is due to manipulation by the dominant classes and institutions.

Like functionalists, conflict theorists tend to focus on macrostructures, but they do not ignore microrelationships. For them, unequal power relationships emerge in all aspects of life, including intimate relationships between spouses or romantic partners. For example, an economically dependent wife may accept a subservient position to her husband even if subjected to abuse and violence. However, conflict theorists accept that some economic and/or family

Box 1.4

A symbol does tend to call out in the individual a group of reactions such as it calls out in the other, but there is *something* further that is involved in its being a significant symbol: this response within one's self to such a word as "chair," or "dog" is one which is a stimulus to the individual as well as a response. This is what, of course, is involved in what we term the meaning of a thing, or its significance.

(Mead, 1934, p. 71)

relationships may be functional, but they question for whom they function. They argue that surely they are functional for and benefit the side that has the most power. Conflict theorists tend to see the existing society as unjust and wish to promote social change towards a more just society.

Symbolic Interactionism

Max Weber's views are in part incorporated into **symbolic interactionism.** Symbolic interactionists are interested in finding out how face-to-face interaction between individuals helps to explain human behaviour and produce shared meaning and stable social systems. The view of symbolic interactionists is similar to that of Weber, in that for Weber, sociology is a science that attempts to interpretively understand social actions, its causes, and its consequences. Weber argued that sociology requires the use of *Verstehen* in order to understand human behaviour. *Verstehen* means empathetic understanding of people's motives and the meaning they attach to their action. Symbolic interactionists pay attention to microstructures, individuals, and agencies.

A well known symbolic interactionist, George Herbert Mead (1863–1931) in *Mind, Self and Society* (1962 [1934]) argued that society emerges from the ability of individuals to refer to themselves as objects and to act accordingly. This is possible because individuals use symbols (language and signs) in order to identify and distinguish themselves. They use self-referent words such as "I" and "me." However, individuals are able to use these self-referent terms because some element of community is embedded in these terms. For example, "I the Canadian," "I the barber," "I the student," and so on, all have social characters. An alien would not know what they mean. Only an English speaking person who understands their significance can know what they mean when they hear them. Therefore, individuals are able to refer to themselves and interact in the society because they use self-referent terms and terms that have some communal status. From this, we can conclude that the self is always symbolically connected to others in the society. Moreover, symbols constrain individuals' behaviour. Canadians, barbers, and students all think and behave according to social values, norms, and constraints associated with these identities (see Box 1.4)

Sherif (1936, 1937) experimented in an autokinetic situation (the apparent movement of a point of light in a light-proof room lacking visible anchorages). He had a group of people sit in a dark room and observe a stationary pinpoint of light that was placed in front of them. Participants, not knowing that the light was stationary, stated that the light was moving in an erratic and random manner. Next, Sherif suggested to them that the light was moving in a horizontal manner and asked them to inform him about the extent of the movement. Subjects modified their understanding and stated that indeed the light was moving back and forth. Finally, after soliciting their views on the length of such movement, Sherif asked them to discuss the length of light with each other. Subsequently, those who had stated that the light was moving a large distance reduced their original estimate, and those who stated that the light was moving a short distance increased their original estimate. The conclusion drawn from this is that Sherif's symbolic assertion that the light moved, and moved in a horizontal manner and distance, was a coercive symbolic construction of individuals' perception. It also meant that individuals construct a disposition to act in specific situations and that the definition of the situation is learned, based on our symbolic experiences. In addition, the mind is a social process arising out of social interactions and changes according to future interactions.

In sum, symbolic interactionists:

- focus on the subjective understanding of human actions and their consequences
- emphasize interpersonal microlevel social relations
- view individuals as reflexive and active interpreters and producers of the society, and
- believe that society does not exist over and above relations between people.

Many social theories followed the lead provided by Marx, Weber, and Durkheim and extended their work. Below, we present a discussion of feminism and a critique of grand- or meta-theories as exemplified in the work of Marx, Weber, and Durkheim.

Feminist Theory

Feminist theory is wide-ranging and is based on views of both conflict and symbolic interactionist theories. It essentially refers to a body of knowledge that aims to offer critical explanations of women's subordination and to undermine and expose it. Feminists are mainly interested in evaluating and explaining why women have less power and resources than men and how to challenge and transform such imbalance. They tend to explain male domination (i.e., **patriarchy**) by examining the structures of society, power relationships, and conventions. Eichler (1985), one of the leading Canadian feminists, articulates the four basic pillars of feminist theory. First is that knowledge is socially constructed and women have been generally excluded from the production of knowledge. Second, the existing knowledge, theory, and science are male constructions primarily developed by males, and these constructions tend to justify male positions of power in society. Third, knowledge and science are not impartial and value-free. Fourth, individuals' views, ideas, and perspectives depend on their social locations. Since males and females have different social locations, they look at the world differently, and since men's ideas and knowledge have been the dominant form of ideas and knowledge in social sciences, then women's views, knowledge, and ideas have been ignored. Women must be "bicultural"— they must be able to look at the world both from their own perspective and that of men's perspective—in order to survive. For example, if we consider understanding the world from a slave's and a master's point of view, we notice that the master only looked at the world from his or her own point of interest, while the slave had to pay attention to both the master's desires, wants, and needs as well as his or her own. This example and Eichler's formulation means that women may need to develop ideas and knowledge from their own social position. Although feminists use Marxists idea of dominant and subordinate positions in order to explain gender inequality, they also criticize Marxists for emphasizing only economic production and paying less attention to the social organization of reproduction, such as childbearing, child rearing, and housework. They argue that when we pay attention to the organization of reproduction, the dominant groups are not necessarily just capitalists and upper classes but they are also males.

A discussion of Nancy Chodorow's (1978) book *Reproduction of Mothering* gives us another example of how feminists might explain female subordination. Chodorow is concerned with the social construction of the gender-based psyche: how women become mothers and men become fathers. She states that the organization of family life and child care helps produce men and women who have different "rational capacities." In such an environment, girls experience a lesser sense of separateness from their mother than do boys. Despite turning to their father in order to develop a sense of separateness, girls never complete their separation from their mother. In fact, girls develop gender identity through identification with their mother. Consequently, as adults, women find themselves most comfortable in intimate relationships and seek to reproduce with a man in order to replicate the same triangular emotional configuration as they experienced in childhood by having a baby. Following a line of argument similar to Freud's, Chodorow states that boys undergo a process of sexuality development (see Chapter 5, Socialization) and repress their need for a love relationship. Therefore, for Chodorow, masculine personality comes as a denial of intimate companionship and connections, or a denial of femininity. Boys' painful separation from their mother through repression of Oedipal sexuality is also what pushes males to seek domination when in a relationship. In fact, Chodorow argues that intimacy with a woman evokes fear in men because it (unconsciously) symbolizes their early repression. In other words, boys' hostility toward their mother is entangled with the acquisition of masculinity, which is then generalized toward all women.

Postmodern Theories

What is common to Marx, Weber, and Durkheim is their attempt to develop general, grand-meta theories of society rooted in their understanding of historical development. **Postmodern** theorists call these general theories **metanarratives** and consider them questionable. Postmodern theorists have a strong antipathy toward the suggestion that there is an overall pattern in history. They argue that human subjects, human histories, and meanings are all socially constructed and culturally specific. There is no essential human being, human subject, or even unified human consciousness. Society is far more fragmented than we are told to believe. In fact, postmodernists go so far as to argue that humans are mere images of an image that does not have a base in reality. Humans are simulations, similar to the robot Data in the TV series *Star Trek: The Next Generation*, who are made after an image of human beings, despite substantial plurality of human life. Simply stated, postmodernists argue that philosophers, social scientists, and other scientists are involved in "language games" and that their language game is one among many, none better than the other.

The project of modernity, rooted in the Enlightenment, was to study social institutions, develop a unified and grand theory of humanity, and help improve human conditions through managed social change (emancipation of humanity). David Cheal (1990) used examples from Canadian and international studies and argued that this project is untenable. Relying on Lyotard's writings, Cheal argued that scientific knowledge is based on language games where one group (legislators, editors, etc.) tends to delegitimatize certain knowledge and legitimatize others (i.e.,

paralogy). It is this continuous process of delegitimization and legitimization that by definition makes grand theories impossible to achieve. If we cannot achieve or agree upon a general theory of society, he suggests, we cannot emancipate or liberate humanity. However, according to Bonnie Fox (1990), Cheal's criticism of knowledge as discursive and subjective is untenable. In order to make this assertion, Cheal must use some form of empirical evidence to be able to substantiate his assertion. Yet, use of empirical evidence would question his assertion that knowledge is discursive or is based on a set of ideas that are agreed upon. Fox also questioned the assumption that there is no essential self as argued by postmodernists. By asserting that subjectivity (and therefore self) is a social construct, postmodernists falsely separate biology from nature and present an overdetermined conception of self.

Summary

The titanic transformations of the 17th and 18th centuries were intimately related to the development of the Enlightenment as a period of remarkable intellectual development, where philosophers and social thinkers challenged traditional ways of life and helped produce grand, general, and abstract systems of ideas derived from the real world and aimed at changing that world. It was reasoned that the natural world was dominated by natural laws and that the goal of scientists was to discover these laws in order to use them to change the world for the better. Enlightenment sociologists used the methods of the natural sciences and applied them to the social world to help them discover social laws governing human behaviours.

Sociology is a way of questioning our personal experiences by locating them within a wider historical, cultural, and social structure. This enables us to develop a capacity for critical thinking and helps in our developing of theoretical explanations that are more systematic and encompassing than either personal experiences or the experiences of those close to us. It enables us to relate the microstructures to that of the macro- and global structures. It helps us understand how we are subject to strong social forces that are external to and constraining us. It makes us aware that these traps and controlling forces are human constructions that can in fact be controlled and changed by humans. As such, sociology allows us to reflect on our own interpretation of the world around us and actively and critically participate in making sense of it. It helps increase our awareness that our society has not always been this way, nor will it remain so. Once we realize that it can be different, we may become active in shaping its future and breaking away from those constraining and controlling forces. We may be able to challenge the powerful institutions, agencies, and groups that have benefited from the status quo or have moved it in one or another direction. In order to help us understand the world and critically evaluate forces that shape human society, sociologists develop theories or tentative explanations that are then tested using evidence.

There are many sociological theories and all have been influenced by the work of Emile Durkheim, Karl Marx, and Max Weber. Among these, functionalists focus on the importance of social integration and how various social institution help social order and survival of the society. Conflict theory stresses that these institutions are also responsible in legitimizing a social order that benefits the upper classes, the rich and powerful. They are more interested in explaining factors that help promote social change that benefit all members of the society and not just the ruling elites. These two perspectives focus more on the role of the macrostructures. Symbolic interactionists focus on interpersonal relations and emphasize that human society is constructed through interpersonal relationships among people who actively shape themselves and the society. This perspective emphasizes microstructures. Feminist theory is concerned with gender inequality and male domination. It focuses on the role of both micro and macrostructures in producing and reproducing the unequal relationship between males and females and views that gender equality is also being shaped by the same structures. **Postmodernism** is less of a theory and more of a critique of grand theories. Postmodernists question an overarching theoretical explanation of human society and see it as being more fluid.

Key Terms

Conflict theory: focuses on how social groups have different interests and how such interests produce conflict in society.

Enlightenment: a period in human knowledge when all aspects of human life and work were the subject of critical examination in order to develop an understanding of human society and to further humanity's general progress.

Equilibrium: a state of social harmony and order.

Feminist theory: the evaluation and explanation of why women have less power and resources than men and how to challenge and transform such imbalance.

Functionalism: explanation of a particular social institution by its functions and how it meets the need of the system and/or helps the survival of larger society.

Latent function: the unintended or unrecognized consequence of any institution or social pattern.

Macrostructure: large-scale social structures.

Manifest function: the intended or recognized consequence of any institution or social pattern.

Metanarratives: general or grand narratives or theories that explain everything.

Microstructures: patterns of social interactions in a given situation.

Paralogy: Jean-Francois Lyotard's view on the tendency in scientific research to undermine itself and previous knowledge.

Patriarchy: social organization where males dominate females.

Positivism: the application of natural science methods to social science.

Postmodern: after modernism.

Postmodernism: a theoretical framework that believes knowledge is socially constructed and developed by multiple life worlds, and which questions grand theories.

Social facts: external and constraining social relations.

Social relations: bonding relations that connect individuals to group or society.

Social structure: relatively stable pattern of social behaviour; large-scale and long-term patterns of organization in a society. These organizations are external to individuals and influence their behaviour and thoughts.

Sociological imagination: an imagination that allows for creative thinking, which enables an individual's awareness in relationship to the wider society.

Sociology: a science that constructs theories about social relationships that compose society.

Symbolic interactionism: examines how face-to-face interaction between individuals helps explain human behaviour and produce shared meaning and stable social systems.

Theory: ideas or tentative explanations about social relations.

Verstehen: interpretative understanding.

Critical Thinking Questions

1. Use your sociological imagination and explain why you were able to attend university while many high school students of your graduating year did not.

2. Why do you think sociology is different from other social science disciplines?

3. What kinds of limitations does your role as a student or a brother/sister impose on your everyday behaviour? What happens if you are to act differently than how these roles are structured?

4. How do the perspectives of the natural sciences and other social sciences complement or conflict with that of sociology?

5. What is the difference between microstructure and macrostructure? How do each affect or impose limitations on human success?

6. Looking at people you know, which of functionalist or conflict theories can best explain these people's socioeconomic positions in society? Why?

7. How do social facts constrain human behaviour? Provide examples.

8. Study various social institutions and identify patriarchal examples that limit female success.

9. How would symbolic interactionists study human behaviour?

10. Why are postmodernists skeptical of metanarratives?

Useful Internet Sites

1. Canadian Sociological Association   http://www.csa-scs.ca/

2. Interesting articles and blogs on various sociological topics and issues

                                      http://thesocietypages.org/citings/tag

3. Social Science Dictionary   http://www.socialsciencedictionary.com/

                                      http://bitbucket.icaap.org/dict.pl?alpha=N

4. Social Science Glossary http://www.faculty.rsu.edu/users/f/felwell/www/glossary/Index.htm

5. Guide for writing research paper   http://www.trinity.edu/mkearl/research.html

6. Sociological theory   http://www.trinity.edu/mkearl/theory.html

7. Specific theorists   http://www.sociosite.net/topics/sociologists.php

What Can I Do with a Bachelor of Arts Degree in Sociology?

About Sociology

Sociology is commonly defined as the scientific study of society. It offers the student an educational experience which is both intellectually rewarding and practically useful as a preparation for future career opportunities. It provides the student with the theoretical and analytical tools to better understand the complex social forces which affect our lives, contributing in this way to personal enrichment and more effective citizenship. It is also valuable preparation for advanced study in the social sciences, as well as for careers in the professions, management, education, law, medicine and health-related areas, social work, and communications in both the public sector and private industry.

Career/Job Opportunities

Sociologists are prepared for a wide range of employment opportunities, although few employers look specifically for "sociologists." Your career could involve working with: government agencies or non-government organizations to understand and resolve social issues, Statistics Canada or independent research firms to measure and describe social trends and corporations to address workplace and employee concerns. Sociology graduates acquire transferable skills such as strong knowledge of organizational and group dynamics, appreciation and understanding of cultural diversity, as well as research skills, statistical skills, written and oral communication skills, problem solving skills, and critical thinking skills. In all, "a degree in Sociology provides the background and skills necessary for employment in many fields which require a thorough understanding of research design and data analysis, group processes, organizational dynamics, and social trends."

Source: Red Deer College (2012).

Chapter 2

Sociological Theories

Social Order and Social Change

How does a society ensure the minimum level of order to guarantee peace and security for its members? If a society has developed means to ensure social order, cohesiveness, and stability, why do societies continue to change? What accounts for social change? The answers to these questions are at the heart of sociology, and all great sociologists, particularly the founders of the discipline, have tried to answer these questions.

Early social thinkers such as Thomas Hobbes believed that the most important condition of social stability and order is fear. He pointed to the fact that in their natural state, people are equal; even if one is more powerful than others, he or she can be killed, either by weapon or in his or her sleep. This could result in a fear of all against all or a war of everyone against everyone. Hobbes argued that this constant fear gave birth to the social contract. This contract was based on the agreement for individuals to give up their natural freedom to do whatever they want in exchange for protection against force and fraud. Hobbes's view is heavily criticized by sociologists in that he failed to see that war and peace are both learned and not natural. Nevertheless, he was correct to argue that fear is an important aspect of social order.

In our discipline, Auguste Comte (1798–1857) is well known because he coined the term *"sociology."* At first, he called this new science *social physics*, but he later changed it to sociology. His understanding of sociology is indebted to his intellectual mentor, Claude Henri de Saint-Simon (1760–1825), who had a major and lasting influence on Comte's life and work. The two men quarrelled over Saint-Simon's insistence that society needed immediate reform by the industrialists and bankers. Comte, on the other hand, believed that theoretical work should take precedence over reform activities. Nevertheless, Comte heavily borrowed from Saint-Simon in developing his understanding of social change and social order.

Comte conceived society by analogy with a biological organism. He noticed that though a biological organism has material boundaries, (e.g., human skin), human society does not have boundaries and cannot be maintained by physical means; only spiritual ties can sustain it. Three of the most important sources of these ties are language, religion, and division of labour. *Language* is the vessel in which the thoughts of preceding generations and the culture of the ancestors are stored. Without common language, humans could never have attained solidarity and consensus; no social order or social contract would have been possible. Moreover, *religion* furnishes the unifying principle, the common ground without which individual differences would tear society apart. Religion allows humans to overcome their egotistic propensities and ensures social order. In fact, Comte saw religion as an indispensable source of legitimization of governments. No temporal power could endure without the support of spiritual **power.** Lastly, **division of labour** links humans to their fellows. Each person is dependent on others for their basic needs and wants. Division of labour contributes to human solidarity by creating functional interdependency among individuals or human organisms. Therefore, for Comte, social order and stability was less due to fear and more due to cultural transmission through language, moral legitimization through religion, and interdependency of individuals due to division of labour.

Comte argued that evolution and change in human society has paralleled the evolution of the individual mind. All individuals pass through three stages of development: affective, cognitive, and active. In the *affective* stage, individuals are governed by biologically innate propensities (e.g., instincts of preservation, drive for food and shelter, sexual instinct, instinct of pride and vanity, and instinct of attachment and veneration). In the *cognitive* stage, contemplation, mediation, and deductive and inductive reasoning are important sources of human conduct. Finally, in the *active* stage, courage in undertaking, prudence in execution, and firmness in accomplishment become important.

Comte also argued that just as individuals tend to be devoted believers in childhood, critical metaphysicians in adolescence, and natural philosophers in adulthood, so has human society in its growth traversed these three major stages. Each branch of human knowledge has passed successively through three different theoretical conditions. For Comte, every successive stage in the evolution of the human mind necessarily grew out of the preceding one. Moreover, he stated that these stages correspond to the stages in the development of social organization, of types of social order, of types of social units, and of the material conditions of human life.

Below are Comte's three stages of development in human society:

1. *Theological stage:* In this stage, humans explain events through the will and actions of humanlike gods, spirits, demons, and other supernatural beings. In other words, the human mind, seeking the essential nature of beings—the first and final causes of all effects—supposes all phenomena to be produced by the immediate action of supernatural beings. At the upper end of this stage, priests manage the society and military men rule it. This meant the emergence of hierarchies and specialization of those people whose task was knowledge and power. Comte used examples of Egyptian, Greek, and Roman **polytheism** as the most developed societies in this stage.

2. *Metaphysical stage:* This was basically a transitional stage between the first and third stage. Events were understood in terms of innate essence or original causes. The intellectual focus was on critique of theistic doctrines and emphasis on free intellectual inquiry in order to organize the social world based on its inherent natural causes. This stage, which corresponds roughly to the Middle Ages, was under the sway of churchmen and lawyers. The entity of the state also arose into social prominence at this time.

3. *Scientific or positive stage:* In this stage, science became the major force of knowledge and a method of the search for absolute notions and the origin and destination of the universe. Scholars applied themselves to the study of observable scientific relationships and their laws. This stage was governed by industrial administrators and scientific moral guides. The whole human race became the operative social unit.

Although Comte insisted on the importance of intellectual knowledge for social development, he also included other causes of social change and development. Comte argued that population increase is a major source of social progress and that the increase in division of labour is a powerful force for social evolution. In addition, he saw that the seed of social order was sown in the family. For Comte, the true social unit is the family. It is within the family that the elementary, egotistical propensities are curbed and harnessed to social purposes (for details see Ashley & Ornstein, 1998; Turner et al., 1998; Zeitlin, 2001).

Besides Comte, many other classical philosophers and social scientists have contributed to the development of sociology and explanation of social order and social change. In particular, the intellectual contributions of Durkheim, Marx, and Weber have had a lasting influence. Each of these sociologists became important because, as discussed before, they shaped a theoretical paradigm or school of thought. What follows is a discussion of key aspects of these three classical social theorists based on their own work and those of contemporary sociologists.

Emile Durkheim (1858–1917)

Durkheim addressed the problem of social contract as a mean of social order as formulated by Thomas Hobbes. For Durkheim, every contract requires some non-contractual elements. It requires that parties to the contract agree on moral obligations and rule of law. These obligations and rules are based on traditions that pre-exist contracts. As such, for Durkheim, contracts are not the basis of social order and stability.

Durkheim viewed society as an integrated unit that in some sense is comparable to that of a living organism. Like Auguste Comte, Durkheim argued that the animal organism is governed mechanically, whereas human society is bound together by ideas. This means that society has its own specific properties that are separable from those of its individual members.

In his famous book *The Division of Labour in Society* (1964 [1933]), Durkheim wanted to find out how and why society is possible. In order to answer these questions, he first distinguished between traditional and modern societies. He noticed that modern and traditional societies are different with regards to the kind of social solidarity that governs them. Traditional societies are based on **mechanical solidarity,** which is based on resemblance of parts. That is, individuals differ from one another as little as possible. They feel the same emotions, cherish the same values, and hold the same things sacred. Therefore, society is stable because of a lack of individual differentiation. In traditional societies, every individual is a microcosm of the whole. This means that there exists a **collective conscience,** or a body of beliefs and sentiments that are common to all members of the society. These sentiments are strongly engraved in individual consciousness, preventing them from violating the moral values common to all.

For example, crime is viewed as an act that violates those sentiments that are universally approved and adhered to by members of the society. As such, crime shocks the common conscience, violates community's sentiments, and threatens social solidarity and the very existence of society. Therefore, any crime committed against a person is viewed as a crime against all. The community devises *repressive laws* to severely punish criminals, in order to ensure social order and stability. Consequently, in this type of society, harsh punishment is needed in order to protect social unity of the community. The goal of punishment is to restore unity and protect and reaffirm the collective conscience.

In contrast, modern societies are based on **organic solidarity,** where consensus results because of differentiation. Everyone is free to believe, to act, and to desire according to their own preferences. However, they are dependent on each other for survival due to a high level of division of labour. Therefore, solidarity stems not from a common belief or sentiment typical of traditional societies but from **functional interdependence** in the division of labour. All individuals are dependent on each other for their contribution to the survival of the society. For example, the carpenter needs the plumber, who needs the police, who in turn needs the teacher, who needs the students, and so on.

According to Durkheim, this type of society tends to be governed by *restitutive or cooperative laws.* The purpose of punishment when a misdeed is committed is to restore things to the previous state or to organize cooperation among the individuals. The point is not to punish but to reestablish the state of things as it should have been in accordance with justice. For example, a person who has not settled his or her debt must pay it. Crime is no longer viewed as being committed against the society but against a specific individual. As can be seen, for Durkheim, as against Hobbes, in both traditional and modern societies, social contracts are only valid and effective if society authorizes and sanctions the necessary obligations for these contracts.

Durkheim argued that the development of society is correlated with the progressive displacement of the repressive by restitutive laws. The higher the level of social development, the greater the relative proportion of restitutive laws compared to repressive laws. Social development itself is a function of increasing differentiation and division of labour. The causes of social division of labour and differentiation in a population are due to the *material* (the number of individuals in a given space) and *moral* (the intensity of communication between individuals) density of the population. As population increases, people are more likely to become closer in space and to communicate with each other. This ensures shared knowledge of skills and abilities, which in turn allows the expansion of division of labour by knowing who does the best job and efficiently. With differentiation, people need each other for survival. This is called functional interdependency of parts. Therefore, Durkheim's general law is that division of labour in society varies in direct ratio with the volume and density of the population.

However, as division of labour increases, so does individualism, which means that the pervasiveness of the collective conscience in society declines too. But if the collective conscience declines, why is society still possible? Why does it not break down? Durkheim argued that individualism actually strengthens another element of the collective conscience: the *cult of the individual.* That is, the expansion of the division of labour creates an entire system of rights and duties that link modern individuals in durable ways, focusing upon the worth and dignity of the individual rather than the collective. These rights and duties slowly become formal laws with systematic codification. Thus, in a society with a high division of labour, each individual contributes to the survival of society and individuals interact in accordance with their obligations to others and to society as a whole. This dependency and obligation become the moral glue, rules, and regulations that bind the self-sufficient units together. Therefore, the

26

growing individualism is positive, even necessary, as long as it does not destroy both morality and social solidarity (see Giddens, 1971).

The destructive source of this morality is exemplified in anomic and forced divisions of labour. When there are genuine regulations that guide the interactions between people, there is no problem of division of labour, as people recognize one another's obligations and contributions. For example, when there is **equality of opportunity,** individuals can occupy appropriate social positions based on their ability and skills. However, if there is moral deregulation or normlessness, **anomic** division of labour develops. In anomic forms of division of labour, the normative standards of behaviour are either weak or non-existent. This produces lawlessness and economic crisis. For example, when there is extreme poverty or inequity in wealth, principles that tend to justify moral regulations disappear, and people become unhappy, resulting in conflict and social problems. Similarly, if rules are unjust, *forced* division of labour develops. This is when self-interest becomes the guiding principle of powerful people, preventing others from a just position in society that is appropriate to their level of skills and abilities. This again compromises social solidarity which could result in conflict.

It is important to note that for Durkheim, social contract is valid and effective if both sides freely and equally consent to the contract. However, if the parties to contracts have unequal power, one party in the contract will suffer unjustified injury. For example, due to inheritance of private property, social contract is often signed unjustly, for it entails contract between the unequal. Durkheim suggested that under both anomic and forced division of labour, the state should manage problems by generating appropriate moral and just regulations or laws, ensuring fair play, moral responsibility, and mutual obligations (see Grabb, 1990).

Karl Marx (1818–1883)

Marx's writings are extensive and include more than 40 volumes, some of which are philosophical and others political. Marx stated that the history of all previous societies is a history of class struggle (see Box 2.1). This means that in any class-based society, there are people and groups who are unequal in wealth, power, and resources. Those who have more tend to dominate those who have less, and the latter struggle to minimize or eliminate such domination. He started from a truism that in order to live, we must produce, and in order to produce, we must work. This truism results in three central facet of his theory:

- human labour (i.e., work) is the most important central human activity separating humans from other animals
- those who control the production process also tend to control other aspects of human life
- when human productive activity or labour power is controlled by others, humans lose their humanity and become alienated.

For Marx, humans create themselves and their environment through theoretical and practical activities. They create tools through which they manipulate nature and control it, and in doing so, they modify their relationships with fellow human beings, resulting in their own transformation. In other words, in the course of human social activities, human consciousness changes and "self" develops.

Marx divided human societies into **modes of production.** In each mode of production, human activity and the relationship between them is organized differently. Each mode of production includes forces and relations of production. **Forces of production** include land, capital, and labour, while **relations of production** refer to how these forces of production are owned (privately or collectively), how they are distributed (equally or unequally), and how agents of production relate to each other through ideology and the state (peacefully or antagonistically).

Five great modes of production include primitive communism, slavery, Asiatic modes of production (in the East) or feudalism (in the West), capitalism, and advanced communism. The first and the fifth modes of production (primitive and advanced communism) are classless societies, whereas the three in the middle (slavery, feudalism, and capitalism) are class-based societies.

Under primitive **communism,** land and resources were plentiful and the population small. Therefore, there was no need for private ownership of land or resources. Moreover, human

28

knowledge, experience, and skill were not at the stage to be able to produce more than they needed for survival. People worked collectively, with minimum division of labour, and consumed the result of their labour collectively.

As population increased skill and experiences of people increased too and division of labour expanded. People started to produce more than they needed, and **surplus products** appeared (i.e., production outpaced consumption). The accumulated surplus product was passed from one generation to the next, and some individuals started to have more accumulated wealth than others. Moreover, as population increased, tribes came into contact with one another. This resulted in wars between tribes over scarce resources. The victorious tribe confiscated the wealth of the defeated tribe and enslaved its members. These slaves at first belonged to the victorious tribe as a group and not to a specific individual. However, with increasing wars, specialized armies and leaders were created. These leaders slowly started to confiscate the wealth and appropriate the slaves for themselves and thus established hierarchies and the class system. This was a fundamental change in the social organization of production. Those who had wealth and slaves became the dominant group, while the slaves and propertyless became the subordinate groups. Therefore, the first historical social system, **slavery,** was based on classes of *masters* and **slaves.** For Marx, **class** is defined in terms of individuals' relationship to the organization of production. Those who own and control key elements of production (e.g., slaves, land, tools, capital, etc.) constitute the dominant class (slave owners), and those who do not own the means of production constitute the subordinate class (slaves). Although masters and slaves were the most important classes in this period, there were also classes of merchants who were not directly involved in production but were involved in its distribution. As well, there were groups of state officials and military personnel who protected masters and their wealth.

Under the slave mode of production, there was no distinction between the work needed for survival of the producers and the extra work **(surplus labour)** that was appropriated by the slave owners. Whatever the slaves were able to produce belonged to the masters. Even the children and partners of slaves belonged to the masters. Masters could do whatever they wished with the slaves, their families, and their belongings. However, masters provided some means of subsistence (e.g., food) to slaves because they did not want to lose their "tools of production." Slaves were considered a fixed part of the means of production. They did not have any formal or legal freedom; they were simply considered "talking animals." Since slaves did not have any legal existence, there was also no compulsion for them to work more than they needed.

29

Therefore, masters used force in order to make slaves work and produce more. As can be seen, slavery was an inefficient mode of production. To ensure that slaves worked and did not escape, masters needed to hire or pay for many other people to oversee them (e.g., security and state officials). Nevertheless, many slaves escaped or worked less.

Marx argued that numerous factors resulted in the destruction of slavery and emergence of **feudalism.** Among these factors were the disintegration of the Roman Empire and continual wars between tribes. The disintegration of the Roman Empire resulted in many semi-nomads becoming tied to the land and turning into cultivators. Continuous wars resulted in many free peasants asking large landowners for protection, and in turn, the landowners received the peasants' land rights. These peasants became bonded serfs. Similarly, kings granted certain nobles subjects and large parcels of lands in exchange for the nobles' loyalty to the king against rivals. Finally, the defeat of peasants in wars meant that many of the new nobles and lords acquired large amounts of land belonging to the defeated peasants, and the peasants themselves became serfs. **Serfs** were a group of people who worked on the landlord's land and kept a share of the output for themselves. For example, serfs might have produced and kept one-third of the product for themselves and gave the remaining two-thirds to the landlord. In this case, one-third of the output was considered the serfs' **necessary labour** for their own survival, with two-thirds surplus labour given to the landlord. Surplus labour or surplus product was either paid as rent, in cash, or in kind to the landlord, or as tax to the king for use of the land.

It is evident that serfs had more control over the means of production than slaves. Serfs were able to buy oxen or a parcel of land if they worked hard. They were more motivated to be productive than slaves. In addition, they were not bought and sold individually as were slaves. But, if the landlord sold the land, serfs were also included in the bargain; they were sold along with the land collectively. Therefore, serfs had limited freedom. Slaves were put to work by force, whereas serfs had to work because of *tradition* and *legal pressures.* Finally, although feudalism was more efficient to the landlord than slavery was to the slave owners, the former had problems too. There was little motivation for serfs to work beyond the minimum. Their experience was that whatever they had produced, a large share went to the landlord or to the king. This inequity diminished their incentives to work. Moreover, as cities and industries emerged, many serfs left the lords' domain and went to work in the cities.

The third and final class-based society for Marx was capitalism and the **capitalist** mode of production. This system of production emerged in the 13th century Europe, and by the 16th century, feudalism had almost disappeared in Europe. **Capitalism** is based on a process that separates direct producers (serfs, small farmers, etc.) from their means of production. This separation occurred when serfs and peasants who had some control over or owned the means of production lost this control or ownership and became workers. Marx's reasons for this change are multifaceted. We already discussed the tendency of serfs to leave for the cities looking for work. Similarly, various economic crises resulted in free peasants borrowing against their land in order to buy consumer goods and tools of production, leaving them unable to pay their debt and hence losing their land. They became landless peasants searching for jobs in the cities. Development of money relations in rural areas meant that peasants produced for the market and thus increased their dependency on the market, which subjected them to market crisis and fluctuations. Looking at the classic case of England, Marx pointed to the importance of state policies such as the **Enclosure Act** in forcing many peasants off their land, which was intended for sheep-grazing for the expanding wool-based industries.

Under capitalism, workers are not bonded to the land. In fact, there is no legal pressure for workers to work either. But work they must. Not having any ownership of means of production to exchange in the market for their basic needs forces workers to sell what they do own, which is their labour power (their ability, creativity, etc.). Therefore, workers have *formal freedom* in that they are free to sell their labour power to whomever and whenever they wish, but they must sell it in order to survive. This means that they are under *economic pressure* to work and produce. Fear of losing their job and of the resulting hunger plays a key role for workers' compliance, as does fear of the state, which is entrusted with the power to protect private property and stability. Finally, ideology plays an important role in ensuring workers to comply with the work contract. The ideology of hard work as means of success and respect for inheritance and private property are the two pillars that ensure compliance. What is important here is that workers do not necessarily think that they are exploited in the way that slaves or serfs were. Slaves gave all their production to their master, and the serfs gave a portion of their work or product. Both slaves and serfs were to observe and conceptualize the fact that they were obviously exploited by their master or lord. Workers got paid for their work, and if they worked harder they got paid more, so on the surface there was no clear **exploitation** that workers could point to. Marx went deeper and argued that the form of exploitation that workers encounter is more serious because it is disguised as wages paid for work performed. The fact is, Marx pointed out, that workers produce more than they get paid for. This is true for several reasons:

- Modern factories enable workers to produce considerably more than is necessary to cover the cost of their subsistence (i.e., their wages). Whatever the workers produce over and above their wage is surplus product and is appropriated by the capitalist as profit.

- By lengthening the workday or using two or three shifts, employers make sure that workers produce more per day, which minimizes the cost of production.

- By reducing wages or creating competition among workers (for example through racial or gender division and discrimination), some workers are paid less but produce the same as or more than others.

- By speeding up the process of production through rationalizing the organization of work (e.g., assembly line production, computer use, etc.) and introducing new machinery, employers ensure that workers produce more during the same period of time.

These sources of exploitation are some of the reasons that workers experience **alienation** or become involved in work stoppage, sabotage, and rebellion. Recall that Marx started from a truism that in order to live, we must eat, and in order to eat, we must produce. Therefore, production of human needs and wants is the first historical social act that also fundamentally differentiated humans and animals. True, animals also produce, but animals produce instinctively and for their immediate use. Humans produce universally, for many generations to come, and they produce creatively. In the process of production, human beings use their labour power and their creativity to modify nature. The outcome of their creativity is their product (i.e., the object). It is possible that humans lose control of their creativity or their object of creation. Marx argued that once they lose control over their product in terms of how and when to produce it, or if their product is taken away from them, humans become alienated from their labour power, their creativity, their humanity, their species-being.

According to Marx, over-exploitation, frequent economic crisis, and increasing alienation will shake the foundation of capitalist society and result in a new stage in human history. **Class conflict** will increase. It even may become international where all workers of the world will become united against the capitalists (as in the Occupy Wall Street movement or Arab Spring). According to Marx, capitalism, like all other modes of production, will be replaced with a new social system (i.e., **socialism**) either peacefully or violently, more likely the latter. Some societies will increase social services and decrease work hours as human productivity and automation increases. With automation, private ownership of means of production will lose its legitimacy in that there is no justification for some having most if not all wealth and others none if no one is working. Other societies may undergo violent changes through persistent class conflicts. Once the capitalist system is overthrown, socialism emerges, where private property is eliminated and workers have control over the process of production. Once private property is eliminated, there will be no need for the state or government, because according to Marx, the state exists in order to serve the interests of the dominant classes over the interests of the subordinate classes. If there is no private property, there are no classes and no need for the state or government. This introduces the advanced communist stage. At the communist stage, *people work according to their ability and take from the society according to their needs.* This also means there is no need for the market since people only produce and consume what they need. This is possible because of the expansion of technology, machinery, and robots, which can do most of the necessary work. People can become, to paraphrase Marx, *hunters in the morning, fishers in the afternoon, and philosophers at night.* The division of labour would also disappear since people would then be multifaceted producers. This marks the end of alienation (powerlessness to control one's own creativity) and the beginning of communism.

Marx had a multidimensional explanation of social order and change that varied from one mode of production to other. In general, he presented a dialectical model where the economic structure triggered changes in the human relations, which in turn affected the economic structure. Class struggle played as the engine of social change, while ideology and religion played both as mechanisms for social order and change.

Max Weber (1864–1920)

Weber's work can be viewed as an intense debate with Marx and Marxists. Whereas Marx offered a theory of capitalism, Weber developed a theory of the process of rationalization and through that an explanation of capitalist development. For Weber, the principle characteristic of modern society is **rationalization,** which is expressed by a widening of the sphere of relation to goals. He was interested in explaining why institutions of society are becoming more rational in the West (i.e., institutional rationalism), but not in the East. By institutional rationalism, he meant formal rationality (i.e., a concern for the actors making choices of means and ends). But these choices are made in reference to universally applied rules, regulations, and laws. These rules, regulations, and laws are, in turn, derived from large-scale organizations and structures (e.g., bureaucracies). According to Weber, **bureaucracy** is a typical example of rationalization. This type of rationality is also called "purposively rational" conduct. Here, an individual's rationality assesses the probable results of a given act in terms of the calculation of means to an end. In securing a given objective, a number of alternative means of reaching that end usually exist. The individual, faced with these alternatives, weighs the relative effectiveness of each of the possible means of attaining the end and the consequence of securing it for other goals that the individual holds. Thus, one can apply the rational application of scientific knowledge to any activity. In modern days, you can see this in fast-food restaurants such as McDonald's, where both the customers and the workers are led to seek the most rational means to ends. McDonald's restaurants epitomize the rational means by which a worker can dispense and customers can obtain food quickly and efficiently (see Ritzer, 1992).

In developing his discussion of bureaucracy, Weber was also challenging another aspect of the Marxian thesis. For Marx, the development of capitalism meant the concentration of the wealth in few and fewer hands and the concurrent separation of the direct producer from the means of production (i.e., proletariatarianization). Weber agreed with Marx that wealth is becoming more concentrated and the producers are becoming separated from their means of production under capitalism. However, he argued that there are parallel changes taking place in several other social spheres. For example, in bureaucracy, civil servants have been separated from the means of administration, and in the military, soldiers have been separated from the means of violence. Under the tribal and feudal systems, soldiers possessed their own weapons and were economically able to make or purchase them. Nowadays, they can't afford to own their means of violence because machineries of war are too expensive and are concentrated under state control. Similarly, the huge bureaucratic machine is now concentrated under the control of few and fewer corporations and organizations. Take the example of scientific research. Previously, scientists were lone researchers each working in the basement, garage, or cellars of their house. In contrast, modern research has become too expensive, as scientists work in collaboration, research thousands of subjects, and require expensive laboratories, requiring huge budgets supported by corporations and governments. Power and decision-making in these large bureaucratic organizations are concentrated in few and fewer hands and the actual rank and file have little control over means and process of production and decision-making. They, too, are alienated. Weber argued that, given the population increase and expansion of division of labour and expertise, it would be hard to imagine that any new social system, including socialism or communism, would be able to eliminate the iron cage of bureaucracy. He insisted that no complex industrial society can overcome the problem of the bureaucratization.

Weber's main concern, the same as Marx's, was the nature of capitalist enterprise and the specific characteristics of Western capitalism. Their similarity of interest and Weber's continuous debate with Marx's arguments resulted in some scholars indicating that Weber's whole life was concentrated on a dialogue with Marx's ghost.

Both Marx and Weber stated that the emergence of the free workers as a group separated from their means of production is important for the development of capitalism. They differed in what was most important for such an historical transformation. Weber sought his explanation in differences in religions of the Western and Eastern world and the importance of the ***Protestant Reformation*** for the development of capitalism in the West. In this way, Weber searched for a religious explanation of this transformation, whereas Marx was mainly interested in economic forces.

Weber saw religion as an attempt by people to find an explanation for the suffering they experienced in the world. Thus, for him, religion developed out of a need to explain inconsistencies in society that separated reality from an ideal existence. Weber noticed that the answers to these inconsistencies were of two kinds:

1. **Other-worldly mystics** (associated with Eastern religions, Buddhism, Hinduism) view salvation as being achieved through the separation of one's self from body. Mystics reject the world that people can perceive with the fine senses as illusionary. Individuals are encouraged to escape from pain and suffering through mental detachment from the world.

2. **Inner-worldly ascetics** (e.g., Protestantism) agree that most problems stem from physical involvement in the world, but they suggest a different solution. They argue that it is not the world that causes suffering but the doubt and temptation that lie within each individual. Therefore, ascetics suggest that the world and body can be mastered and disciplined so that doubt and temptation can be defeated. Thus, the inner-worldly ascetics escape suffering by living in the world in a disciplined manner.

Now that we are familiar with Weber's classification of world religions, we can discuss his famous book, *The Protestant Ethic and the Spirit of Capitalism*. In this book, Weber focused on the attitude of economic individualism, which helped break down traditional feudalism. Weber opened the book by stating a certain statistical fact: Modern European business leaders and owners of capital, as well as skilled labourers and technically and commercially trained personnel of modern enterprises, were overwhelmingly Protestant. This was also the case in the early 16th century, where the early centres of capitalist development were strongly Protestant. In order to explain the correlation between Protestantism and capitalism, Weber analyzed the content of Protestant beliefs and assessed their influence on the actions of believers and their economic activities.

He argued that traditional workers worked as much as necessary in order to earn and meet their usual needs. In contrast, modern workers seek more and more money, even after making enough for their usual needs. Moreover, they do not spend this extra money for luxurious consumptions. Therefore, he concluded that the spirit of modern capitalism is characterized by a unique devotion to earn wealth and to avoid using the earned income for personal enjoyment. He related this capitalist spirit to the **Protestant ethic** and argued that Protestants are concerned with the idea of a **"calling."** Weber further noticed that the concept of a calling came into being only at the time of the Reformation. According to Protestants, the calling of an individual is to glorify God through the conduct of day-to-day life.

Weber took the example of John Calvin (1509–1564), a French theologian, in order to make his point and highlighted three major aspects of Calvinist doctrines:

1. "God does not exist for men, but men for the sake of God." Therefore, humans must glorify Him on earth.
2. Humans are unable to know the divine truth. Only God knows.
3. All humans are predestined and their actions cannot influence the divine judgement.

Thus, believing in predestination meant that humans, priests, or laypersons could not intercede with God to produce their salvation (notice the difference with Catholicism where priests can grant absolution). Two conclusions were derived from this:

- An individual should consider him or herself to be one of the chosen. Any doubt signifies imperfect faith and therefore lack of grace.
- The most appropriate means to develop and maintain the necessary self-confidence that an individual is one of the chosen is through intense world activity.

Thus, for Calvinists, the performance of hard work became regarded as a "sign" of election—not a method of salvation. Hard work was a method of eliminating doubts in salvation. Consequently, believers saw labour as the highest positive ethical salvation.

Weber also argued that according to Calvinism, accumulation of wealth as an enticement to idle luxury was unacceptable. Calvinists instead reinvested the wealth acquired through hard work, because material profit acquired through the pursuit of duty in a calling was highly recommended. As a result, if individuals worked hard and succeeded in their calling, they would interpret their success as a sign of salvation. They would ask themselves rhetorically: "Would God let me succeed in my calling if I was not one of the chosen? Since I succeeded, I must have been one of the chosen."

Therefore, hard and diligent work was useful for believers in several ways. First, it kept individuals busy, preventing them from thinking about their suffering in this world and their faith in the next world. Second, it helped them succeed in the work they were doing, allowing them to become rich. Finally, since they were not able to spend their newly acquired wealth for self-consumption, they reinvested it in business activities. Therefore, a new breed of psychologically motivated entrepreneurs—also known as capitalists—was formed. Weber concluded that the origin of the capitalist spirit is found in the Calvinist religious ethic. He argued that there is an "elective affinity" between Calvinism and the economic ethics of modern capitalist activity (see Giddens, 1971; Zeitlin, 2001).

Summary

Sociology's birth as a discipline goes back to the work of Aug⟨...⟩ emphasized the role of language, religion, and division of labour. He saw relig⟨...⟩at holds members of the society together and language as a vessel that ensures the cu⟨...⟩ne past is transmitted to that of the present generation. Division of labour ensures interdependency and solidarity of individuals. Durkheim followed Comte's reasoning but argued that the expansion of division of labour is due to an increase in population, which brings in contact disperse individuals. In their early history, humans were not differentiated and this lack of differentiation helped their solidarity, mechanically. However, with an increase in population and consequent expansion of the division of labour, humans became more differentiated and dependent on each other, which also furnished their solidarity, organically.

Marx argued that there is no unifying pattern of social order and change in human society, but that order and change was dependent on modes of production of human economic needs, which also gave birth to social institutions ensuring social order. The social order was generally built by and benefited the dominant classes who owned the means of production of human needs during slavery, feudalism, and capitalism. Specifically, the shift from feudalism to the present mode of production (i.e, capitalism) was possible because the majority of people became workers without any property to exchange in the market for their subsistence. The only thing they had was their labour power or creativity, which they were forced to sell for wages. In the process, the capitalists became rich and richer benefiting from the creativity of workers. This has resulted in solidarity of workers asking and pushing for change towards equality. For Marx, the engine of social change must be sought in the struggle among haves and have nots, rich and poor, oppressor and oppressed. Weber agreed with Marx on the importance of a wage-labour system, but also emphasized the importance of ideology for social change and order. For example, he saw the development of capitalism as being rooted in the Protestant Reformation that created a new breed of individuals who saw hard work as their religious calling in order to glorify God on earth. Not only, these individuals worked hard but also saved their wealth and invested it to make more wealth. As can be seen, for Weber, this new breed of individuals is the capitalist entrepreneurs whom help with the accumulation of wealth.

Key Terms

Alienation: the term, as originally used by Karl Marx, refers to loss of control over one's work and product. It is a feeling of powerlessness from other people and from oneself.

Anomie: according to Emile Durkheim, anomie is a condition in which society provides little or no moral guidance for individual actions. A state of normlessness.

Bureaucracy: a rational organization designed to perform tasks efficiently.

Calling: a religious duty. The term was used by the Protestants to refer to one's occupation as a religious duty.

Capitalism: a system of production in which a small group of people own the means of production, while a large group of people who do not have access to those means of production have to sell their labour power in order to earn enough to subsist. The pressure to produce tends to increase innovation and technological development, yet helps produce unemployment, poverty, and inequality.

Capitalist: in Marxism, it refers to an individual or a group of people who own the means of production (capital, raw materials, factories, tools, etc.) and who hire workers in order to produce products to sell for profit.

Class: generally, it means an individual's relative location in a society based on wealth, power, prestige, or other valued resources. Marxists view class as individuals' relationship to the organization of production. Weberians refer to class in terms of individuals' access to life chances.

Class conflict: antagonism between social classes in a society. Marx used this term to refer to the struggle between capitalists and workers because of their clash of interests.

Collective conscience: a body of beliefs and sentiments that is common to all members of a society.

Communism: a social system where there is no private ownership of the means of production and no state; all members of the society are economically, politically, and socially to be equal.

Division of labour: task specialization of economic activities.

Enclosure Act: law passed in England to clear the land for sheep-grazing.

Equality of opportunity: a view that all individuals should be given an equal chance to compete for higher education, status, and jobs.

Exploitation: the process by which members of one class (e.g., capitalists) extract surplus value or surplus labour from members of another class (e.g., workers).

Feudalism: a social system prevalent in the Middle Ages where land and resources are owned by the nobility, state, and landlords, and main producers are attached to the land.

Forces of production: various means used to produce necessary and surplus products in each mode of production.

Functional interdependency: interdependency of individuals in the division of labour where each would contribute to the benefit of others and society through the task that they perform.

Inner-worldly ascetics: thinking that most problems stem from physical involvement in the world and that doubt and temptation within the individual causes suffering.

Mechanical solidarity: according to Emile Durkheim, it refers to shared morality among members, helping social bonds in traditional societies.

Mode of production: ways in which the production process in each social system are organized.

Necessary labour: the amount of work needed to meet one's basic needs.

Organic solidarity: according to Emile Durkheim, the social bonds created due to interconnectedness in division of labour.

Other-worldly mystics: viewing salvation as being reached through the separation of one's self from body.

Polytheism: beliefs in many gods.

Power: refers to one's ability to influence others and reach a goal even against opposition from those who are subject to power.

Protestant ethic: a belief system among Protestants that according to Max Weber, includes hard work in order to glorify God on Earth. Also a belief in predestination.

Rationalization: Weber's term for the movement towards the development of human thought based on systematic accumulation of evidence as in the form of impersonal authority common in bureaucracies.

Relations of production: the social relationships that organize and dictate the distribution and ownership of forces of production.

Serfs: group of people who worked on the landlord's land and kept a share of the output for themselves.

Slavery: economic organization in which some individuals are the property of other individuals.

Slaves: group of people who can be bought and sold at the owner's wish.

Socialism: an economic system in which the means of production are collectively owned.

Surplus labour: the labour used to produce products over and above what is needed for subsistence.

Surplus products: the products produced over and above what is needed for subsistence; when production outpaces consumption.

Critical Thinking Questions

1. Why did Marx argue that exploitation of workers under capitalism is more hideous than that of slaves or serfs?

2. What are the key explanations of social change according to Marx, Weber, and Durkheim?

3. How does the explanation of Marx and Weber on the development of capitalism differ?

4. How does Durkheim differ from Comte in his explanation of social change and social order?

5. How important is "theory" in sociology? Why are the views of Durkheim, Marx, and Weber theoretical?

6. Why do you think that the expansion of division of labour is important for social development and for social stability?

7. How is Auguste Comte's explanation of human intellectual development similar or different from his explanation of the social development of human society?

8. How different or similar are modern day workers and capitalists when compared to what was described by Weber in early capitalist development?

9. What are the differences between alienation and anomie?

10. Is there an essential self? Is there a fixed and coherent essence to individuals? Alternatively, is there not a fixed individual self? Are all individuals socially constructed and are they constantly being reconstructed? Discuss.

11. Are scientists and sociologists involved in language games? If so, how?

12. What is (was) the modernity project? Has science failed to improve human conditions?

13. To what extent is our social reality socially constructed? Which theory accounts best for the social construction of reality? Why?

14. What are the functions of education? Explain how each function works.

Chapter 3

Sociological Research Methods

Positivism and Research

One of the most important aspects of research is application of scientific methods to research. You may recall that Auguste Comte coined the term "sociology." It is not a surprise that sociological methods are to some extent similar to his vision of doing research. He wanted to shape the science of society similar to that of the natural sciences in an attempt to explain the past development of humankind and to predict its future.

Comte argued that, similar to the natural sciences, sociology can draw on three types of methods (**observation,** experimentation**,** and comparison) in order to set the task of explaining the laws of progress and social order. Although he acknowledged the importance of observation and use of experimentation for understanding the social world, he viewed the most important scientific method of inquiry to sociologists to be that of comparison. For example, the method of comparing humans to animals gives us precious clues about the first germs of social relations. Of course, comparisons within the human species are even more central to sociology. Comte insisted that the sociological method of inquiry is distinct from the natural sciences by its fourth method, the historical method. Historical comparisons throughout the time in which humanity has evolved are at the very core of sociological inquiry. Sociology is nothing if it is not informed by a sense of historical evolution.

Auguste Comte's philosophy of knowledge is called *positivism.* Essentially, for positivists, scientific explanation is both deductive and inductive. A **deductive** explanation attributes events to a general law. One starts from an abstract concept or a theoretical proposition and moves toward concrete events or empirical evidence. For example, recall that Durkheim's general law was that division of labour increases in relation to the increase in moral and physical density of the population. Thus, the antecedent conditions (e.g., moral and physical density of the population) explain the phenomenon in question (i.e., division of labour). Researchers can then empirically test this general law by evaluating levels of division of labour in different countries, or in the same country across time, in order to see if division of labour varies in those places or time with moral (intensity of communication) and physical (number of people in a given location) density of the population. An **inductive** explanation starts from specific observation of an event and moves toward a theoretical proposition. Recall that Durkheim noticed that men, single individuals, and/or Protestants are more likely to commit suicide than their counterparts. From these observations he concluded that suicide rates vary inversely to individuals' integration to society.

Positivists suggest that there are two main approaches for evaluating a theory. **Confirmation** involves use of empirical evidence in order to provide support for the truth of a scientific theory. **Falsification** involves use of evidence to show that a theory is actually incorrect. The falsification method is advantageous to the confirmation method because if a theory is confirmed, it is not known if it is supported by evidence since the next research project may reject it. On the other hand, if a theory is falsified through evidence, the theory is inaccurate because it was rejected at least once. In sum, for positivists, a theory is scientific if it can be tested. That is, scientific and non-scientific theories can be distinguished through their use of empirical evidence.

Role of Values in Research

How do sociologists select a topic, do their research, test a theory, and/or make judgments about certain relationships? Sociologists, like all other people, live in this world and are therefore subject to some common values and beliefs. This means that their values can influence their subject matter of interest such as the study of education, poverty, inequality, globalization, politics, crime and deviance, family, gender, or race/ethnic relations. Similarly, their values may also influence what sociological methods they use, which theoretical framework they employ to help explain their research findings, and how they interpret the results of their research. In order to control the role of values on their research, sociologists follow a series of research steps, keeping in mind that their values need to be checked in each of these steps (see Box 3.1).

Since Comte's time, sociological methods have evolved. Some sociologists, including Max Weber, have argued that methods of studying human subjects are different from those of studying natural objects. The difference is due to the fact that human subjects play an active role in the inquiry process when compared to objects in natural sciences which do not influence the process of inquiry. Similarly, social and cultural values play an important role in determining what questions are to be asked, what subjects are to be studied, and how to interpret the findings.

Box 3.1 Research Steps

1. **Select a topic.** Sociologists may select topics such as social inequality, crime, mate selection, social networking.

2. **Ask questions.** They may ask questions such as why men earn more income than women, why the rich are getting richer and the poor are becoming poorer, or why some people commit suicide and others do not.

3. **Review the literature.** They assess what they know, consider what they don't, and acknowledge the work of theorists and researchers that have addressed the same topic.

4. **Develop an appropriate research design and method.** They may decide on using quantitative or qualitative methods—they may rely on experiment, surveys, observation, and/or use of existing statistics or archives.

 5. **Collect data.** Use the appropriate method and design and collect the relevant data through content analysis, questionnaires, interviews, observation, experiment, etc.

6. **Analyze the data.** They may use a statistical technique or immerse themselves in the collected data and reveal some patterns that show how the phenomena of interest are related to each other.

7. **Explain the findings.** They use an appropriate theory and explain the findings as well as show how the findings are consistent or inconsistent with alternative theories.

8. **Report the findings.** They need to report and publish their findings so that the public, policymakers, and other scientists can read, apply, or critique it.

Weber argued that sociologists should focus instead on *empathetic understanding* as the only way of studying human subjects. Weber defined sociology as a science that is interested in understanding human action, its cause, and its consequences. He argued that understanding human motives, values, attitudes, and behaviours is possible if we develop an empathetic understanding ("*Verstehen*" in German) of those motives. Thus, like the visitor from outer space, we must penetrate into the minds of our actors to understand the world as they do. Consider: if you see a man who is chopping wood, you tend to interpret this as meaning that he wants to get fuel for his fire. If you observe a person who has burst into tears, you tend to interpret that this person must have just suffered a bitter disappointment. We understand that the captain went down with his ship because we view him as faithful to his idea of honour. We understand that a mother may punish her child because the child was behaving badly. We understand that children respect their parents because of custom and tradition. In all these cases, we explain an event by the subjective meanings we associate to the human actions.

You have noticed that though positivism is dominant in the social sciences, it is only one among many methods of scientific research. Moreover, various methods can be used to complement our understanding of the social world. All methods of research are used in order to find satisfying explanations for aspects of human reality. This understanding is achieved through the use of theories: statements and explanations applicable to the widest possibility of phenomena. In the end, however, such general statements must be testable.

We should also remember that scientific exercise is cultural. The scientific community decides what problems are important, the best ways of testing a theory or interpreting the evidence, and which theory is most correct. Furthermore, government agencies, corporate groups, and publishing companies all have a hand in deciding the merits of a research project and explaining certain evidence. Some research projects are not funded or are not published because interest groups may not think the project is important. As such, gatekeepers and cultural limitations could be important in deciding what is scientific or not.

Quantitative Research Methods

Sociological research is either quantitative or qualitative. As alluded to above, **quantitative** research is based on methods modelled after the natural sciences. It uses methods of experiment, observation, and comparison. Sociologists interested in quantitative research often use concepts such as dependent and independent variables. A **variable** is simply the observable equivalent of a concept and is formed by a range of different observable values. For example, the concept gender is often measured by the variable of sex, which is generally deemed to have two categories: males and females. Income is measured in dollars. Political party affiliation in Canada consists of Liberal, Conservative, Bloc Quebecois, New Democratic Party, and others. A variable that can be changed by another variable is called a **dependent** variable. A variable that causes change in another variable is called an **independent** variable. Thus, for example, we can say income causes well-being. In this case, income is the independent variable and well-being is the dependent variable. If our **causal** statement is correct, then a change in income should produce a change in well-being. As another example, we may state that students whose parents have higher education are more likely to have higher education themselves. In this example, parents' educational level is the independent variable, and students' educational level is the dependent variable. We immediately notice that a causal phenomenon comes before the outcome. That is, **temporal order** is an important aspect of causal order—the cause must come before the effect. As well, we notice that the proposition that parents' education is related to their offspring's education points to an **association** between the independent (parents' education) and dependent variable (offspring's education). That is, the two phenomena are said to be related to each other.

Finally, in establishing a causal order, we should make sure that the relationship between the independent and dependent variable is not **spurious,** meaning that both variables are caused by something else. For example, one may argue that cohabiters are more likely to abuse their partner than married people. However, this may not be due to cohabitation, per se. Cohabiters and violent individuals are both generally younger. Thus, after we control for the effect of age, we may notice that the effect of cohabitation on violence disappears because younger individuals are more likely to be both cohabiters and abusive. Therefore, we can say that age "causes" both cohabitation and abusiveness. The original relationship between cohabitation and abuse was thus spurious—it was a mirage because it ignored the fact that both variables are caused by a third variable (e.g., age). On the other hand, if after controlling for the effect of age, we notice that the original relationship between cohabitation and abuse still persists, we say that the original relationship is not spurious and that the **hypothesis** that cohabitation causes abuse is supported (see Box 3.2).

Box 3.2 Spuriousness

After control for a variable	Pattern	Next Step	Theoretical Implication	Next Step
No change	X causes Y	Ignore control variable	Hypothesis is supported	Select another control variable
Weak or no relationship	Spurious relationship	Include control variable	Hypothesis is rejected	Focus on the effect of the control variable

Experimental Design

Experimentation is most commonly used by physical scientists, but it is also employed by psychologists and sociologists. It is the ideal method of establishing precise causal relationship between variables by controlling other variables. The purpose is to hold constant all forces that affect the phenomenon under investigation and isolate the effect of cause or independent variable. In an experiment, the most important issue is **randomization.** It means giving individuals or subjects equal chance of selection to both experimental or control group by randomly assigning individuals into one of the groups. Alternatively, the two groups should be matched on a list of characteristics that might affect the outcome of the research (e.g., height, weight, sex).

In a classical experiment, two groups are identified. Individuals in the *experimental group* are subjected to the treatment or independent variable, while individuals in the **control group** are not subjected to the treatment or independent variable. Once individuals are assigned to the experimental and control groups, we may test them on the issue of importance for our research: the dependent variable **(pre-test).** Then, after subjecting the experimental group but not the control group to the independent variable, we test both groups again **(post-test).** The effect of the independent variable can be measured by the difference in the amount of change between the two groups when comparing the pre-test to post-test.

Why do students sitting in the front of the class get higher marks than those who sit at the back? Is it because those who sit in front are smarter, better able, and more interested than those sitting at the back? Or, alternatively, is it that those who sit in front are not that different from other students except that proximity to the teacher may result in more eye contact and attentiveness? Dooley (1984) tested these alternative questions. After students chose their seat in the first class, the professor asked them to sit in the same seat for three weeks, after which he tested them (pre-test). He noticed that students sitting in front of the class did better. Then he mixed them up randomly making students in the front sit at the back and those at the back sit at the front. He tested them again after three weeks (post-test). Comparing the results of pre- and post-test Dooley noticed that changing student seating made little difference. This supported the first hypothesis that better able and more interested students sit in front and do better. However, students participated more by asking questions and getting involved in class if they sat at the front of the class in both tests. This also suggests that closeness to the professor is an important **predictor** of class participation.

Although the experimental method is very useful in establishing causal relationship by controlling other variables, it is limited in that we cannot control all relevant variables in an experiment. Moreover, it is questionable that a generalization can be made from an artificial experiment to a setting that involves behaviours in a complex social relationship. Furthermore, subjects may guess the purpose of the experiment and modify their behaviour in order to please or trick the researcher. Finally, the experimenter may consciously or unconsciously modify the results. In the example above, could it be that the professor interacted differently with students between the first and second test?

Social Surveys

Surveys are the most common method sociologists use in order to study large numbers of people. Surveys are the most popular because of the new technologies that allow for efficient sample selection and data processing. In a survey, we need to know what we want to study (the dependent variable) and what we think is related to it and/or affected by it. Then, we develop a questionnaire that asks questions about all of the relevant variables. Some of the questions can be *close-ended,* which solicits specific answers of yes or no, agree or disagree, placement in specific age or income groups. Other questions can be *open-ended* where respondents are given the opportunity to answer what they feel or believe without limitations. In developing the relevant questions, one should avoid jargon, vagueness, emotional language, leading questions, and double negatives. Moreover, threatening and sensitive questions should be asked after the respondent has developed some level of trust with the interviewer. More important, questions must be rooted on the conceptual models of a specific theory.

Questions should be a valid indicator of what we wish to measure. **Validity** refers to the match between the instrument or question and the theoretical concept. Sometimes we may not be able to capture a theoretical concept by one question. Here several questions are needed. As an example, we may think of social class as measured by a combination of education, occupation, income, wealth, prestige, and/or ownership. If so, each and all of the questions that solicit these issues should be in our questionnaire. We should also be concerned that our measurement method consistently yields similar results whether by the same researcher in a different time or place or by different researchers. This is the issue of reliability. **Reliability** refers to the dependability and replicability of results by the same or different researchers.

Once we develop valid and reliable questions, we need to ask these questions from a population of interest. Since it is too expensive and time-consuming, researchers often do not direct the research questions at all members of the population of interest but at a *sample* or a segment of the population. A sample can be *random,* where everyone in the population will have

49

about equal chance of being selected. This means that our sample is representative of the population and thus the results of our study can be generalized to that population. In order to have a random sample, we need to have a list for the total population, like the telephone book or voting registry. Once we have a complete list of the population, we can select 1 to 5 percent of the population, more or less, depending on the size of the population, our research need, and cost. We can, for example, select every 100th name on the list, or instruct the computer to randomly generate the desired sample. A sample can also be **non-random,** whether *convenient* (e.g., people in a mall or in a line-up to a movie) or **snowball** (e.g., the first respondent introduces his friend whom introduces her aunt or someone with specific characteristics of interest, and so on). Since snowball and convenient samples are not random and are non-representative of the general population, they are not generalizable to the population.

Once our sample is selected and our questions are developed, we need to administer our survey by asking questions through telephone, mailing the questionnaire, and/or conducting face-to-face interviews at the respondents' place of residence or work. Each of these methods has some strengths and weaknesses. Both telephone interviews and self-administered questionnaires are relatively inexpensive, but the response rate is generally low. Face-to-face interview is relatively expensive but results in a higher response rate than the other two methods. Moreover, if a question is ambiguous to a respondent, it can be explained in a face-to-face or telephone interview but not in a self-administered questionnaire.

Survey research is advantageous to the experimental methods in that a large number of variables can be controlled or held constant, something we cannot do easily in an experiment. For example, if we are interested in knowing why some students do better than others and we think this has to do with who sits in the front or the back of the class, in addition to finding out about their marks, we can also ask about their sex, age, study habits, class background, attentiveness to teacher, amount of time spent studying at home or library, whether they work for pay and, if so, how many hours, and so forth. Then, in a multivariate model, we can evaluate the effect of class seating on their marks and control for some or all of these relevant variables. This means that we can hold constant the effect of other variables except for where they sit in class.

Conceptualization and Operationalization

You may have noticed that the two main processes of measurement are conceptualization and operationalization. **Conceptualization** is the process of refinement of the construct that matches the abstract theoretical concept. This means that we spend some time thinking and consulting the literature as to how best to define our theoretical concept with clear, explicit, and specific meaning and without ambiguity and vagueness. Theoretical concepts are abstract ideas. In order to test them, we need to define them in ways that allow them to be measured. **Operationalization** is the process of linking a theoretical concept and definition to specific measures and questions. Researchers need to be exact as to what question to ask and how to measure the concept. Thus, a researcher interested in measuring the conflict theory idea of social class needs questions that illicit individuals' ownership of means of production, control of labour-power, and management of the production process, while a researcher interested in measuring functionalist theory ideas about social class would ask questions related to income and prestige and so on.

Other Data Sources

Instead of collecting our own data, there are easier ways of testing many sociological hypotheses. The existing Censuses and General Social Surveys (GSS) collected by Statistics Canada contain many relevant variables for sociological inquiries. The use of such data is not only cheaper for researchers, but many of the methodological issues discussed above have been managed by skilled researchers. Statistics Canada data sets are very reliable and include a large sample size (e.g., GSS) and/or the whole population (censuses) and are publicly available. Censuses are done every 10 years (all of the population) and five years (a sample of the population). GSS surveys are done almost every other year and are topic specific (time use, crime and victimization, labour force dynamics, ethnic diversity, etc.). A quick search of the Statistics Canada website will direct you to the available data, census and survey methodology, and questionnaires.

Data Analysis and Statistics

Once quantitative sociologists have reviewed the literature, developed a theoretical hypothesis, selected appropriate methods, and gathered the relevant data, they need to analyze the data in order to confirm or reject their hypothesis. There are various statistical techniques that help researchers summarize their research, test their hypotheses, and discuss their findings. These techniques are highly specialized and require some knowledge of mathematics and statistics. The brief below will help students understand information and tables provided in most sociological research articles and/or books.

Sociologists often summarize information by showing the **frequency** distribution of their findings. For example, if there are 20 male subjects and 30 female subjects, then we can say that 40 percent of subjects are males (= 20 * 100/20 + 30) and 60 percent are females (= 30 * 100/20 + 30). Sometimes, sociologists summarize information by showing the **mean,** also known as the average. The mean is a common measure of central tendency and applies to variables that are ranked and the distance between the categories is equal. These variables may or may not have a true or absolute zero point. If such variables do not have a true zero point, they are called **interval** variables (e.g., IQ, Fahrenheit). On the other hand, if they do have a true zero point, they are called **ratio** level variables (e.g., income in dollars, Kelvin scale). Many mathematical calculations can be done with interval and ratio measures (addition, subtraction, division, etc), which makes them easy to work with. For example, $10 is half as much as $20 and a quarter of $40. In order to calculate the mean, we simply add the frequencies and divide it by the number of categories in the data. For example, if one person has $20, another $50, and yet another $140, then their mean income of these three individuals would be $70 (= 20 + 50 + 140/3).

Other times, sociologists are interested in knowing how dispersed individuals' or groups' scores are from their mean. Here, they may be interested in variance on standard deviation. **Variance** is simply a measure of the differences between the individuals' score and their mean: the higher the variance, the more the dispersion of individuals from their mean. The square root of variance is called **standard deviation** which standardizes the variance and makes it more interpretable than would be the case with variance.

Sociologists sometimes analyze two or more variables at the same time. For example, they may wish to know how many males versus females have a university education and how many have a college education. This is done through **bivariate** analysis: examining the relationship between two variables. Other times, sociologists would like to know the effect of one variable or phenomenon on another when they take into account the importance of other variables or phenomena. That is, they would like to know the net effect of a variable, holding the effect(s) of other variable(s) constant. This is done through **multivariate** analysis. Sociologists use many different multivariate techniques. Due to their complexity, we will not discuss these techniques here.

Although quantitative research is popular, it is just one among many methods of research. Critics have argued that quantitative analysis does not give us an in-depth understanding of the phenomenon. For example, in a survey, researchers may just read into the answers the respondents have provided and find the pattern that they want to find. Moreover, the wording in a questionnaire may be interpreted differently by different respondents, thus minimizing the reliability of their responses. The interviewing method of asking questions directly in one-to-one situations may solve some of the problems, for example by clarifying meanings and correcting ambiguities; however, the problem with this interviewing method is that there may emerge interviewing bias by unskilled interviewers. The respondents may also provide types of answers that they think may please the interviewer. Therefore, sociologists also use qualitative methods of data collection.

Qualitative Methods

The **qualitative method** is a popular way of collecting information that is used mostly by symbolic interactionists, phenomenologists, ethnomethodologists, a large number of feminists, and some Marxist scholars. It uses a variety of methods for collecting data. The conceptualization, operationalization, and measurement often occur in the data collection process and not in the planning stage, as is common to the quantitative method. Although qualitative researchers may use numbers to report their findings, most of their report includes the written or spoken words and actions of their subjects. The process of research is highly flexible and does not follow a set style. It involves dialogue and interaction between the researcher and subjects, followed by reflection on the process and findings. Researchers spend significant amounts of time with subjects in order to understand how they construct social meaning and how they reason for doing certain things. They gather large quantities of detailed information and ensure an in-depth understanding of the research phenomenon from the subjects' point of view.

Qualitative researchers rely on interpretative methods of investigation. Interpretative method is a technique of collecting information based on the viewpoints of the person(s) under study. The focus is on the subjective meanings and perceptions of the subjects themselves. For example, in the method of **participant observation,** subjects are observed in their own territory and studied on their own terms. Unlike survey research, questions are not structured and closed-ended. Researchers are flexible and open to changing conversation and emergence of previously unthought patterns of interactions. Researchers are involved in intimate and prolonged field experience in order to identify reappearing patterns among the subjects. They also reflect on their own involvement in order to identify and minimize the effect of their own values, perceptions, and interests in the research process. They must evaluate the credibility of their findings by appraising their own level of involvement, familiarity, theoretical knowledge, and investigative skills. Researchers also provide detailed notes on their methods of data gathering, analysis, and interpretation. Finally, they present the evidence in the form of words, images, documents, observations, themes, motifs, and generalizations.

If you were to study the reasons that students get high or low marks as a qualitative researcher, you may need to spend a significant amount of time with some of the students. For example, let's go back to the students, some tending to sit at the back and others preferring to sit in the front of the class. You need to ask them to describe in their own words their study habits, their family encouragements or discouragements for learning, why they like to sit at the back or front of the class, why they think that they get high or low marks, what they think of their teachers, and what kind of interaction they have with teachers, staff, and other students. You would take extensive notes or record the conversation. You would keep asking them to describe their learning process until a pattern emerges. Then, you could report any emerged pattern by using some of the students' own explanations of why they get high or low marks or sit at the back or front of the class. You would reflect on their description, provide new types of knowledge that we did not have before, and potentially build a theory from the ground up. Other researchers might use the depth of knowledge emerging from your observation and build quantifiable measures for further research and broader generalization.

Qualitative researchers assess the value of a research by the **trustworthiness** of the data. There are four aspects to the trustworthiness of research. **Trust value** refers to the confidence of researchers in the truth of the study's findings. It means that peer reviewers and/or the participants consider the results to be credible. It also means that the researcher has reflected on his or her own bias. **Applicability** refers to the degree to which findings can be applied to other contexts or groups. *Consistency* refers to the degree to which the findings are consistent if replicated. Finally, **neutrality** refers to the extent to which findings are the result of the participants and conditions of research and not the result of other influences (see McGloin, 2008; Tuckett, 2005).

Despite the depth of knowledge that may emerge from qualitative research such as participant observation, it is a time-consuming activity because researchers may need to be involved with the subjects for months or even years. Moreover, there is a potential danger for the researcher to **"go native."** In a classic participant observation research that is published in a book entitled the *Street Corner Society*, William Foote Whyte (1943) spent three and a half years with a group of unemployed immigrants in Boston in the 1930s. He infiltrated the Cornerville gang by befriending Doc, the leader of the Norton street gang (see Box 3.3). Although Doc knew that Whyte was researching the gang, other members were told only that he was writing a book. Whyte lived for 18 months with an Italian family, learned Italian, established contacts, participated in their daily activities, attended church, and played sports, and discussed sex and baseball. But he noticed that he was "going native," losing research purpose and becoming a non-observing participant, and therefore moved away. The result of this research was an extensive study of the social structure of the slums.

Another potential problem with participant observation is that the results are hard to *replicate* because researchers' experiences are unique. As well, it is possible that extensive involvement with subjects could alter subjects' behaviours. This is also an ***ethical*** issue. One of the sociological researchers' main ethical codes is that subjects should not be damaged by research. The researcher must ask if extensive involvement with subjects and potentially altering their behaviour would affect the subjects so that their original management of life becomes questionable, and they may not be able to function properly. Another ethical code is that subjects must agree and have the right to refuse participation in the research. To whom does the participant observer ask permission when doing community research? Should they ask permission from the community leader? Can the leader speak for everyone else? But if the permission is asked from only the leader, how could other members agree or have the right to refuse participation? Should each person in the community be consulted? These issues are both related to the research code of ethics but could also affect results. For example, if only some of the subjects in a community agree to be studied, the results may be biased in favour of those who wished to be researched.

Another qualitative method that would overcome some of the ethical issues discussed above is content analysis. In content analysis, researchers use the existing texts, documents, newspapers, letters, diaries, government reports and the like to search for a pattern that is either expected as a pre-determined hypothesis or "fish" for a new pattern (for a summary comparison of quantitative and qualitative methods see Box 3.4).

Box 3.3

As I began hanging about Cornerville, I found that I needed an explanation for myself and for my study. As long as I was with Doc and vouched for by him, no one asked me who I was or what I was doing. When I circulated in other groups or even among the Nortons without him, it was obvious that they were curious about me.

I began with a rather elaborate explanation. I was studying the social history of Cornville ...I was seeking to get a thorough knowledge of present conditions and then work from present to past. I was quite pleased with this explanation at the time, but nobody else seemed to care for it. I gave the explanation on only two occasions, and each time, when I had finished, there was an awkward silence. No one, myself included, knew what to say...

I soon found that people were developing their own explanation about me: I was writing a book about Cornerville. This might seem entirely too vague an explanation, and yet it sufficed. I found that my acceptance in the district depended on the personal relationships I developed far more than any explanations I might give.

(Whyte, 1943, p. 300)

Box 3.4

Quantitative Research	Qualitative Research
Positivist	Anti-positivist
Deductive	Inductive
Tests hypothesis	Focuses on meanings
Large sample size	Small number of subjects
Statistical data analysis	Detailed and thematic description
Design is decided in advance	Design is developed as research progresses
Numbers and statistics for the data	Words, pictures, and objects form the data
Precise and objective measurements	Interpretative and subjective measurements
Reliable and generalizable	Consistent and applicable
Validity	Truth, value, and neutrality
Researcher is detached from the study	Researcher is immersed in the study

Summary

Sociological research involves a painstaking process of asking relevant questions, gathering data, checking values, testing and building theories, and reporting results. In doing research, one or both sociological methods are used. Quantitative methods focus on large groups of people in order to test theories and generalize to a large number of people. The focus is on behaviours and attitudes that can be measured. Qualitative methods focus on in-depth investigations of small groups of people or events with the goal of gaining insight that may be used for better understanding of a broader generalization. The focus is on emotions, attitudes, and behaviours that cannot easily be measured but that still allow us to acquire a deep insight about human life. Both methods can explore the same phenomenon but from different perspectives. In both methods, researchers interact with the theory, and in each step, theory guides them and/or is modified through the research process. You may have noticed that social scientists gather and use information, data, and evidence in a variety of ways. Whatever methods and types of research they use, depending on the theoretical perspectives and the major questions that are the focus of the study, they tend to follow certain steps, as identified at the beginning of this chapter.

Key Terms

Applicability: the extent to which the qualitative data can be applied to other contexts and settings.

Association: an empirical relationship between two or more phenomena or variables. A change in one variable is statistically related to a change in another variable.

Bivariate: involving two variables.

Causality: the stated relationship between two or more variables where the predictor and predicted are identified.

Conceptualization: the process of refining the mental construct that represents part of the world.

Confirmation: involves the use of empirical evidence in order to provide support for the truth of a scientific theory.

Control: a statistical term that refers to holding constant all relevant variables except for the one that we are interested in, to see its effect.

Deductive: attributes events to general law.

Dependent variable: a variable that can be changed by another (independent) variable.

Experiment: a research method that investigates the cause and effect relationship in a controlled environment.

Falsification: involves use of evidence to show that a theory is actually incorrect.

Frequency: a statistical term referring to number of similar events or categories.

Go native: the extent of involvement of researcher with the subjects that could result in the loss of objectivity.

Hypothesis: an unverified statement of the relationship between two or more variables.

Independent variable: a variable that causes change in another (dependent) variable.

Inductive: starts from the observation of an event and moves toward theoretical proposition.

Interval variable: a ranked variable with equal distance between categories.

Mean: statistical term used to describe the sum of all the scores divided by the number of scores.

Multivariate: a method of studying a phenomenon by explaining it through two or more variables.

Neutrality: the extent to which the qualitative data are the result of conditions of research.

Non-random sample: non-representative sample, convenient or snowball.

Observation: a method of discovery that searches for similarities and differences based on observation of subjects or events.

Operationalization: specification of and assignment of values to a variable.

Participant observation: a systematic method of involvement and observation of people's routine activity.

Post-test: second test of subjects.

Prediction: a method of scientific research that allows researcher to predict future events based on events occurred in the past.

Pre-test: first time test of subjects.

Qualitative method: a method of gathering information that is not numeric and that includes participant and nonparticipant observation and historical-comparative research.

Quantitative method: a method of gathering numeric information, based on methods of natural science. It uses methods of experimentation, observation, and comparison.

Randomization: random assignment and selection of subjects where each has an equal chance of being selected.

Ratio variable: a ranked variable with equal distance between categories and a true zero point.

Reliability: consistency and repeatability in a measurement.

Snowball sample: non-representative sample where subjects are selected through their relationship of or reference by other subjects.

Spurious relationship: an apparent though false relationship between two or more variables that is in fact due to a third variable.

Standard deviation: measure of dispersion based on deviation from the mean.

Survey: a method of data collection that selects a portion of the population.

Temporal order: a principle of causal order where the cause of a phenomenon must take place before its effect.

Trust value: see trustworthiness.

Trustworthiness: researcher's confidence in the truth of the study's findings in qualitative data.

Validity: actual measurement of what is intended.

Variable: Observable equivalent of a concept that can be measured.

Variance: a measure of dispersion around the mean.

Critical Thinking Questions

1. Among all types of sample techniques, which one allows for generalizations about the population? Why?

2. As a participant observation researcher, how could you establish a relationship with your subject and yet maintain your value neutrality?

3. Why do some participant observers have a tendency to "go native"?

4. What role does theory play in doing research?

5. Among the various sociological methods, which appeals to you most? Why?

6. Select a topic of interest. What would be the steps for researching this topic?

7. What specific research method do you think is appropriate for studying the topic you chose above?

8. What is positivism?

9. What are the limitations of positivism as applied to human or social behaviour?

10. Discuss differences in validity and reliability issues in qualitative and quantitative methods.

11. How would you know if the stated relationship is spurious?

12. How would you conceptualize and operationalize social class?

Useful Internet Sites

1. Experimental design http://www.socialresearchmethods.net/kb/desexper.htm

2. Participant observation http://faculty.chass.ncsu.edu/garson/PA765/particip.htm

3. Survey ethics http://www.srl.uic.edu/srllink/srllink.htm#Ethics

Chapter 4

Culture

Immediately after birth, humans, unlike animals, are subjected to cultural and learned behaviours that enable them in time to stand on their own and survive without their parents. Animals are social, too, and communicate with each other, but they are not cultural. Their communication and behaviour are primarily instinctual. On the other hand, humans need to learn, invent, produce, build, adapt, and adjust to their immediate environment. Sociologists call these totally learned and transmitted complex ways of life *culture*. Language (signs and symbols), itself an aspect of culture, is an important means of cultural transmission. Language requires shared cultural conceptions and meanings to be able to associate symbols, letters, and words with emotions, attitudes, behaviours, and objects. The association allows transmission of culture. It is because of the shared conceptions and meanings attached to words and symbols that the reader can generally grasp the same meaning that an author displays through the words in books. Loss of a language is strongly associated with the loss of the culture to which the language belongs. When large groups of people live in the same area, sharing a culture and interacting with each other, they constitute a **society.**

In everyday life, you might notice that some people do not follow society's norms or that their values and norms are different from yours. For example, some may think that eating frog legs is a sign of high culture, whereas others view it with disdain. In some societies, premarital sex is acceptable and is a test of love and compatibility, whereas in other societies, the same behaviour is viewed as promiscuity and even prostitution. What these examples suggest is that people adhere to different cultural values, beliefs, and norms. In this sense, **culture** refers to a set of values, norms, mores, laws, and so on that prevail in a given society. **Values** are abstract principles, which in and of themselves are neither true nor false, neither good nor bad. They are cultural conceptions about desirable goals that result in judgment of actions. Equality, justice, freedom, diversity, compassion, respect, and order are some of the values that we may be encouraged to have. However, these values only have meaning in relation to their opposites. Equality has meaning in relation to inequality, and such meaning differs by place, time, and context. For example, during slavery, slaves were subject to the will of the master. They were bought and sold without having any rights. At that time, slavery was acceptable, at least among the slave owners. In modern times, we look at slavery with disdain and refer to it as our dark past.

Once values become institutionalized, they are referred to as norms. Institutionalization of norms means that they are supported by an organized system of social relationships. An **institution** includes highly standardized behaviours with supporting attitudes and values that have traditions and rituals. Every society requires certain basic institutions for its survival (see

Box 4.1

Five basic social institutions that regulate values, norms, and behaviours include:

Family: issues related to marriage, divorce, childbearing and child rearing, housework, and maintenance of the family.

Religion: issues related to prayer, faith, morality, place of worship.

Education: issues related to learning, schooling, knowledge, science, and innovations.

Economy: issues related to investment, banking, capital, productivity, and growth.

Government: issues related to welfare, public work, tax, laws, policing, and war.

Box 4.1).

Norms are standard rules and expectations about what we should or should not do. To be quiet during a lecture in class and to wash your hands before dinner are both norms. Norms are not necessarily stable. They change over time. For example, before the 1960s, it was the norm not to have premarital sex. Now the norm has changed. The new norm is that if you have premarital sex, you should have safe sex. One specific type of norm are *folkways,* which govern everyday behaviour. They are not formalized but shape behaviours such as walking on the right side in the pedestrian walkways, something based on tacit agreement between the users of public space. **Mores** (pronounced "MOR-AYS") are a much stronger set of norms. They must be followed because they are the most cherished principles and are essential for the survival of a society. For example, there are strong mores against murder and eating human flesh in all cultures. Once norms become formally written and legislated, they become **laws.** Today there are laws against slavery, incest, and genocide. Therefore, generally, all laws are based on norms, and all norms are based on values. In contrast, not all values are norms, and not all norms are laws.

Culture is more than values, norms, and laws. It includes both material and nonmaterial aspects of a society. Material cultures such as houses differ from one society to another. Some houses are made of wood, and others are made of bricks. Some societies have TVs, DVDs, computers, cars, and planes, and others do not or have them to a lesser degree. It is important to remember that all shared products of a society, material or nonmaterial, are part of that society's culture.

Descriptive beliefs are ideas about what was, what is, and what will be. They may be right or wrong, but nevertheless they shape our values. If we say God or Allah made the universe, we are merely describing how the universe was made. This description shapes our understanding of the world we live in and justifies its existence or its future through the act of a supreme being. **Normative beliefs** are ideas about what must be, ought to be, or should be. They also shape our values and behaviours. If we say that a Christian should attend church every Sunday and a Muslim should attend the mosque every Friday, we are expressing normative beliefs. Although religious books and teachings are filled with normative beliefs, such beliefs can exist in its secular form, too. The statements that the gap between rich and poor should be reduced or that hard work should be rewarded accordingly are both examples of a more secular form of normative beliefs.

Ideology

Another important aspect of a culture is **ideology.** It is an emotionally charged set of descriptive and normative beliefs and values that tend to justify or question various social institutions of that society. Ideologies are commonsense beliefs to which people adhere. They are not necessarily wrong, but they tend to be incomplete and biased. Whether an ideology justifies or questions a specific aspect of the society, it is always a one-sided method of inquiry that fails to see, consider, and/or understand the situation of the opposite group (see Box 4.2) As an example, the ideology that success is due to hard work tends to justify blaming the unemployed as lazy or stupid. It fails to see the opposite view that unemployment is due to economic crisis often created by profit-motivated actions and/or poor economic planning. Ideologies are social products and are generally framed, understood, and enforced within a specific culture. Ideas about religious beliefs, customs, fashions, magic, and superstitions are solely human social products and vary from culture to culture. As Box 4.2 shows, most people or about 75 to 85 percent of people in Canada, the U.S., and Sweden tend to be reformist in their ideological orientations, seeking gradual changes in their society.

Box 4.2

Ideologies are commonly expressed in a continuum and are generally divided into three broad categories:

Conservative ideologies tend to support and protect the status quo, the way things are.

Reformist ideologies tend to seek some minor modification on the status quo, such as improving the taxing system, employment insurance, or the health care.

Radical ideologies tend to suggest and seek fundamental change to the status quo such as the replacement of the capitalist system with a new and more egalitarian system. It is also called counter ideology.

Percentage of people agreeing with different types of ideology by country

Types of Ideology	Question	Canada	U.S.	Sweden
Radical	Society must be radically changed	7.0	6.6	4.4
Reformist	Society must be gradually improved by reform	77.7	75.1	85.5
Conservative	Society must be valiantly defended	15.3	18.3	10.1

Source: World Values Survey (2009).

Dominant ideology refers to beliefs and practices that help and support the interests of powerful, social, economic, and political groups in society. This concept is rooted in the Marxist tradition which states that economic elites who own most of the wealth and means of production in a society also control the political apparatus and means of ideological production and reproduction such as media. By controlling the means of ideological production, they also reproduce their values so they become the values of others (see Box 4.3). The evidence in Box 4.4 shows that, despite some differences, a common trend among capitalist democracies is to support income inequality and competition and be skeptical of government's ownership of businesses.

Box 4.3

Marx on Dominant Ideology: "The ideas of the ruling class are in every epoch the ruling ideas, i.e. the class which is the ruling material force of society, is at the same time its ruling intellectual force. The class which has the means of material production at its disposal, has control at the same time over the means of mental production, so that thereby, generally speaking, the ideas of those who lack the means of mental production are subject to it."

(Marx, 1976, p. 67)

Box 4.4

Average support for some aspects of dominant ideology*	Canada	U.S.	Sweden
Support for inequality	5.82	6.08	6.11
Support for government ownership of businesses	4.39	3.71	4.79
Support for competition	7.18	7.52	7.61

    * Least support = 1, most support = 10
Source: World Values Survey (2009).

Subculture and Counterculture

The forgoing suggests that cultural values and beliefs may not be uniform and predominant in all segments of the society. Some groups or segments of the population may accept some of the dominant culture prevalent in a society but also have their own distinctiveness. These distinctive groups are called subcultures. A **subculture** is a group of individuals who share the dominant culture but also have their own distinctive values, norms, and behaviours.

You can see examples of subculture by looking at occupations, generations, provinces, or student groups. Each of these groups share the overall culture of the society but also has their own distinctiveness. Lawyers, medical doctors, scientists, students, younger generations, and Quebeckers are generally distinctive in their values, beliefs, behaviours, and rituals when compared to other segments of the population. You may rarely see an elderly person wearing a jean with holes, while among the youth this may be a sign of **status.** When a segment of the population deliberately opposes some aspects of the larger culture, we call them **countercultures.** The anti-establishment student movement in the 60s is an example of counter culture, as are hippies who challenged the dominant definition of sexuality and appearance, or the Occupy Wall Street movement that challenged capitalist concentration of wealth. Many liberation movements are at first countercultures, but once they succeed, they become the dominant culture.

Role of Culture in Human Achievement

Culture is one of the most important elements of human society, distinguishing us from animals. It allows individuals to learn values, norms, laws, new discoveries, and products from the past, share what they have learned with others, and transmit them to the next generation and other societies. Animals act instinctively and start anew in each generation. Humans, in contrast, produce culture (material and nonmaterial) and pass it to the next generation. In turn, culture produces people and the future generations. Imagine trying to learn how to hunt with spears, to build a house, a car, a plane, the space shuttles, or probes in order to travel between planets. If we were to rely on each generation starting from scratch, none of these things would have been possible. Accumulation of culture across generations resulted in the unprecedented success of humans when compared to other species.

In order to appreciate the importance of culture, we need to travel back in time. We can demonstrate this by the evolution of planet Earth, the human species, and their various activities. Scientists believe that Earth was formed about 4.7 billion years ago and the first organisms emerged about three billion years ago. It took about another two and half billion years until the earliest land animals emerged.

One of the first important events in the human evolution was the emergence of mammals about 180 million years ago. Mammals have an exceptional capacity to learn from experience, something that we almost entirely rely on. The second important event was the emergence of higher primates, about 70 million years ago. They are our immediate ancestors. They lived in groups, were highly sociable and intelligent, were extremely vocal, and had sensitive hands that enabled them to use their thumb and place it opposite to their forefinger. Their sensitive hands enabled them the capacity to have a firm and precise grip, which in humans helped in food-gathering, hunting, sewing, writing, and other dexterity-based activities. Moreover, their capacity to use and manipulate sounds helped the development of symbols and human language. Most primates are tree dwellers and spend much of their lives above the forest floor. These include apes and monkeys. Apes are the closest relatives of modern humans. They differ from humans in that their movements are mostly through swinging from branches and trees to branches and trees.

The third important event was that some primates diverged from their tree dweller relatives by being forced to leave the trees most likely due to drastic climate changes or forest fire that resulted in the destruction of forests and creation of open savannahs. These primates became ground dwellers, and those who were strong and adaptable were able to adjust to the new situation. As they moved on their two legs and used their arms less, their legs became longer and arms shorter compared to the body length of their ape relatives. Humans as *homo erectus* emerged about two million years ago and moved out of Africa into Mesopotamia and Asia about one million years ago, then further to Europe about half a million years ago. *Homo sapiens* emerged about 200 thousand years ago. About 40 thousand years ago, *Homo sapiens* outnumbered and outsmarted their Neanderthal predecessors and forced them into extinction. Humans moved into North America only about 12 thousand years ago and to South America about 10 thousand years ago. Modern humans have a larger brain size (about 1,350 cc) than apes (about 500 cc).

Despite the fact that at birth human offspring are not physically stronger than many other animal or primates, they end up being the most powerful beings on Earth. There are several reasons for human success. Although gestation period is generally the same for most apes (gorillas, orangutans, chimpanzees) and humans (between 230 to 260 days), human development is substantially accelerated at the end of the gestation. The human brain is substantially larger than that of other primates at birth—the human brain size at birth is about 400 cc, compared to our closest relative chimpanzee with a brain size of 200 cc at birth. The large brain size helps the infant child learn, through the relationship with family and others, a significant amount of knowledge and experiences that is accumulated in many generations

Humans have the tendency for year-round sexual accessibility, and human infants are dependent on their parents for a long time. These traits tend to promote strong bonding relationships, increase the learning potential of children, and expand the division of labour. Through environmental adaptation, learning from past experiences, and generational transfer of knowledge, humans were able to use new tools, but more importantly, they became tool makers. They became actively involved in the production of tools, which helped their survival and subsistence. They laboured and produced their means of subsistence, which they created themselves by means of cooperation. Production brought members of society close together, where they cooperated to produce each other's needs. Being together meant that they communicated with each other orally, symbolically, and ultimately through a specific language. Language and communication resulted in the capacity for abstract thinking and reasoning. Since most human vocabulary consists of words where the sounds have little intrinsic connections with the objects they denote, humans needed to learn the meanings of these objects through conventional symbols shared by members of the society. Language allowed humans to acquire socially produced and symbolically shared knowledge and experiences of the past generations, and then produce more. Each generation did not need to start from the scratch by repeating trials and errors of the past generations. If each generation was to learn anew, humans would have not been able to go to the moon. Through language, humans learned the past socially accumulated knowledge and experience. Labour and language also meant further development of division of labour and goal-oriented activities. At first, men were involved in hunting and women in food gathering, young became warriors and old became educators and cultural transmitters to children. Later, the division of labour expended based on skill, experience, and speed of production. By now, humans were well underway in producing more than they needed and so they began accumulating and saving for drought and winter seasons and for their offspring.

Humans' ability to use and make tools, to communicate through language and symbols, and to cooperate resulted in the expansion of the division of labour and accumulation of surplus product for unexpected events and times. These capacities accelerated their environmental adaptation and increased their ability to produce their or future generations' means of subsistence. These skills helped humans to mutually support each other and mutually benefit from the labour they performed; thus, they were able to control their natural environment. They became masters of their own destiny rather than being enslaved to nature like their predecessors.

The above evolutionary changes resulted in the use of tools (about two million years ago), use of fire and organized hunting (about half a million years ago), development of arts (about a quarter million years ago), creation of funeral performance as well as fishing (about 100 thousand years ago), development of sewing (about 30 thousand years ago), expertise in farming and the formation of the earliest civilization (about 10 thousand years ago). The extensive evolutionary time period allowed humans to adjust and adapt to their environment and transmit their new skills, techniques, behaviours, and rituals to the next generation. This process was not linear and similar in all regions. For example, Mediterranean areas alone were responsible for the discovery and distribution of 32 out of 56 large-seeded grass species. Dogs, sheep, and goats were domesticated about 10 thousand years ago in Southwest Asia, while donkeys and horses were domesticated about four thousand years ago in Egypt and the Ukraine respectively. Indo-European languages date back to six to eight thousand years, while the Tibetan language dates back to about six thousand years ago (for details see Diamond, 1999).

Ethnocentrism and Cultural Relativism

The aforementioned discussion also points to the diversity of human culture. This diversity cannot be understood if we look at others just through our own way of life—**ethnocentrism.** We also need to adopt an outsider's point of view—**cultural relativism.** That is, we need to recognize that other cultures cannot be judged by our own cultural standards. For instance, we may not like that the Japanese criticize us for abandoning our elderly by leaving them apart from the family and in old-age homes. Yet we criticize the traditional Inuit culture that left the aged to die in the snow. We may be quick to view our religion as the one true faith and others as full of superstitions. We brag that our soldiers are brave and state that the soldiers of the enemy are inhuman or terrorists. These examples suggest that it is often hard to view one's own culture objectively. One of the reasons for such ethnocentrism or for a sense of cultural superiority is that it tends to develop social cohesion, faith, and confidence in one's culture. These, in turn, build a close-minded thought process that prevents us from looking at other cultures from their point of view.

Culture Shock and Cultural Diffusion

The diversity of human culture sometimes results in **culture shock** where one's own cultural views become profoundly questioned when one encounters another culture. Imagine how some Europeans and Muslims may think when encountering each other's dress code, sexual behaviours, and interaction with the elderly and parents. Similarly, such diversity may result in cultural diffusion through interaction. Nowadays, we notice that Chinese and Italian foods have become more common on the North American and European dinner tables, as it is more common to see McDonald's, Coca-Cola, or Mexican food finding their way into Asian and African eating habits.

Cultural diffusion started early in human society, when food, language, writing, printing, industries, clothing materials, and other cultural objects moved back and forth between different countries through trade, sometimes peacefully and other times through wars and invasions. The diffusion of spices exemplifies a past that included war while that of *I Love Lucy* and *Gossip Girl* may be more peaceful diffusions. Given American economic worldwide domination, it is not a surprise that we see American pop culture such as rock music or Coco-Cola becoming universal cultural items. When we see that Starbucks has spread into a predominantly tea-drinking China, we can attest to the cultural diffusion of the American ways of life. **Cultural diffusion** means the spreading of a culture, blurring of cultural boundaries, and borrowing of cultural elements from another society. Many societies fearful of losing their own culture attempt to limit such cultural imperialism. In Canada, the Canadian Radio-Television and Telecommunication Commission is mandated to protect Canadian talent and creativity by limiting exposure of the non-Canadian content on television. In other countries, this task is given to their heritage ministries and or other institutions. Cultural diffusion does not just mean adoption and use of the specific cultural items from another culture; it also means the spread of a way of life. **McDonaldization,** or melding of cultures, similarity of cultural expressions, and the spread of fast-food services is strongly resisted by the French who prefer fine cuisines, slow eating, a bottle of wine, and a prolonged conversation over the dinner table. Similarly, the spread of the American style of one-place shopping such as in supermarkets or superstores means a destruction of small businesses.

Multiculturalism

Given constant increased communication between different cultures and cheap and speedy transportation, people tend to move from one place to another for economic, social, and political reasons. This means that most societies are populated by people of different cultures. In order to accommodate such diversities, governments often have enacted multicultural policies. In Canada, **multiculturalism** is built on the three pillars of social justice, civic participation, and identity (specifically, a sense of belonging to Canada). The success of multiculturalism in Canada and elsewhere and whether it is a source of identity formation or division is subject to intense debate. The same events are used by both proponents and opponents to justify or question the merits of multiculturalism. The riots in Paris, France and London, England can be used to justify the failure of multiculturalism or conversely to seek legislation to ensure equity and justice among different ethnocultural groups.

Cultural Comparison: Canada and the United States

People often develop a better understanding of their own culture and society by comparing themselves to others. Canadians, for example, have a tendency to compare themselves to Americans. Canadians view themselves as polite, shy, and timid, while they view Americans as nationalistic, loud, and disrespectful. In recent times, however, there are signs that Canadians are as nationalistic and loud as their neighbour to the South (see Box 4.5 for a beer commercial aired in the spring of 2000).

Other examples include T-shirts stating that "Canada kicks ass" or "Canadian girls kick ass." The popular rock song "American Woman" by the Guess Who is arguably an anti-American song written by Canadian musicians. Although these examples suggest that Canadians are becoming more similar to their American neighbour by being loud and nationalistic, it is not clear from these examples if this similarity has been there in the past or is even present now. To know this, we need comparative sociological studies.

Seymour Martin Lipset (1963, 1965, 1986, 1990, 2001), one of the eminent American

---

Box 4.5

"The Rant," a spot for Molson Canadian, featured a young man known only as "Joe," who stands on stage before a screen which flashes Canadian images while he outlines what makes Canada unique. Joe begins his rant shyly, hesitantly, but slowly gains confidence, building to an heroic crescendo and climaxing with the tag line, "My name is Joe, and I am Canadian!"… Within days of its release, "The Rant" was being discussed in media across the country (and beyond), parodied on the radio, and repeated live to cheering crowds at hockey games.

(Millard, Riegel, & Wright, 2002)

---

sociologists, has been involved for decades in comparing Canada and the United States. He has argued that Canada and the United States differ from each other on the basis of a five-value system that he called the American Creed: **liberty, egalitarianism, individualism, populism,** and **laissez-faire.** Lipset has argued that the root of these differences is in the American Revolution, which produced enduring cultural differences between the two countries. The Canadians are exemplified by the United Empire Loyalists, who left the United States as an opposition to the American Revolution and in support of the Empire (Britain). Thus, Canada was born out of counter-revolution, whereas the United States was born of revolution. In a series of articles and a book, Grabb, Curtis, and colleagues (2005) have provided evidence that there is little U.S./Canada difference in these core values. Michael Carroll (2005) takes up this debate and argues that this debate is irresolvable because each side has come to the table adhering to unacknowledged ideology in terms of which is the best type of democracy: Canadian or American. Lipset believes that the American democracy is best, while Grabb and his colleagues believe that the U.K. and Canadian democracies are the best. Box 4.6 shows that there are more similarities than differences between Canada and the United States but also that the American value system seems to be more different from UK values when compared to the Canadians.

Box 4.6 Values and Beliefs by Country

	Canada %	U.S. %	U.K. %	France %	Sweden %
Trusting values					
Most people can be trusted	42.8	39.3	30.5	18.8	68.0
I trust my family	98.1	97.6	97.9	95.5	99.6
Gender values					
When jobs are scarce men should have more rights to a job than women	14.4	6.8	16.3	18.1	2.0
Men make better political leaders than women do	18.3	24.7	19.7	21.2	7.7
Men make better business executives than women do	11.3	16.4	16.9	14.3	7.5
Approves of woman as a single parent	46.4	52.2	33.5	62.3	49.1
Political beliefs					
Interested in politics	52.6	59.1	44.1	36.8	59.4
Willingness to fight for country: yes	60.4	63.1	61.5	61.1	85.8
Personal beliefs					
I decide my goals in life by myself	87.2	81.8	87.2	77.6	95.3
I have freedom of choice and control	86.1	86.8	83.2	68.7	91.1
Religious beliefs					
A religious person	66.7	72.0	48.7	47.0	33.5

Source: World Values Survey (2009).

Summary

Culture consists of values, beliefs and ideas as well as the material objects we have inherited from the past that have helped to produce and reproduce us. It is the most important glue creating solidarity among members of the society and the reason for unprecedented success of human society. Culture could also be a source of conflict and divisions if there are cultural differences among segments of a society or among various societies.

We can also look at culture theoretically by explaining how the four broad sociological theories explain culture. Functionalists view culture as meeting a need such as helping with the survival of human society. Conflict theorists view culture as the production and reproduction of value and belief systems of the dominant groups, serving their own interests. Symbolic interactionists view culture as being actively created and recreated through interaction. Feminists pay attention to how femininity and masculinity are created in order to mostly serve men's interests.

Key Terms

Counterculture: deliberate opposition to some aspects of the broader culture.

Cultural diffusion: blurring of cultural boundaries through intrusion of cultures.

Cultural relativism: the practice of judging a culture by its own standards.

Culture: a set of values, norms, mores, and laws, and so on that prevail in a given society or part of it.

Culture shock: an experience in a profound questioning of one's cultural view.

Descriptive beliefs: ideas about what is, was and will be.

Dominant ideology: a set of emotionally charged normative and descriptive beliefs that prevail in society and are consistent with that of the dominant groups.

Egalitarianism: a belief in political, economic, and social equality between people (e.g., each person to be treated equally under the law).

Ethnocentrism: the practice of judging members of another cultural group by one's own cultural standards; a belief in superiority of one's own culture.

Ideology: a set of charged normative and descriptive beliefs that justify and/or challenge the existing order of society.

Individualism: contrast to egalitarianism; the right of individuals to challenge important beliefs and institutions.

Institution: highly standardized behaviour with common traditions, rituals, and supporting values.

Laissez faire: nonintervention of the state into economic activities; greater liberty of trade and business.

Law: a set of formally codified legal rules or norms that either forbid or permit specific behaviours or relationships among people.

Liberty: conditions in which individuals have immunity and are protected from arbitrary exercise of authority or power.

McDonaldization: George Ritzer's view on melding and spread of the fast-food industry into traditional cultures.

Mores: set of norms that must be followed because the survival of the society may depend on them.

Multiculturalism: policies designed to ensure cultural and ethnic maintenance of ethnic groups and to promote equality of opportunity for all ethnic groups in Canada. Social justice, identity, and engagement are the three pillars of multiculturalism.

Normative beliefs: ideas about what must be, should be, and ought to be.

Norms: institutionalized values.

Populism: a view that espouses direct political participation of the people in the government.

Society: an interacting group of people with shared culture living in the same territory.

Status: the relative prestige or position of an individual and its negative and positive perception by others.

Subculture: a distinctive culture within a broader culture.

Values: abstract principles that guide human actions.

Critical Thinking Questions

1. What are the key elements of being Canadian, and how are these distinguishable from American culture, if at all?

2. Think about values and ideas related to mate selection and behaviour and identify some of the differences between you and your friends and acquaintances from different cultures. Why do you think there are differences?

3. What is the "best" sort of democracy? How does one come to an understanding of the "best" democracy? Can and should democracy be imposed on other countries by wars and invasions? Why?

4. Think of your everyday life and itemize various cultural elements that you encounter in a day. What and how many are these? Classify them based on the key concepts provided in this

chapter.

5. What are some of the rules and codes of conduct for students in your college/university? Are they poorly or inconsistently enforced? What are some of the potential consequences of these rules or codes of conduct if they are inconsistently enforced?

6. How do various cultural elements encountered in question 4 constrain you? Can they also be liberating?

7. Think of various ideas that prevail in Canada. Are any of them part of the dominant ideology? If so, how do they affect social justice or equality?

8. Provide examples of cultural shocks you have encountered. Why do you consider them to be cultural shocks?

9. Has multiculturalism been successful in Canada? Why?

10. Why have humans been more successful than other species inhabiting the planet Earth?

Useful Internet Sites

1. A critical look at culture and media   http://rburnett.ecuad.ca/

2. Cultural resources   http://www.sociosite.net/topics/culture.php

3. Definition of culture   http://anthro.palomar.edu/culture/Default.htm

4. What is culture? Foreign Affairs and International Trade Canada

http://www.dfait-maeci.gc.ca/cfsi-icse/cil-cai/whatisculture-questlaculture-eng.asp

5. PowerPoint on culture

http://www.truworld.ca/__shared/assets/culture_in_the_classroom13174.pdf

6. Culture from Aboriginal's perspective

http://www.aboriginalconstructioncareers.ca/toolkit/what-culture-and-why-does-it-matter

Sociological Example: Three Views of the Downing of Flight 655*

Introduction: Research Purpose

Recall that culture entails a set of values, norms, ideas, beliefs, and laws that prevail in a given society. Culture is learned and transmitted from one generation to another through language or other means of communication. An important aspect of a culture is ideology. Ideology is an emotionally charged set of descriptive and normative beliefs and values that tend to justify or question various social institutions of a society. Ideologies are commonsense beliefs to which people adhere. They are not necessarily wrong, but they tend to be incomplete and biased. Whether an ideology justifies or questions a specific aspect of a society, it is always a one-sided method of inquiry that fails to see, appreciate, or understand the situation of other cultural groups. At any given time in a society, one type of ideology tends to be more dominant than others.

Dominant ideology refers to beliefs and practices that help and support the interests of powerful, social, economic, and political groups in society. This concept is rooted in the Marxist tradition which states that economic elites who own most of the wealth and means of production in a society also control the political apparatus and means of ideological production and reproduction such as media. By controlling the means of ideological production, they also reproduce their values as that of others. If a dominant ideology that prevails in one society is different from the ideology of another society, ideological **ethnocentrism** tends to develop. In order to understand the importance of distinctive dominant ideologies or ideological ethnocentrism, we need to compare two or more countries. For example, we can perform a natural experiment by comparing two or more countries' views on a specific event. This comparison will help us in better understanding our culture and society.

---

* Based on Nakhaie and Pike (1995, pp. 309–311).

A Natural Experiment ?

On July 3, 1988, an Iranian passenger plane (Flight 655) was shot down by an American warship patrolling the Persian Gulf; all passengers (290 people) on board this flight were killed. How did the American and Iranian media present this event? What about the Canadian media? If portrayal of this same event by the media in these three countries is different we can point to different **hegemonic** (or dominant) ideologies of these countries.

Theoretical Explanation

Most scholars believe that the media present a distorted image of reality. There are several different ways that media's presentation can be explained:

- Media gatekeepers such as owners or editors tend to have a specific view of the world, and they tend to select editors or journalists with similar views.
- The primary motive of media companies is to make profit; therefore, media tend to present views that are consistent with their audience, readers, and advertisers.
- Media gatekeepers and journalists are immersed in the culture in which they have been socialized and therefore present views that are consistent with this socialization.
- Journalists and editors are socialized in the media organization with past history and practice, so those past practices ensure conformity of the new employees.

These explanations can be synthesized into a view consistent with the cultural or hegemonic ideology model discussed above. This model highlights the importance of the prevailing ideology in a society that helps reproduce itself. The hegemonic ideology shapes both the working of the media and the reproduction of values, norms, and ideologies. According to this model, the social structure, relations of production, profit motives, as well as institutional goals can exert a powerful influence on the everyday work of journalists and media institutions because these agents are already socialized into, and subsequently tend to reflect, the existing social arrangements (see Rachlin, 1988). The work of journalists and the media is constrained by and reflective of a society and the socialization that takes place within it. Therefore, the distortions in media reports do not represent deliberate attempts to skew reality but are instead reflections of the society's culture, attitudes, beliefs, social structures, economics, and politics. This hegemonic ideology is present in all of the major institutions of society and often produces cultural ethnocentrism. Culturally ethnocentric perspectives tend to reduce media and reporter consideration of alternative viewpoints.

The hegemonic ideology model has been criticized for presenting an overly simplified version of the effect that ideology has on the media and journalist activities. More specifically, this model fails to acknowledge the potential for dissent from the dominant ideology as it presents these worldviews as unified and unchallenged forces while presenting journalists as passive agents promoting the dominant ideology. While dominant ideology often plays an important role in shaping how journalists perceive the world and report on events, there are certainly instances in which the media has challenged state and societal views. This is because journalists are in fact active rather than passive agents. Journalists do not simply reiterate the dominant or official account of events. So if a specific ideology is pervasive in a society and media agents are active and not passive agents of the news, then how do they process issues and events that are contrary to the dominant views?

In order to answer this question, we need to look at the literature that evaluates deviants' and criminals' vocabulary of motives. In this regard, the work of Skyes and Matza (1957) is instructive. According to Skyes and Matza, individuals who commit deviant acts often engage in a process of rationalization or **"techniques of neutralization"** that allow them to interpret their own violations in a way that is acceptable to their internalized cultural ideology. For instance, an offender may "deny responsibility" for their actions by attributing the act to forces outside their control. They "deny the victim," by arguing that the injury is not wrong in light of circumstances. They may even "blame the victim" by arguing that the victim was responsible for the event. This process of rationalization allows the offender the ability to deny that their act was criminal or deviant in nature and therefore still adhere, in their own mind, to the dominant moral values of the society.

Therefore, when journalists encounter situations that challenge their beliefs and morals, they may use methods of rationalization that are very similar to the techniques of neutralization used by deviants. This allows journalists the ability to diminish their doubts and render accounts of an event justifiable and acceptable according to the standards of their dominant ideology. For instance, the dominant ideology of a journalist's country may tell them that killing people is wrong; however, a journalist may interpret and present their nation's military actions against an enemy country as necessary and justifiable, while at the same time they may interpret and present similar military actions made by another nation against their own country as being inhumane and barbaric. This "double standard" is rationalized by the journalists through developing a "stigma theory," which accounts for a person's (or a social system's) inferiority, imputing to them a wide range of imperfections. This rationalization then allows differential treatment of persons or societies (see Goffman, 1963).

Previous Research

There have been several previous studies that have explored hegemonic ideology and media accounts of events. Rachlin (1988) analyzed newspaper and magazine articles from the United States, Canada, and Cuba that pertained to the destruction of Korean Flight 007 by a Soviet fighter. This plane was shot down in the darkness over the USSR (the Soviet Union of Socialist Russia, prior to 1980) airspace in a militarily sensitive area where an American spy plane had just been spotted. Therefore, there is a possibility that the Russian pilot or air controller could have made a mistake. However, during this time period, the United States deemed Russia to be an "evil empire," and American journalistic accounts of this event reflected this view accordingly. The American journalists failed to consider alternative explanations for the destruction, choosing to only favour explanations provided by American leaders, and the American view of the event was presented as being the complete and accurate story. If views different from the dominant or hegemonic views were presented to the American journalists, they often assessed these contrary views as lacking legitimacy and consequently quickly discounted them. They were presented as being distorted and manipulated.

In another study, Entman (1991) explored the news coverage surrounding Flight 007 and the media coverage of Iranian Flight 655. His findings not only confirmed Rachlin's thesis but also revealed that the American journalists lessened the importance of their country's attack on Flight 655. The American journalists reported that the incident was the result of a technological mistake. In comparison to the American media's coverage of Flight 007, the coverage surrounding Flight 655 was presented in a manner that was more neutralized and less humanized. For instance, while the American media presented the Korean passengers as victims, the media failed to grant similar victim status to the Iranian passengers.

Research Importance and Questions

While previous research has explored media reports of the Iranian Flight 655 incident, this research did not take into account the active participation of the reporters in rationalizing the event to be congruent to their own dominant culture. For this purpose, we need a comparative framework. We need to compare media coverage in different countries. What follows is comparative analyses of the rationalization process of media in the offending country (United States), the victim country (Iran), and a neutral third-party country (Canada).

Research Questions

1. How do the national hegemonic ideologies affect media accounts of Flight 655?
2. How do the media rationalize and neutralize the Flight 655 event?

Based on the theoretical model, we can hypothesize that the journalists of the offending, victimized, and neutral countries would rationalize their accounts of the event in order to make it correspond with their dominant ideology. A clear divergence in the American and Iranian media accounts of the event was expected because Iran and the United States have very different dominant or hegemonic cultures, whereas Canada and the United States are generally similar. At the time of this event, Iran viewed the United States as the "Great Satan," which previously helped overthrow a democratically elected Iranian prime minister in the 1953 coup d'état, destroyed Iranian oil platforms, and provided military and reconnaissance help to Iraq in a war that was initiated by Saddam Hussein of Iraq against Iran. The United States, on the other hand, viewed Iran as a threat because of its independence, its anti-imperialist revolution, and the 1979 hostage crisis. Canada can generally be considered a neutral country in that it was not involved in the downing of Flight 655. However, due to its cultural and geographical proximity to the United States, Canada's dominant ideology is more similar to the United States than to Iran.

Requirement for Testing the Relationship

In order to conduct this study, an influential national newspaper from each of the three countries was selected. *Keyhan* (Iran), *The New York Times* (NYT, U.S.), and *The Globe and Mail* (G&M, Canada) were each analyzed for a period of two weeks (Monday, July 4 to Saturday, July 16, 1988).

A content analysis was used to explore the importance of hegemonic ideology as well as the journalists' rationalization process. The analysis included evaluation of issues such as the overall coverage (space, number of articles, front page articles, and pictures pertaining to the event), identification of the responsible agent for downing Flight 655, identification of motives (deliberate, understandable, or a mistake), and responsibility (criminalization, neutralization, and humanization).

Do the Findings Support the Hypotheses?

Keyhan wrote more articles about the incident than the NYT and G&M combined; it also included more relevant photographs than the two Western newspapers. *Keyhan* gave more prominence to this event than other papers. Its coverage was 7.6 times more than NYT and 9.9 times more than G&M. There were also important differences between how the news sources reported on the event (see Tables 4.1.1, 4.1.2, and 4.1.3). *Keyhan* claimed that the event was a deliberate act by the United States and presented the downing of Flight 655 as "criminal" (66.6 percent) and "barbaric" (20.1 percent). It also viewed it as "a tragedy" and a "massacre." The victims were presented as "martyrs" (53.2 percent), "innocents" (20.8 percent), or children (20.8 percent).

Table 4.1.1 Value Identification of Downing Flight 655*

	Keyhan	*New York Times*	*Globe & Mail*
Presented as			
Deliberate	130 (29.3)	39 (13.2)	28 (21.1)
Understandable	12 (2.7)	46 (15.5)	8 (6.0)
Mistake	41 (9.2)	83 (28.0)	36 (27.1)
Fault of Victim	15 (3.4)	75 (25.3)	37 (27.9)

* Numbers in parentheses are the ratio of act mentioned to one square metre (m^2) of coverage of the event in the paper.

Source: Nakhaie and Pike (1995, pp. 309–331).

Table 4.1.2 Neutralization of Downing Flight 655*

	Keyhan		New York Times		Globe & Mail	
	#	%	#	%	#	%
Tragedy	255	61.6	42	26.4	42	31.5
Incident/event	56	13.5	78	49.1	70	52.6
Travellers/passgr./civiln.	53	12.8	16	10	13	9.8
Victims	50	12.1	23	14.5	8	6
Total	414		159		133	
Per m² of coverage	93.3		53.7		100.2	

* Number of times act mentioned in these terms, and percentages.

Source: Nakhaie and Pike (1995, pp. 309–331).

Table 4.1.3 Criminalization of Downing Flight 655*

	Keyhan		New York Times		Globe & Mail	
	#	%	#	%	#	%
Criminal/crime	451	66.6	11	17.2	12	30
Barbaric/inhuman/atrocious	141	20.1	11	17.2	6	15
Terrorist act	33	4.9	3	4.7	5	12.5
Massacre/murder	37	5.2	7	10.9	8	20
Kill	15	2.2	32	50	9	22.5
Total	677		64		40	
Per m² of coverage	152.7		21.6		30.1	

* Number of times act mentioned in these terms, and percentages.

Source: Nakhaie and Pike (1995, pp. 309–331).

In contrast, the NYT identified the event as "understandable," a "mistake," an "incident," or an "'accident." The NYT reports also tended to blame the victim by incorrectly stating that the plane did not properly transmit a signal. The NYT also rarely attributed personal or human attributes to the victims. Overall, NYT media presentations transformed Iran (the victim) into a nation deserving of injury, denied it the right to be a victim, and even blamed it for the event.

Finally, the immediate news coverage in the G&M was very similar to that of the American media, as it relied heavily on American news sources and "objective" Canadian officials to make sense of the event. These officials categorized the event as a "defensive action" and made an effort to discredit the Iranian versions of the incident. Over a period of time, reports began to emerge in the Canadian news that challenged American accounts of the event. Overall, American articles were more likely than Canadian articles to present the event as an understandable mistake or to blame the victim.

It is important to note that the Western journalists faced a moral dilemma when trying to neutralize the Iranian attempts to criminalize their actions, as the United States had previously criminalized the USSR for the destruction of Flight 007. To neutralize this dilemma, journalists emphasized official statements that denied any similarity and tried to highlight key differences between the two events. In addition, the Western media solved their moral dilemma by reporting and discounting Iranian sources on the issue. In contrast, the American destruction of Flight 655 was deemed by *Keyhan* journalists to be more hideous than the Russian destruction of Flight 007.

Finally, mention should be made of the newspapers' use of maps. One of the maps in *Keyhan* showed the explosion of the plane in Iranian water space and within the international air corridor. This and other maps informed the reader of U.S. responsibility and the concomitant victimization of Iran. Maps in the NYT were used to place the blame on the Iranian plane and emphasize that the shooting may have been a mistake. The first map showed a small plane exploding outside the international air corridor in the Persian Gulf. The second map did not show a plane, but an arrow pointed to the site of the plane wreckage outside the international air corridor. If the plane is depicted as being small and outside the international air corridor, then it is hard to distinguish the type of plane. It is therefore easy to see that the ship's crew made a mistake by viewing it as a smaller military jet and not a commercial plane. The map in the G&M showed the Persian Gulf (no ship, plane, or missile) with the plane route from Iran to Dubai.

What Can Be Concluded from the Findings?

This study shows that media reports do not reflect the reality; instead, they reflect an event's significance to national values, government, tastes, politics, worldviews, and social relations. For instance, Iranian media never entertained the possibility that the downing of Flight 655 was an accident. Due to the recent cultural ideology of Iran, which was built on a general distrust of American **imperialism,** its media emphasized the deliberate nature of the attack. This political culture as well as facts of the event led to far less opportunity for Iranian journalists to deviate from the dominant official line, in comparison to a somewhat wider albeit slight freedom of deviation for American and Canadian journalists.

The impact of hegemonic ideology was also apparent in the G&M news coverage. While the G&M initially provided coverage that was very similar to that of the NYT, this was likely due to the Canadian newspaper's reliance on American media and political sources. As previously noted, over a period of time, accounts began to emerge in the G&M that served to challenge American accounts of the downing of Flight 655. For example, international agencies, consistent with the Iranian version of events, confirmed that the plane was shot down in Iranian water space. This divergent news coverage supports Hackett's (1991, p. 129) argument that Canada lacks "a monolithic dominant ideology" and Hiller's (1991) argument that Canadian history and culture identity somewhat oppose American policies and the U.S. "melting pot."

What Are the Possible Policy Implications?

The implication of our discussion on culture is that we should be critical of many of our everyday commonsense beliefs. We need to evaluate their ideological underpinnings, which may justify the existing order of the society without having scientific foundation. Ideology as an element of culture has a capacity that help presents a false portrayal of reality as truth. Such ideological views produce a cultural blind spot that sees no need for a critical evaluation of one's own ideological views.

Given such an ideological blind spot rooted in a culture, as sociologists, we may want to pause and reflect on various assertions such as the idea that humans are aggressive or acquisitive by "nature" or that we have an instinct for survival or sex. We may realize that some individuals are aggressive and acquisitive, whereas others are less so or not at all. Some people commit suicide, others remain celibate for life, and yet others go on hunger strikes. If these attributes were "natural," we should not be able to find variations in these attributes by people and across cultures. As sociologists, we need to challenge the ideological basis of our explanations. For example, if we believe that people are "naturally" aggressive and acquisitive, then it does not make sense to strive for more equality or a just society. This is because it can be argued that because of their "nature," some people become powerful and rich while others end up powerless and poor. Any struggle against inequality could be considered a struggle against nature. However, we can challenge the "naturalness" of social statuses by showing that some of the people who were poor and powerless ended up rich due to certain social circumstances beyond their making, or on the contrary, rich and powerful people end up poor and powerless due to economic and political crises. Our argument does not deny the importance of nature. It merely shows that many of the so-called natural aspects of our life are actually socially constructed. In this sense, nature and nurture/culture complement each other. Nature provides us with the raw materials that can be shaped by culture in many different directions, depending on the social circumstances.

Key Terms

Dominant ideology: a set of emotionally charged normative and descriptive beliefs that prevail in society and are consistent with that of the dominant groups.

Ethnocentrism: the practice of judging members of another cultural group by one's own cultural standards; a belief in the superiority of one's own culture.

Hegemony: a type of domination. The subordinate classes' consensus to the dominant class is achieved through control over their thinking process; ideological control.

Imperialism: an economic, political, and military system that has no geographic limit and dominates a vast area of human society.

Techniques of neutralization: justification and rationalization of deviant behaviour.

Critical Thinking Questions

1. Why do journalists tend to present views that are consistent with a nation's dominant cultural views?
2. What function does it play when journalists' or even academics' view is consistent with the dominant culture? What about if their view is inconsistent with the dominant culture?
3. Under what conditions do journalists tend to present views that are reflective of reality? Why?
4. Looking back at the downing of Flight 655, do you think that American journalists intentionally distorted the presentation of this event?
5. Why do you think Canadian, American, and Iranian journalists saw and presented the same event differently?
6. Think of journalists in Ontario and Quebec. How would you think they would present Quebeckers' separatist tendencies? Why?

Chapter 5

Socialization

How do helpless babies survive and grow to become full participatory members of society? Can children develop cognitive, emotional, and behavioural social attributes without help from family, peers, schools, and media? The answer to the second question is no. Children learn a language, develop identity, selfhood and survival skills, manage everyday life, communicate with others, play roles according to social expectations, adjust to changing situations, and develop selfhood. The human self is not within the human anatomy and cannot be observed. Nevertheless, it is real and is developed in interaction with other members of the society. The process of developing selfhood, learning these attributes, and becoming a participant in society is called **socialization.** It includes the acquisition of values, norms, motives, beliefs, and knowledge in informal and formal settings (e.g., family and peers or schools and religious institutions respectively). Socialization includes cognitive, emotional, and behavioural development and is subject to biological inheritance, environment, culture, and unique experiences. Biological inheritance tends to affect intelligence, looks, height, and weight; physical environments may affect motivation and aspiration; culture tends to influence values, beliefs, ideas, and behaviours; and group experience with peers and family or unique experiences such as rights violations have long-lasting influences on personality development.

Importance of Biology and Environment

Does biology create destiny? Although biological inheritance is important in development of intelligence, looks, height, and weight, personality development is largely due to environment and social forces. Sociologists emphasize the importance of nurture or the social environment for maturity and behavioural development, but they do not ignore the importance of nature or biology. Recent research shows that the space devoted to sexual drive is two and half time larger in men's brain than in women. Similarly, a larger portion of men's brains than those of women is devoted to aggression. The section of the brain devoted to emotion, language, and memory is larger in women than men (Brizendine, 2006). These differences, developed over million years in human evolutionary process, may account for some of the differences in men's and women's cognitive and language skills, expression of emotion, and aggression. However, studies of identical twins shows that when brought up in diametrically different social environment, twins scored significantly different in IQ tests, and when they were brought up in a very similar environment, they scored very similarly in such tests. It is estimated that 20 percent to 30 percent of IQ is associated with shared environmental effects. Individuals with high IQs tend to have been brought up in intellectually stimulating families (see McGue & Bouchard, 1998).

We can take the example of sexual behaviour among adolescents as a way of showing the interplay between nature and nurture, biological and social forces. Udry (1988) was interested to find out the effect of biology and social forces on sexual behaviours of adolescents. He studied a representative sample of 102 males and 99 females, drawn from grades 8, 9, and 10 in a public school system of a medium-sized southern U.S. city. He measured sexual behaviour by frequency of intercourse, masturbation, heterosexual behaviours, arousal tendencies, sexual thoughts, and the plan to have sex in the near future. Biological forces were measured by the adolescents' hormonal levels (testosterone, androstenedione, progesterone, dehydroepiandrostrone, etc.). Social forces were measured by the adolescents' commitment to conventional institutions such as the importance of religion and school and involvement in conventional activities such as church attendance and sport. He also included measures such as friend encouragement, mother permissiveness with respect to premarital sex, family interaction, family size, and socioeconomic status. His research showed that social forces have a strong effect on sexual behaviours with the effect being stronger on boys than girls. He also showed that biological forces were strong, again the effect being stronger for boys than girls. Each of these forces contributed about equally to the explanation of the sexual behaviours, though both forces together showed a stronger effect on boys' than on girls' sexual behaviours. Yet the combined effects were stronger (see Box 5.1).

Many environmental factors have a long-lasting effect on socialization, while others

Box 5.1

A sociological model of social control leads to a reasonably convincing explanation of the control of sexual behaviour. A separate biological model also produces convincing results. But the combination of these in a biosocial model produces results that are far more interesting than either alone and leads to new insights concerning social influences.

(Udry, 1988, p. 717)

modify the importance of biology on personality development. In this respect, Weiss (1994) reported on the wealthy position of the American Vietnamese who were evacuated from Saigon in 1975 and the near-poverty position of Vietnamese who arrived since the late 1980s. Weiss suggested that earlier immigrants arrived during a period of economic prosperity, while recent immigrants arrived during economic recession, when jobs are scarce, there is a housing crisis, and federal refugee assistance in the U.S. has dropped from 36 months of benefits in 1975 to only eight months. Weiss also reported that earlier Vietnamese arrivals were from North Vietnam with a higher work ethic, contrasting with recent South Vietnam arrivals (see Box 5.2). The evidence of differential access to opportunities suggests that although the genetic makeup of the Vietnamese are generally similar, environmental forces and economic timing have significant effects on their chances of acquiring wealth. In addition, unique experiences also had significant effect on these Vietnamese. Weiss (1994) noted that the recent arriving Vietnamese experienced the horror of imprisonment, with negative psychological consequences such as depression and stagnation. These environmental, social, and unique differences were all responsible for the differences in inequality among the Vietnamese.

Box 5.2

The Northerners among the refugees..., were weaned on harsh weather and infertile soils and are known for their rigorous work ethic. The native Southerners, in contrast, have for centuries been thought to exude the attitude of a people who were "born with a spoonful of rice in their mouths."

(Weiss, 1994, p. 32)

Role of Social Isolation

We can also look at the case of children who have been isolated for a long period of time and identify their progress when they were subject to social care. Kingsley Davis (1947) reports two examples of children kept in isolation, which are informative for our purposes. Anna was born illegitimate on March 1 or 6, 1932. Due to fear of a shrewd, stern, hard-driving, and calculating grandfather, Anna was kept on the second floor of the house in an attic-like room for nearly six years. Anna's mother worked hard on the farm and fed Anna virtually nothing except for cow's milk. When discovered and removed from the farm, Anna was extremely undernourished with skeleton-like legs and a bloated abdomen. She did not have an ability to walk, was unable to feed herself, had no sense of gesture, or glimmering of speech. Two years after her discovery, Anna had progressed to the point that she could walk, feed herself, and understand a few commands, but she still could not speak. Three years after her discovery, her food habits were now normal, she could dress herself, and finally began to develop speech at the level of a two-year-old child's. She died a year later in June 22, 1942. By then she was able to follow directions, string beads, build with blocks, talk in phrases, try to carry a conversation, and help other children. Although Anna's isolation prevented her considerable mental development, nevertheless once under some care, she somewhat was able to mature.

Isabelle (pseudonym) was also born illegitimate to a deaf and mute mother. Both were kept most of the time in a dark room isolated from the rest of the mother's family. She was discovered at the age of six and a half, nine months after the discovery of Anna. Isabelle could not communicate with her mother except by means of gestures. Her behaviour towards strangers was like that of a wild animal and manifested it with fear and anxiety. Once under proper care, she underwent a process of learning more speedily than normal. By the time she was eight and a half years old, she reached a normal educational level. That is, she covered in two years the stages of learning that normally take six years. By the age of 14, she had passed the sixth grade in a public school.

What are the differences and similarities between Anna and Isabelle? Both started in isolation, exhibited a low level of intellectual development, and both reached a higher level of maturity after their discovery. Isabelle was able to reach a normal level of development after two years of being under proper social care while Anna, even after four and half years of social care, was marked as inadequate. However, Anna's and Isabelle's level of care after discovery was different. Isabelle, unlike Anna, received prolonged and expert attention. This resulted in development of speech in Isabelle at an early stage that ensured her subsequent development (see Box 5.3).

Box 5.3

Consideration of Isabelle's case serves to show, as Anna's case does not clearly show, that isolation up to the age of six, with failure to acquire any form of speech and hence failure to grasp nearly the whole world of cultural meaning, does not preclude the subsequent acquisition of these. Indeed, there seems to be a process of accelerated recovery in which the child goes through the mental stages at a more rapid rate than would be the case in normal development.

(Davis, 1947, p. 437)

Of course, another difference between Anna and Isabelle is that Anna had comparatively minimal interaction with other people. Although, Isabelle's mother was deaf and mute, she was nevertheless able to communicate with her daughter through gestures, comfort her when needed, and spend a significant amount of time with her.

Human are born with innate mechanisms that underlies a unique competence for language. However, these innate mechanisms must be activated through exposure to language at an early age, such as before puberty. If they are not triggered by the environment, they appear to atrophy. This may be exemplified in the case of Genie. Genie was discovered at age 13 and half in California after being isolated in a small room and not been spoken to by her parents since infancy. Despite the fact that she was placed under professional care in an attempt to learn language and other skills, Genie never learned to speak a fully developed language. She did acquire some language, but failed to learn the kind of grammatical principles that Noam Chomsky, a well known American linguist, distinguishes as the language of humans as against animals.

A similar inability to develop language was evident in the case of Victor, the "wild boy" of Aveyron. Victor was discovered at the age of 12 after living in the forest of Aveyron in France in the late 18th and early 19th centuries. Victor was under professional care to learn language, but he also never learned to speak more than a few single words (see Curtiss 1977 for detail).

Again, it is important to remember the lack of social interaction, the absence of affection, and the inhuman environment that Genie and Victor experienced. For example, for 12 years, Genie lived in near total isolation, naked and left to sit on her potty seat day after day. At nights, she was caged in a crib that had wire-mesh sides, and she often experienced malnutrition.

Studies of monkeys by Harlow and Harlow (1962) and Harlow (1971) show how important social interaction and affection are for personality development. Harlow studied rhesus monkeys that were raised in various conditions of isolation from their mothers and other monkeys. These monkeys, once returned to their group, exhibited passivity, anxiety, and fearfulness. They did not mate with other monkeys either. Harlow further experimented on these monkeys by exposing them to a soft cloth-covered replica of a monkey representing a "mother" and another replica made up of wire mesh and a wooden head but which offered milk. Harlow noticed that the monkeys that were raised in isolation went to the wire-covered monkey to get milk but spent far more time with the mother replica that was covered with soft cloth. That is, these monkeys tended to develop attachment based on a need for comfort and intimacy more than for milk. They were less likely to exhibit emotional distress, even if the soft-cloth replica provided less milk than the wire-mesh replica. In contrast, the monkeys that only used the wire-mesh replica were unable to interact normally with other monkeys. Harlow also noticed that absence of a real mother did not produce emotional distress as longs as monkeys were surrounded with other infant monkeys.

Primary and Secondary Socialization

As humans grow up, they are first subject to **primary** agents of socialization. In the early years of life, children are unaware of themselves. The only knowledge of the world and themselves is sensory and based on touching, feeling, hearing, seeing, and tasting. Even these senses have little meanings because children have not learned a language to be able to interpret their senses. Family is an important primary agent of socialization that helps with language development and interpretation of the world. It helps with the development of personal and gender-based identity and helps instill cultural values and norms. Peers become the next important primary agent of socialization. Compared to when they are exposed to and interact with their peers, children have far less control of their personality development when subject to the early influence of the family, which acts as the figure of authority. Peers influence is more voluntary and democratic, both because some aspects of children's cognition, emotion, and behaviour are already developed when they first encounter their peers but also because peers encounter each other on more or less equal settings. Generally, at this stage, children develop an idealistic perception of the world because they are taught about Cinderella, fairy tales, purity, sweetness, and honesty. Family and peers operate in an **informal** setting when compared to the *secondary* agents of socialization that operate in a more **formal** setting. Schools and workplaces are formal institutions and are guided by well-articulated rules and regulations. In these settings, children, now grown to be youth and adolescents, learn to adjust into new situations. They learn about the role expectation of an occupation, establish a family, and operate under impersonal and often strict rules and regulations. Overall, secondary socialization is more realistic since individuals learn about occupations, government, corruption, crime, domination, and war.

Socialization is a continuous process, and individuals are subject to personality development even until they are at the death bed. Here, they may learn to die with "dignity" and accept their mortality. Of course, socialization is not linear and sometimes individuals need to be **re-socialized**, as when joining the army. In these settings, individuals' early personality is subjected to initiation rites and/or shaped so that they may accept authority without question and even kill if needed.

Theories of Socialization and Personality Development

Behavioural Theories

Ivan Pavlov (1849–1936) is credited with the **classical conditioning** theory of socialization (see Pavlov, 1927). His experiment suggests that individuals learn attitudes and behaviours in relation to certain stimuli. He noticed that dogs salivate *(unconditioned response)* at the sight of meat *(unconditioned stimulus).* Subsequently, he experimented by ringing a bell *(conditioned stimulus)* every time he gave meat to a dog for a period of time. Then Pavlov rang the bell without providing meat to the dog. He noticed that the dog salivated when the bell rang even if meat was not present *(conditioned response).* Do humans similarly learn based on stimuli? Do you automatically look at your car's speedometer or push the brake when you see a police car? Do you feel hungry at 12 noon? If the answer to these questions is yes, then perhaps your responses may be due to the fact that you have been conditioned in relation to a stimulus (e.g., police, time). It needs to be stressed that it is the social relations that may condition us to behave one way or another. For example, we eat at socially appointed times and consume culturally selected foods in an appropriate manner.

Other forms of conditioning operate through rewards for good behaviour and punishment for bad behaviour, as suggested by Skinner (1953) and Thorndike (1913). Some other aspects of children's learning process at the early stage may be more due to imitation (Bandura & Walters, 1963) than conditioning. Children tend to learn language by imitating parents and peers. Nevertheless, even though children learn the sounds of words through imitation and repetition, the meanings of words are learned through interaction with members of their society.

Psycho-Social Theory

Sigmund Freud (1856–1939) argued that biology plays an important part in human development. However, humans do not act instinctually. They respond to basic drives, such as love and survival. He identified three elements of human personality: id, ego, and super-ego. According to Freud, all humans are born with certain innate drives that seek pleasure. These drives could include eating, touching, or other diffused sexual or physical pleasures. He called the innate drives that seek pleasure the id. The **id** is filled with energy and strives to bring about the satisfaction of the instinctual needs and observance of pleasure principle. Infants also develop strategies of satisfying the id's desires. Freud referred to the sum total of all strategies that seek to please id as the **ego.** For example, infants may experience responses to crying such as getting attention, getting picked up, and getting food. In this case, the ego has found a strategy of gratifying the id's desire for attention, comfort, and food. The ego is physically related to the id. With socialization, a part of the id becomes the ego, which mediates between the id and the outside world. The id does not change through the passage of time, but the ego, modified by the influence of the external world, changes. Therefore, the ego's proximity to and relationship with the external world is what distinguishes it from the id. The ego's roles are to repress those impulses that are incompatible with reality, delay gratification of impulses, or change the mode of gratification. In a sense, one role of the ego is to replace "pleasure principles" with "reality principles." Freud argues that the ego has three masters: the id, the external world and the super-ego.

Formation of the **super-ego** is related to the origin of conscience and the development of ideas and beliefs that inhibit the id's desire. It is the metamorphosis of the parental relationship and the influence of those who have stepped into the place of parents such as teachers. "The super-ego is the representative for us of every moral restriction, [it is] the advocate of a striving towards perfection" (Freud, 1964, p. 98). The super-ego helps the individual to experience guilt for transgressing or even wishing to transgress social and moral restrictions. An example, which is perhaps fitting of Freud's concern with sex, is if you are walking down the street and see a very attractive person of the sex you are oriented towards. What goes through your mind? Freud would say that perhaps your id may want to have sex with that individual. Your ego will find a strategy of meeting the id's desire by, for example, "wining and dining" that person. However, your super-ego may jump in, make you feel guilty, and encourage you to take a "cold shower." In this case, individual wish fantasies and related impulses are repressed, thus pushing them back or keeping them in the subconscious. The repression of the id's desires as the price for the advancement of civilization, according to Freud, may result in incalculable biological and psychological damages in the forms of deep unhappiness, mental disorder, or other discontents. You may notice that, according to Freud, the super-ego is important for socialization, without which human civilization would not have been possible. Without a super-ego, individuals may be significantly more prone to steal, injure, and kill other individuals. A world without the super-ego would be like the Hobbesian "war of all against all." Therefore, the role of the super-ego is to inhibit all kinds of socially harmful strategies that the ego may imagine in order to satisfy the id's desires.

How does the super-ego come about? According to Freud (1964), all children pass through three sexual stages. This simply means that as children grow, different types of physical activities give them pleasure. Thus, at the *oral* stage (0 to 18 months), the act of sucking; at the *anal* stage (one and half to three and half years), the act of excreting; and at the *phallic* stage (three and half to six years), the act of playing with their genitals is pleasurable to children. Freud argued that toilet training is the classic example of conflict between the id, ego, and super-ego. Freud was most interested in the third (phallic) stage. During this stage, the male child, who tends to view his mother as his **"love-object,"** notices that he has a competitor—his father. The child also notices that this competitor is very powerful and more than twice his size. According to Freud, this observation allows the child, consciously or subconsciously, to think that his father will retaliate against him by preventing his id's pleasure. Since the child is at the phallic stage, he conceives this retaliation as being directed at the source of his pleasure, his genitals, with the possibility of castration. The child, fearful of castration (or what Freud calls **castration anxiety**), abandons his desire for his mother as his love object. He can only possess his mother vicariously through identification with his father and becomes much like him. Here, the super-ego is the voice of the father within the boy. As he grows up, he replaces the desire for his mother with a desire for another female as his mate. This transformation, in Freud's opinion, formed the development of the prohibition of incest, which in turn lifted human beings out of biological relations into social relations.

Freud argued that the development of femininity is different from that of masculinity. Compared to the development of personality in boys, the development of girls into "normal" women is more difficult and more complicated. Both boys and girls at first take their mothers as their "love-object." Boys are forced to abandon mother and identify with father for fear of castration. But girls are already castrated. Girls, by observing the genitals of the other sex, notice the difference with that of their own and feel that they have been wronged often declaring that they want to "have something like it too" and thus becoming the victim of **"penis-envy"** (Freud, 1964, p. 159). Freud argued that the discovery of being already castrated may result in three alternative personality development in girls:

- sexual inhibition and neurosis
- masculinity complex, and

- normal femininity.

At first, she turns to her father as the love-object, which in Freud's mind means that it is a wish for the penis that her mother has refused her and which now she expects from her father. The hate for her mother disappears when she realizes that all girls and women lack a penis, and therefore she will never have a penis. She identifies with her mother and vicariously acquires her father's penis. Later in the process of developing normal feminine personality, the desire for a penis is transformed into the desire for having a baby, especially a little boy (see Box 5.4).

The preceding may suggest that for Freud women are not equal to men. In contrast, Freud discussed at length and questioned the image of "passive" women and "active" men by pointing to some classes of animals where females are stronger and more aggressive and that even in humans "a mother is active in every sense towards her child" (1964, p. 148). Freud is criticized by feminist scholars for his view that depicts humanity in male terms. He portrayed women as immature because they lacked a penis. Why didn't Freud argue that men are immature because they lacked a uterus? Couldn't males undergo a process of "uterus envy"? Moreover, it is not

Box 5.4

In a boy the Oedipus complex, in which he desires his mother and would like to get rid of his father as being a rival, develops naturally from the phase of his phallic sexuality. The threat of castration compels him, however, to give up that attitude. Under the impression of the danger of losing his penis, the Oedipus complex is abandoned, repressed and, in the most normal cases, entirely destroyed, and a severe super-ego is set up as its heir. What happens with a girl is almost the opposite. The castration complex prepares for the Oedipus complex instead of destroying it; the girl is driven out of her attachment to her mother through the influence of her envy for the penis and she enters the Oedipus situation as though into a haven of refuge. In the absence of fear of castration the chief motive is lacking which leads boys to surmount the Oedipus complex. Girls remain in it for indeterminate length of time; they demolish it late and, even so, incompletely. In these circumstances the formation of the super-ego must suffer; it cannot attain the strength and independence which give it its cultural significance...

(Freud, 1964, p. 163)

clear whether or not the sample of the people that Freud used to draw his conclusions is generalizable or if his work can be applied to the modern world. His sample was based almost entirely on Austrian upper-class women who lived in the sexually repressed 19th century. Finally, Freud's view that *biology is destiny* suggests that personality development ends after the phallic stage. Research has shown that socialization and personality development are life-long processes. Nevertheless, Freud's research and theory on the unavoidable tension between the "instinctual" needs and social forces significantly influenced and became a foundation of the future research on development of personality. For example, Herbert Marcuse extended Freud's theory by pointing to the fact that humans have endured painful social arrangement by engaging in work and production in order to satisfy their needs. Work occupies a large portion of human existence wherein pain is tolerated and pleasure is suspended. In the process, most working people suffer regimentation and pain, but the result of their work is appropriated by the powerful people (slave masters, feudal lords, military chiefs, kings, nobles, and owners of capital). Therefore, according to Marcuse, not only the socialization process suppresses human's organic needs and results in suffering, but so does unequal social organization of distribution of society's resources and production surpluses (Marcuse, 1961). Therefore, for Marcuse, the unequal social organization of production makes humans suffer more than they must due to socialization and the advance of civilization.

Sociological Theories

Jean Piaget

Piaget (1896–1980) was also interested in knowing how humans learn to think and understand the social world (see Delaney, 2005; Muuss, 1996). He was more interested in explaining the development of intellectual capabilities of children such as reasoning, perceiving, remembering, and calculating. He argued that such cognitive development is a function of the internal maturity and development of the mind as it interacts with the social environment. Moreover, he believed that children pass through concrete stages of cognitive development and that they must pass through an earlier stage to be able to get to the next level. Children may pass through these stages at different speeds, depending on their intellectual ability or sociocultural forces. He identified four stages:

1. *Sensorimotor stage* occurs up to the age of two. At this stage, human senses play important roles in experimenting with the world. Children learn through seeing, hearing, touching, and feeling the important objects and individuals in their life. This stage has six sub-stages. At first, children are involved in inborn reflexes such as sucking. Second, their actions may become more voluntary such as grasping. Third, their actions may have some intention such as repeatedly making a bell jingle. Fourth, their action is means-ends oriented, such as searching for a lost

object. Fifth, they develop some form of "object permanency" by searching for an object that may have been moved. Finally, there emerges the possibility of thought before action. They may investigate whether a hole is large enough for a toy to pass through before attempting to do so.

Therefore, at first since they lack language, they don't "know" that they exist as a separate object. They are unaware that they can manipulate objects so that, for example, a toy can make a sound. The world for them is chaotic and has no permanence. If an object or a person cannot be felt, seen, or touched, then there is no reason for children to believe that the object or person can exist outside their senses. Once children start to look for the missing toy or person, at the end of this stage, they have reached an important cognitive achievement. They tend to view the world as more stable, permanent, and predictable.

2. *Preoperational stage* (around two to seven years of age) is when children start to have a more stable conception of the world. They learn new concepts based on their perceptual experiences. They still have no understanding of quantities, weight, speed, or causality and do not know the reason why things happen. They are unable to perform many simple intellectual operations. They are unable to count and may think that the larger of two objects is heavier. If a cookie falls and break into pieces, children may think that there are more cookies because the pieces give this appearance. Similarly, they think that there is more milk in a tall glass than a short but wide glass, even if both have an equal amount of milk. They may insist that they are in Toronto but not in Ontario because they can't comprehend that one is included in the other. Nevertheless, they are beginning to deal with more complex issues. They can manipulate objects, express thoughts, and ask questions. They increasingly learn the language; therefore, they can think in terms of real events or objects even if these things are not present. They have a perception of events and processes because they see and interact with their parents or someone else who meets their needs every day, repetitively. At this stage, children are extremely egocentric; they can only look at the world from their own point of view. They have not yet learned to play various social roles.

3. *Concrete operational stage* occurs around the age of seven or eight to approximately puberty. At this stage, children are able to look at the world from a concrete, but not abstract, position. Their knowledge is directed at the reality. For instance, they may understand death by experiencing the loss of a pet, without having an understanding of death or life in general. That is to say, children do not have a philosophy of death and dying. Nevertheless, they don't need to learn through trial and error because they can mentally perform concrete operations. They are

able to do some simple operations and to understand concepts such as weight and numbers. They can classify objects based on their given classes. For example, they can order toys by their size or colour. They start to realize that shaping Play-Doh or clay into a ball or pancake does not alter its mass, weight, or value. They can take the role of others and thus look at the world from other people's point of view to some degree. They have now moved from being egocentric to being sociocentric. They can play games and manage to understand generalized and organized roles and rules.

4. *Formal operational stage* starts about the age of 12, approximately adolescence. This is a stage of formal and abstract thought. Adolescents are able to understand and develop theories and explanations and are able to form their own opinions. They can manipulate and solve problems and can have utopian ideas.

As children pass through these stages, their mental processes become more logical, more abstract, more complex, and more flexible and reflexive. They start to "think about thinking" (Piaget, 1962, p. 145), layering knowledge, visualizing alternative combinations, controlling events in the mind, and thus constructing new knowledge and possibilities. In operational thinking, reality is in the foreground and possibility the background; in the formal operational stage, possibility has become the foreground and reality has become simply one of many possibilities (Muuss, 1996).

Piaget seems to suggest that children in all societies pass through all these four stages of cognitive development. Others have suggested that, even at about 30 years of age, many may not reach the last stage (see Kohlberg & Gilligan, 1971). Moreover, the developmental process varies from culture to culture. Children will not be exposed to formal thinking in a culture where there is no formal education. Similarly, children may not develop a more global worldview if a culture does not have access to books, TV, or the Internet.

Charles Horton Cooley

Cooley (1864–1929) is a prominent symbolic interactionist. He argued that the social origin of self is based on individual's interaction and communication with others and is reflected in a person's consciousness. Society, on the other hand, is the imagination people have of one another. Self and society are not separable. He saw self as being developed by adopting other

Box 5.5

As we see our face, figure and dress in the glass, and are interested in them because they are ours, and pleased or otherwise with them according as they do or do not answer to what we should like them to be, so in our imagination we perceive in another's mind some thought of our appearance, manner, aims, deeds, character, friends, and so on, and are variously affected by it.

(Cooley, 1964, p. 184)

people's attitudes and views towards oneself. He illustrated this reflected character of self by comparing it to a looking glass (see Box 5.5).

He called this process of taking other people's view and attitudes as the **looking glass self,** which helps the development of self in three processes:

1. the imagination of how we appear to others,

2. the imagination of how others judge us, and

3. one's emotional or self-feeling, such as pride or mortification, towards that imagination.

Of course, the first two elements are important in the early years of child personality development. Since self is not sufficiently developed, the child is more easily influenced by family, the play group of children, and the neighbourhood, or what Cooley called the *primary groups.* Members of this group are linked with each other in a close intimate environment which includes selflessness, human warmth, sympathy, and affection, and thus the group is the universal breeding grounds for cooperation and solidarity. It is in the primary group, Cooley believed, that the human self or "nature," which did not exist at birth, comes to existence and will decay in isolation. So, if the primary groups consider the child to be handsome or intelligent, the child's self-confidence increases, and if they suggest that specific clothing colour looks good on the child, the tendency will be higher to wear clothing of that colour. Through multiple exchanges of imaginations and evaluations of the child's mind and those of others multiple individual perspectives, an organic congruent and consistent self is developed. As the child's personality develops, the last element, one's emotional or self-feeling, become more prominent, and thus the individual might be less susceptible to the social influences.

George Herbert Mead

Development of a sociological explanation of socialization is heavily indebted to the work of George Herbert Mead. Other scholars had emphasized biological instincts, economic interests, and survival instincts, among others, for human development. Mead, in *Mind, Self and Society* (1962), instead emphasized the symbolic nature of the human world. According to Mead, symbols (e.g., language, signs) allow us to have a conception of ourselves and others, as well as of life and death. Such abstract concepts enable us to reflect on ourselves, to communicate and be communicated to, and to judge and be judged. For example, in the case of Hamlet, who ponders "to be or not to be," he is attempting to play the multiple roles of executioner and victim, murderer and murdered, judge and jury. In order to answer this question, Hamlet must have a symbolic conception of himself, others, death, and dying. He must be aware of his place in the world and be able to judge himself in order to decide whether or not to execute himself (see Ritzer, 1996).

The ability to think and reflect on oneself, to become an object to oneself, is decisively a human capability, allowing humans to achieve self-consciousness. To develop self-consciousness or look at oneself from others' point of view is the most important aspect of human consciousness; it is social consciousness. Hamlet's mind, in asking the question, clearly presupposes a social process of linguistic and symbolic meaning of life and judgment about it. Humans' ability to think and reflect abstractly and to share the outcome of their thoughts and reflections with others is a quality that is found in no other animal. A dog can pick up a specific scent, but the dog cannot communicate this scent to other dogs because dogs, like other animals, do not have abstract symbols. Symbolic communication or language allows humans to reflect and explore alternative courses of future actions without actually acting on those possibilities. They allow humans to have a distinctive social entity independent of (though related to) their physical organism.

At birth, individuals do not have a self-concept. They do not even have a conception of a lack of self-concept. As they acquire symbols (e.g., language and signs), they develop self-referent concepts such as **"I"** and **"me."** These concepts not only enable individuals to distinguish themselves from others but also allow them to bond to a community. "I" is the unpredictable and creative aspects of the self. It is the manifestation of human impulse and needs. It is the actual process of overt action and a key source of novelty and self-actualization. "I" enables individuals to project themselves into the future. One cannot catch oneself as an "I," for one cannot be aware of oneself as one thinks, speaks, or acts. By the time one tries to catch the "I" in thinking, speaking, and acting, it has become a memory; it is now "me," looking back at "I." Lacan's famous statement that "I am where I do not think," points to this illusiveness of the "I." "Me" is the reflective process and is organized around the attitudes of others. It represents the internalization of the values of society. It is the social self and is consciously responsible.

In order for individuals to develop a self-identity that allows them to be connected to society, Mead argues that individuals pass through three stages.

1. *Preparatory stage* is the stage of imitation. Children mimic the behaviour of their **significant others** (e.g., mothers). By copying adults, children become prepared to take adult roles. For example, a two- or three-year-old child may want to get the attention of her mother by calling out, "Mom." The mother, working on the computer, responds "Wait a minute, I am working on my thesis." Several minutes later, the mother calls up to the child, "Jill, come, supper is ready." The child, playing a game on her toy computer, without having a conception of *thesis*, responds "Wait a few minutes, I am working on my thesis." Similarly, a child may pretend to read the newspaper as she sees her mother or father reading the paper, but she or he may even hold the newspaper upside down.

2. *Play stage* is when children learn to take roles and learn others' points of view. Children develop self-awareness by taking such social roles as that of a mother, a father, or a storekeeper, among others. They may play with a truck or doll and act as a truck driver or a parent. They may play with their toy tea set and serve tea to themselves or become a storekeeper and sell goods to themselves.

3. *Game stage* is when children learn to take general and multiple roles. Thus, in playing baseball, they learn to be a pitcher by relating to the runner at first base and the batter who stands before them, but they also relate to the catcher, the infielder, the outfielder, the manager, the advertisers, and the fans. In this stage, children learn to symbolically relate themselves to the **generalized others** and to place themselves in their community.

According to Mead, it is therefore false to argue that either society or individuals have primacy over the other. Rather, individuals emerge out of a society that exists prior to them, but the very existence of society presupposes self-conscious individuals. In Mead's opinion, individuals and society are welded together as parts of a common process.

If Freud can be criticized for his biological determinism, Mead can be questioned for his social behaviorism. There is no room for biology in Mead (see Box 5.6).

In his study, "On Becoming a Marijuana User," Howard Becker (1953) highlighted the importance of the learning process. Becker suggests that there is nothing intrinsically pleasurable about using this drug. In other words, becoming "high" is not just due to smoking marijuana. Those who start using marijuana must learn the relevant techniques, the interpretive framework, and the rationale of becoming a smoker. They must learn to interpret their feelings and sensations created by the drug. Becker interviewed 50 marijuana smokers and found that most beginners thought that the effects were frightening and unpleasant. They were calmed down by experienced users who told them that such effects were normal. The experienced users stated to the new user: "The same thing happened to me," or that "You'll get to like that after a while." In other words, a favourable definition of the experience by others introduced a feeling of

Box 5.6

A person is a personality because he belongs to a community, because he takes over the institutions of the community into his own conduct. He takes its language as a medium by which he gets his personality, and then through a process of taking the different roles that all the others furnish he comes to get the attitude of the members of the community, Such, in a certain sense, is the structure of a man's personality... Selves can only exist in definite relationships to other selves. No hard-and-fast line can be drawn between our own selves and the selves of others, since our own selves exist and enter as such into our experience only insofar as the selves of others exist and enter as such into our experience also. The individual possesses a self only in relation to the selves of the other members of his social group; and the structure of his self expresses or reflects the general behavior pattern of this social group to which he belongs, just as does the structure of the self of every other individual belonging to this social group.

(Mead, 1962 [1934], pp. 149–156)

enjoyment into the not-so-enjoyable act of smoking marijuana.

The same is true for acquiring a taste for consuming oysters, frog legs, sushi, or vodka. Smokers will learn to interpret feelings of dizziness, thirst, scalp tingles, and misjudgment of time as being "high" and will attribute pleasure to these feelings. You may have heard a drug user or an alcohol drinker brag that, "I was so high that I did not know where I was for a long time," or "I was so drunk that I lost my jacket and was bruised all over." These experiences are not necessarily pleasurable. Drug users and alcohol drinkers learn to interpret them positively. These examples do not mean that drugs or alcohol do not have any effect on the human body;

rather, the example suggests that we learn to interpret the effect positively or negatively through our social relationships.

Agents of Socialization

By now, you may have noticed that socialization is a life-long process, and that in the process of being socialized, a child encounters many agents of socialization (family, peer groups, schools, and mass media). These agents exert a powerful influence upon the individuals in the development of selfhood and their ability to participate in the social life of their community.

Family is the first and most important agent of an infant's personality development. This is because most of the early personality develops in a family environment and because children at this stage are powerless. There is no other external influence that may balance the persistent and strong influence of parents and siblings on the child. For example, there is a very strong correlation between parents' and offspring's religious beliefs as well as their political attitudes and ideas.

Children are not only exposed and learn from their parents but also from their siblings. Siblings imitate and act as role models for each other. Parents and siblings are the first "looking glass" for children where children learn how smart, handsome, beautiful, big, or crazy they are, influencing their self-esteem.

Children in different social classes learn different tastes and desires in food, clothing, cars, housing styles, and musical inclinations. They develop different values, beliefs, motivations, and aspirations. For example, research shows that middle and upper classes are more likely to be competitive and future- and goal-oriented, while lower and working classes are more likely to be present- and means-oriented (see Richer, 1982). Lower-class people have higher unemployment and less money and thus end up with relatively poor diet, shelter, education, and health. This means that their children's potential skills and intelligence cannot be fully realized and developed. Their children tend to develop a feeling of insecurity and powerlessness with a lower self-esteem. Similarly, ethnic groups differ in personality and socialization process. Some ethnic cultures have more authoritarian, strict, and punitive attitudes towards the socialization of their children compared to others, and they also differ in how they react to boys' or girls' needs, desires, and tempers. Both social class and ethnicity are shown to be related to language skill development (see Box 5.7).

Peer groups are the second potent socialization agent, and their importance has increased in recent decades because more families rely on two or three employed income earners. Since family socialization has been losing its influence, peers, schools, and media seem to have been gaining importance in terms of personality development. At a young age, children are very sensitive to their friends' opinions and would like to "fit in." Therefore, they are more likely to develop roles such as leader or follower, work on cooperation and competition, and use their peers as role models and an appropriate source of comparison.

Peers influence each other in many ways. Take the previous example of marijuana use. Wister and Avison (1982) studied 355 students at an Ontario university. They noted that group pressures were important agents in influencing students' use of marijuana. They noted that users

Box 5.7

Betty Hart and Todd Risley (1995) spend one hour every month in the home of 42 families as their children were growing up from one to three years old. They focused on three economic level families: professional, middle and working class, and low income, both black and white. They recorded every word spoken by parents and children. They noticed that by the age of three professional parents have spoken 35 million words to their children compared to 20 million words by the middle and working class parents and only 10 million words by the lower class families. Similarly they noticed that by the age of three the children of professional parents had a vocabulary which was more than twice that of the lower class children. This means that by the time these kids entered the school, they already had significantly different linguistic tools and conversational culture from each other allowing differential bases to build success in reading and mathematics. In another similar study, Christopher Jencks and Meredith Phillips (1998) evaluated the vocabulary of blacks and whites in the U.S. They found that even within the same social class, black children typically had smaller vocabularies than their white counterparts.

(Hart & Risley, 1995; Jencks & Phillips, 1998)

had significantly higher and denser social networks where friends condone or encouraged smoking marijuana than non-users. Moreover, the higher the positive attitudes of friends about using the drug, the higher the consumption level of users. Of course, this study cannot establish causality, since it is possible that drug users selected friends who were users themselves. In a study of 1419 Finnish secondary school students, Kiuru et al. (2010) showed that youth tended to select friends with similar levels of tobacco and alcohol use. Nevertheless, in the case of alcohol use, adolescents did tend to adopt the drinking behaviours of their friends. This suggests that selection and peer socialization were both at work.

Schools are the third important and durable agent of socialization. Schools provide skills and formal knowledge; they also help with anticipatory socialization. In schools, children learn to rehearse roles in advance. They learn the predominant values and beliefs of the society at large such as an ethic of individual responsibility, respect of authority and the rule of law, and judgement based on universal criteria. Children and youth learn to look at the world from the point of view of the "generalized others" and not just the "significant others" as was the case with family and friends. Teachers and textbooks interpret the world based on a more universal criteria and help with skill and knowledge acquisition useful for labour market involvement. Teachers and textbooks are also important in that they tend to interpret the world based on the predominant cultural values of a society, sometimes in a distorted way (see Box 5.8).

The effect of education is not limited to primary and secondary textbooks, teachers, or schooling. Students seek higher education primarily to improve skills, get a degree and a job, and, consequently, to improve their standard of living. But does higher education have other functions? Does it help students to question inequities? Or alternatively, does education ensure that students support the existing social order, which may be unjust? If education has any effect on student attitudes, does the effect vary by different disciplines? Are some disciplines more critical of social injustices than others? Guimond et al. suggested that higher education has a liberalizing effect. They also provided national and international evidence that supports this assertion (Guimond, Palmer, & Begin, 1989).

Media (television, radio, computer, Internet, telephone, newspapers, magazines, books, movies, tapes and records, etc.) as another agent of socialization is an impersonal communication source that tends to influence a large audience. Media shapes values through news, documentaries, crime reports, police stories, and commercials. It helps develop or perpetuate subcultures such as pop music, dance, fashion, and fads. Children, youth, and others use media for entertainment, identity formation, sensation-seeking, coping and dispelling negative emotions, and identification and connection with a larger culture and network of peers. The varieties of use of media tend also to influence children's and adolescents' socialization process. Such use of media helps with the development of a conscience, role preparation, and performance and cultivation of meanings of what is important, what is to be valued, and what is to be lived for (Arnett, 1995).

Box 5.8

Barbara Ransby (1992) relied on the historical records of the Christopher Columbus "discovery" of the Americas and studied thirty social study textbooks, published between 1966-1990. She showed that these history textbooks encourage school children in the U.S. to view Columbus as a great hero, as the Admiral of the Ocean Sea who, in 1942, sailed the ocean blue. She showed that in these books, Christopher Columbus is portrayed as a symbol of the virtues of rugged individualism and a ruthless pioneering spirit. She argued that the portrayal of Columbus in these books is racist and justifies a bloody legacy of rape, pillage, plunder, and genocide as a "necessary evil" for the sake of progress and Western civilization. These textbooks portray the inhabitants of the "discovered" world as "heathens" that needed to be Christianized, "savages" that need to be tamed, and "inferior" men and women to justify their exploitation and subjugation. Ransby pointed that similar justifications were also used for the invasion of Iraq and the murder of thousands of Iraqi civilians. The justification for invasion of Iraq was that they can't help themselves and need the help of Western world, through invasion, so they might have democracy.

(Ransby, 1992, pp. 79–86)

Although the role of media in personality development is not well established, the experimental studies point to its powerful influence. Posavac et al. (1998), in three experiments, studied the effect of media on females' self-image. They asked female undergraduate students to view for 10 seconds each slide of female fashion models (experimental group) and automobiles (control group). They noticed that exposure to media images of attractive female fashion models is capable of causing increased weight concerns among young undergraduate students. This evidence suggests that the females' weight concern results from a social comparison process.

Females use media as a comparison point that depicts society's weight standard. However, they also showed that not all women were subject of the media manipulation. Females who were initially very satisfied with their bodies were as concerned with their weight as their counterparts after being exposed to the media images. This suggests that media may influence children more than adolescents and adults because children's self image is not fully developed and thus they are more susceptible to media manipulation. Moreover, since the short exposure to media images is shown to have a strong effect on females' weight concerns, we can speculate that long exposure to media will have a stronger effect.

Table 5.1 shows the amount of time Canadians spend viewing TV. It shows that, on average, Canadians spend more than two hours per day watching TV and this varies by age and gender. Young males and those over 60 years of age watch more TV than females and middle-aged groups. Note that it does not show the amount of TV viewing for those under 15 years of age. Younger age groups, particularly those under six years of age, watch more TV than any other age groups. In fact, TV is called the "electronic babysitter" for this young age group.

Of course, media also has a positive effect on socialization. It acts as an agent of anticipatory socialization, for example, for role-playing in a future job. Studies show that those

Table 5.1 Television Viewing Per Day by Sex (minutes)

Age Group	Females	Males
15 to 17	127.7	141.0
18 to 19	101.6	108.9
20 to 24	99.1	122.6
25 to 29	97.2	127.0
30 to 34	92.9	110.5
35 to 39	96.1	115.0
40 to 44	88.3	121.1
45 to 49	99.2	139.3
50 to 54	118.7	149.1
55 to 59	123.6	158.3
60 to 64	158.5	170.6
65 to 69	169.3	230.3
70 to 74	206.4	223.6
75 to 79	221.6	236.8
80+	206.6	260.4
Total	124.2	145.5

Source: Adapted from Statistics Canada (1998).

children who watched *Sesame Street* had better reading skills and were more familiar with the alphabet than those who did not. Other programs such as *Fat Albert* and *The Cosby Kids* taught honesty, friendship, and cooperation, and decreased ethnocentrism. Moreover, as discussed above, there are a multitude of media sources and types. This means that children and youth have more choice in what they watch. For example, use of the Internet is far more voluntary and allows children and youth to have a more interactive relationship with media.

Figure 5.1 shows percentages of different Canadian households that used the Internet between 1999 and 2003. It shows that a majority of Canadians and households are now connected to the World Wide Web and use it. Substantial change took place between 1999 and 2001, when the percentage of homes using the Internet rose from 28.7 percent to 54.5 percent. The graph also shows that most of the Internet use is taking place at home and work.

Figure 5.1 Household Internet Use by Location of Use

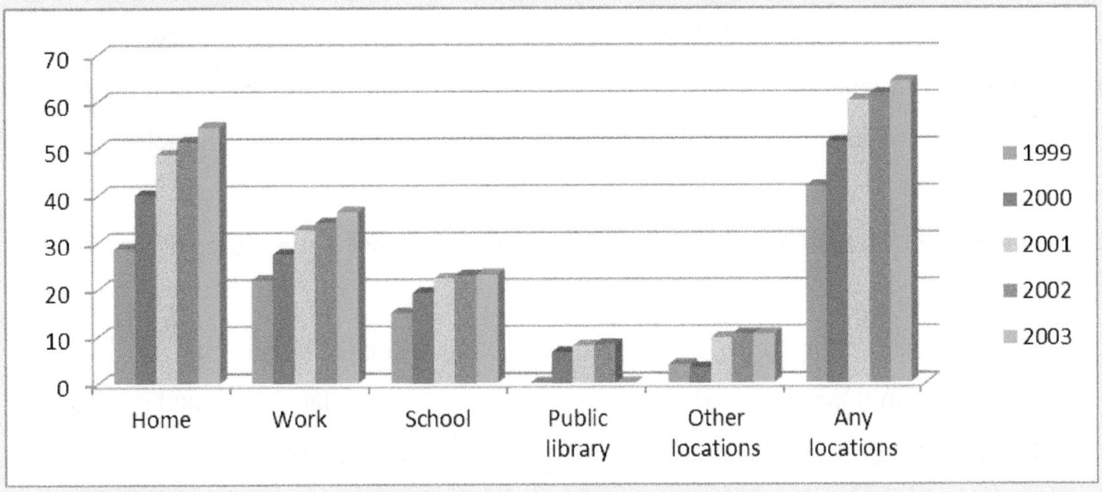

Source: Statistics Canada (2002).

Summary

Socialization is a long-life process through which individuals learn the values, norms, and ideas of society and how to participate in it effectively. It involves learning to accept and embrace the culture of a society. Although there are periods in which children and adolescents resist or oppose the ways of their culture, most people eventually adopt cultural standards. In a way of summarizing this chapter, we can look at how the four broad sociological theories view the socialization process. Functionalists believe that the role of agents of socialization is to ensure that the instilled values, norms, and ideas help produce cohesion and equilibrium. If socialization is done properly, then society will survive. Feminists argue that the role of these agents is to help produce masculinity and femininity and produce inequality through systematic socialization of infant boys and girls. Conflict theorists argue that the process of socialization is a power-based one through which the views, values, and ideas of the dominant groups are perpetuated and reproduced. Symbolic interactionists rely on the ideas developed by Cooley and, primarily, Mead and argue that childhood socialization and personality development is the result of the interplay between the self and society.

Key Terms

Castration anxiety: Freud's term of the male's child's fear of losing his penis.

Classical conditioning: adjustment of behaviour due to modification of stimulus.

Ego: for Freud, it refers to a person's efforts to manage id's pleasure-seeking desires in society.

Formal setting: institutional setting that is guided by well-articulated rules and regulations.

Generalized others: widespread cultural norms and values that guide individuals' self-evaluation.

I: according to George Herbert Mead, "I" is an aspect of the self that is the source of novelty and self-actualization.

Id: according to Freud, it refers to the basic pleasure-seeking desires of human beings.

Informal setting: institutional setting that is not guided by well-articulated rules and regulations.

Looking glass self: the process of taking the views and attitudes of others as one's own personality based on a reaction to the imagination of how other's judge the person.

Love-object: the primary caretaker of infant child whom the child is substantially attached.

Me: an aspect of the personality that according to George Herbert Mead refers to the organized set of attitudes assumed by an individual.

Penis-envy: Freud's term for female child's desire of having a penis.

Primary group: group of people that the infant child is first in contact with.

Re-socialization: learning of new rules and attributes and modification of personality.

Significant others: most important individual(s) in one's life.

Socialization: the learning of certain attributes and becoming a participant in society.

Super-ego: according to Freud, it refers to the internalized values and norms of a culture that keep in check id's pleasure-seeking drives.

Critical Thinking Questions

1. What role does biology play in personality development?

2. How do you account for personality development differences between Anna and Isabelle discussed in this chapter?

3. What are differences and similarities between Freud, Piaget, Cooley, and Mead? How similarly or differently do they explain personality development and socialization? Why?

4. Why might young people become marijuana, alcohol, or tobacco users? Which theory best explains their drug consumption habits?

5. Think of your relationships with your family and friends. How differently or similarly do they impact your personality? Why?

6. How much time do you watch TV or surf the net? Do you think they influence your personality? How? Why?

7. After reading Ransby's (1992) study of the school textbooks in the U.S., how do you think the presentation of Christopher Columbus as a symbol of the virtue of "rugged individualism" and a "ruthless pioneer spirit" has helped the development of the American psyche? To what extent does this psyche justify the invasions of Vietnam, Panama, Afghanistan, Libya, etc.? How might it be responsible for the Americans' "right" to use drones in order to assassinate suspected terrorists who are not proven guilty as required by the law?

Sociological Example: Cognitive Maturity of Children's Economic Knowledge*

Introduction: Research Purpose

Socialization is the process through which children learn a language, develop identity and survival skills, manage everyday life, communicate with others, play roles according to social expectations, adjust to changing situations, and develop selfhood. These societal values, norms, motives, beliefs, and cognitive skills are developed in informal settings (e.g., family and peers) as well as formal ones (e.g., schools and religious institutions). Among various socialization processes, development of cognitive skills or the ability to understand the social world is the most important. Children need to develop intellectual capabilities such as reasoning, perceiving, remembering, and calculating in order to be successful in education and social, economic, and political arenas.

How do children develop theses important cognitive skills? In order to answer this question, we will focus on a sample of Canadian elementary school children's understanding of shop profit and bank interest and pay attention to the internal maturation of children and the social context in which they are raised.

Theoretical Explanation

Jean Piaget (1962) has argued that children's cognitive development is a function of the internal maturation and development of the mind as it interacts with the social environment. Moreover, he believed that children pass through concrete stages of cognitive development and that they must pass through an earlier stage to be able to get to the next level. Children may pass through these stages at different speeds, depending on their intellectual ability or sociocultural forces. He identified four stages:

1. *Sensorimotor stage* occurs up to the age of two.
2. *Preoperational stage* occurs around two to seven years of age.
3. *Concrete operational stage* starts around the age of seven or eight and lasts approximately until puberty.
4. *Formal operational stage* starts about the age of 12, around adolescence.

* Based on Nakhaie (1993, pp. 147–160).

As children pass through these stages, their mental process becomes more logical, abstract, complex, flexible, and reflexive. They start to visualize alternative combinations and are able to control events in the mind, thus constructing new knowledge and possibilities.

Recall that Piaget has argued that children in all societies pass through all these four stages of cognitive development. Others have suggested that, even at about 30 years of age, many may not reach the last stage (see Kohlberg & Gilligan, 1971). Nevertheless, there is a general agreement among developmental theorists that the development of cognitive skill is correlated with age. Moreover, the developmental process, although age-related, varies from culture to culture and depends on the social context in which children grow. We would like to test Piaget's theory by focusing on children's cognitive conception of shop profit and bank interest.

Previous Research

Previous research on the relationship of children's understanding of shop profit and economic interest shows the following:

- children have an underdeveloped understanding of shop profit until the ages of nine and 10 (Berti et al., 1986);
- up until this age children understand shop economics in terms of *reciprocity,* often found in their personal dealings in friend and family relationships (Furth, 1980);
- the concept of profit is not usually fully understood until about the age of eleven (Furth, 1980; Jahoda, 1979);
- this understanding is greatly influenced by children's exposure to economic experiences such as trading (Jahoda, 1983; Ng, 1983); and
- European and New Zealand children "lag" behind children in Hong Kong in understanding this relationship (Ng, 1985).

In short, much previous research has pointed to the role of childhood experiences and socialization in various cultural settings as well as age maturation in explaining children's development in understanding profit and interest. However, previous research has often ignored how particular social agents play a role in maturation. Psychoanalytic and social learning theories place substantial emphasis on the instrumental role of primary caregivers as the causal agents influencing a child's social conceptions and understanding and in the child's acquisition of values (Turiel, 1978). Within the family, the mother generally takes the majority of the child-rearing role and thus is the main social agent that influences child's cognitive development.

Moreover, since mothers in different socioeconomic statuses and educational levels interact with their children differently and help instill different forms of knowledge, it is reasonable to expect that the socioeconomic education of mothers would have a profound effect on children's cognitive understanding of economic issues.

Research Importance and Questions

Research on the cognitive development of children's knowledge of economic institutions has rarely paid attention to children's understanding of profit and even less to their cognition of bank interest. Moreover, research has often ignored how particular social agents play a role in childhood maturation. This paper will therefore build on previous literature by examining how mothers' **socioeconomic status** as measured by their education contributes to children's knowledge of economics.

Research Questions

1. Does the knowledge of children regarding shop profit and bank interest improve as they age?
2. Is such knowledge influenced by their mother's level of education?

Based on Piaget's theoretical model, we hypothesize that as children age, their knowledge of shop profit and bank interest increases. However, since understanding of bank interest is more complex than that of shop profit, age maturation for shop profit should emerge earlier than that of understanding of bank interest. Finally, we expect that the more educated mothers should have more economic knowledge and are more likely to discuss the economic issues with their children than less educated parents. Therefore, we hypothesize that children of more educated mothers will have more knowledge of shop profit and bank interest than those of less educated mothers.

Requirements for Testing the Relationship

The subjects in this study are six- to 11-year-old students from a public school in a medium-sized, service industry-oriented and mostly Anglo-Saxon city in Canada. Three hundred and forty parents of schoolchildren were asked to give their consent for their child to be interviewed. Parents were also asked to answer a short questionnaire providing information on parental socioeconomic background and to note how often they teach their child about the economy (including about money, shop transactions, and banks). In total, parents gave consent to interview 128 children.

Do the Findings Support the Hypotheses?

The findings in Table 5.1.1 show that older children are more likely than their younger counterparts to say that the shopkeeper charges the customer more than what was paid for the goods or say that wages paid to the shop assistant or managers come from the shop profit. Only 4 percent of children younger than seven years of age could understand the concept of shop profit. This percentage increased to 27.9 for children between the ages of eight and nine. There occurred less notable changes after nine years of age. This suggests that economic cognition of shop profit develops mostly earlier in childhood and then levels off. Older children were more likely to attribute the difference between purchase and selling prices to an explicit need by the shopkeeper to make a profit, while the younger children were more likely to consider the shopkeeper's need to pay taxes or workers or to purchase at discount than to state any need of the shopkeeper to make a profit. By the ages of 10 and 11, children seem to have been socialized to accept a "need" for unequal economic exchanges and market relationships that consider profit an important economic activity (see Table 5.1.1).

Consistent with the hypothesis, the understanding of interest on deposits and loans increased significantly with age. Older children were better able than younger children to define a bank, why people deposit their money in the bank, what happens to the money in the bank, and what banks do with the money. Moreover, there was little difference between the younger and the middle age groups' understanding of bank interest (8 percent and 9.3 percent respectively). In sharp contrast, the percentage of older children who showed a full understanding of banking interest substantially increased to 38.3 percent. Comparison of the maturation age regarding understanding shop profit and bank interest points to the complexity of cognition regarding interest compared to profit.

The mother's education was also related to shop profit and bank interest, though more so with respect to interest than profit. The higher the educational attainment of mothers, the higher the likelihood that children would describe a fuller understanding of banking interest. The major

Table 5.1.1 Children's Understanding of Profit and Interest

| | Shop Profit | | | Bank Interest | | | |
	No Understanding %	Transitional %	Full %	No Understanding %	Transitional %	Full %	No. of Cases
Age							
6, 7	84.0	12.0	4.0	68.0	24.0	8.0	25
8, 9	58.1	14.0	27.9	51.2	39.5	9.3	43
10, 11	50.0	20.0	30.0	23.3	38.3	38.3	60
X^2	9.66*			23.49***			
Mother's Education							
Grade 13 and less	62.9	22.9	14.3	48.6	34.3	17.1	35
Undergrad. degree	65.6	12.5	21.9	46.9	32.8	20.3	64
Graduate degree	35.0	20.0	45.0	15.0	35.0	50.0	20
X^2	9.33			10.79*			
Total N	76	21	31	53	46	29	128
Percentage	59.4	16.4	24.2	41.4	35.9	22.7	100

* P <.05, *** P <.001.

X^2 measures the statistical significance of the relationship between variables.

Source: Nakhaie (1993, pp. 147–160).

changes occurred among children whose mothers possessed at least one degree beyond the undergraduate level. There was little difference in children's knowledge of interest and profit if their mothers had an undergraduate or high school degree. Children of mothers with a graduate degree were about twice as likely as those with less educated mothers to say that a shopkeeper pays less for the purchase of goods than the sale price to the customer. These children were also more likely to explain this by noting the shopkeeper's explicit need to make a profit. Detailed analysis showed that 40 percent of children whose mothers had graduate degrees explained the difference between the selling price and the purchase price by noting the shopkeeper's need to make a profit and only 5 percent explained it in terms of cost. None of the children of mothers with the lowest degree of education attributed this to the need for profit, and all explained the difference in terms of cost.

In a **multivariate** analysis that took account of the effect of home language, single motherhood, father's education, and discussion of the economic issues, the most persistent findings was shown to be the independent and statistically significant influences of age and mother's education on the child's understanding of profit and bank interest. Age was the most important factor, closely followed by mother's education. Middle and older children differed significantly from the younger children in their understanding of shop profit. In contrast, children's understanding of bank interest only differed significantly between older and younger age groups. These findings suggest a differential developmental sequence for understanding shop profit and bank interest and also suggest that understanding bank interest is more abstract and complex than shop profit.

What Can Be Concluded from the Findings?

It must be noted that the results are tentative given that our need for parent participation prevented us from drawing a random sample of children. Nevertheless, the social demographic characteristics of the subjects were similar to that of the city, which suggests that the sample is representative of the population.

Overall, our findings are consistent with our hypotheses and with the previous findings which show that *economic cognition* is related to age (see Ng, 1983, 1985; Roland-Levy, 1990) and to **social class** as measured by mother's level of education (Furnham & Thomas, 1984). Some of this earlier research, however, failed to show a **statistically significant** class effect (for example, see Ng, 1983), probably because the samples often included a mostly middle-class pool of individuals with little class variation, or the class variable was not elicited from each parent directly.

Furthermore, there was little progression from the younger to the middle age group in their understanding of bank interest (from 8 percent to 9.3 percent), while the latter's comprehension of shop profit increased substantially when compared to the younger age group (from 4 percent to 27.9 percent). These findings point to an earlier cognitive maturity regarding shop profit rather than bank interest. The finding that 10- and 11-year-old children have a mature understanding of shop profit is in line with European children. Canadian children, scored substantially lower than the Hong Kong children (55 percent; see Ng, 1983, p. 208). A comparison of children's understanding of interest shows that Hong Kong children are more knowledgeable than their Canadian counterparts.

Finally, this study shows that children with mothers who have a high level of education seem to benefit from the transmission of cognitive skills and attitudes, which enabled these children to understand remote and abstract concepts of economics such as interest. The overall contribution of the mother is not necessarily a result of direct parental teaching about the appropriate economic principles and the consequent development of economic cognition among children. It may instead be explained by **cultural capital** (values, traits, and characteristics) of mothers that are transmitted to their children. It may be that highly educated mothers are involved in more positive interactions with their children (Jahoda, 1983).

What Are the Possible Policy Implications?

The findings of this study suggest that in addition to age maturation, the education of mothers is also important to children's understanding of economic relationships. This relationship seems to be due to the highly educated mothers' ability to understand and transmit the more remote and abstract concepts of economic relationships such as the meaning of interest to their children. This suggests that educational and intellectual empowerment of mothers can ultimately help foster advanced maturation in children toward an understanding of economic or other relationships. Such mothers act as role models and spend time with their children, which could enhance their economic knowledge. Therefore, the present findings support the argument that the type of learning environment that the child encounters in the home accentuates the positive element of social cognition. This suggests that children's cognitive development is not just an internal process, but something that interacts with the **social structure** to which the children belong.

Key Terms

Cultural capital: a term used by Pierre Bourdieu to refer to people's assets, including their values, beliefs, attitudes, and competence in language and culture.

Multivariate: a method of studying a phenomenon by explaining it through two or more variables.

Social class: individuals' position in the hierarchical system of inequality.

Social structure: relatively stable pattern of social behaviour; large-scale and long-term patterns of organization in a society. These organizations are external to individuals and influence their behaviour and thoughts.

Socioeconomic status: one's social status in the stratification hierarchy based on education, occupation, and income.

Statistical significance: the probability that the results are similar in the population at large.

Critical Thinking Questions

1. Discuss Piaget's stages of personality development by using examples of children you know.

2. How do social environments influence childhood cognitive development?

3. What other social factors influence childhood understanding of economic relationships according to this paper?

4. How and why does age play a role in childhood understanding of shop profit or bank interest?

5. Why are there differences in cognitive development of children among various societies or cultures?

6. Why is economic cognition of Canadian children not developed as early as that of children in Hong Kong?

7. What role does social class play in cognitive development of children? Why?

Chapter 6

Crime and Deviance

Definition of Crime and Deviance

What is deviant behaviour? Why do people commit crime? Is crime a normal or pathological behaviour? These questions have challenged social scientists, criminologists, and lawmakers for centuries. If we were to examine different places and different times in human history, we would notice substantial diversity in what is considered deviance or crime. For example, if someone kills someone else, it is called murder. If the state kills someone, it is execution. If a soldier kills the enemy, it is patriotism. Likewise, if a Muslim woman dresses modestly and covers her hair and/or body (i.e., *hejab)*, it is a sign of modesty in a Muslim country, but in France, she may be looked with disdain or even prosecuted. Now, if a woman dresses in a short skirt and tank top in France or other European countries, it may be viewed as a sign of women's liberation. But in Saudi Arabia, she may be viewed with contempt and even prosecuted. Sexual relations between men were institutionalized in many Greek city-states, but these practices later became stigmatized and subject to harassment in many democratic countries. Socrates was forced to drink a cup of poison for the charges of refusing to recognize the Gods acknowledged by the Athenian state and for encouraging his students to despise the established laws. Yet he is well respected for his teachings and services to humanity. Galileo Galilei was sent to the Inquisition and placed under house arrest for the remainder of his life for declaring that the Earth is spherical and that it moved around the Sun. He was forced to recant his theory, yet the Earth *does* move around the Sun. Both Socrates and Galileo were punished because what they did was an offence against the public sentiments and average consciousness.

What is important in all of these examples is that it was not the intrinsic quality of these acts, nor the innate predisposition or personality of individuals committing them, that made them deviant or criminal. Rather, it was the definition of those acts by the average sentiments at the time which made them deviant or criminal. As Durkheim would say, they were perceived as deviance or crime because they shock the foundation of the collective conscience and threatened the social solidarity. In fact, deviance and crime may be more normal than abnormal in that they are found in all human societies, past and present. Since we don't know of a society without deviance and crime, then they must be an integral part of the social order. As there are diversities of values and moral beliefs, it is understandable that in all societies, there are people who depart from the established norms.

Generally, we look at **deviance** as a departure from the social norms. When norms are legislated, they are called laws. Although **crime** is an act that is committed by an individual who violates laws decreed by the State to regulate the relations between citizens (Ferraro, 1972, p. 3), **laws** do not necessary represent a consensus of values and norms. In fact, the presence of law may be considered evidence of conflict of values, norms, and interests. If there were a consensus on these subjects, no one would commit an antisocial act, so there would be no need to pass a law against such an act.

Chambliss (1975) argued that laws are *not* a reflection of custom or represent community sentiments. They are a set of rules established by the state in the interests of the dominant classes. This means that a) acts are defined as criminal because they serve the interests of the ruling class; and b) members of the ruling class can violate these laws with impunity, but if they are violated by the subordinate classes, violators will be punished severely (see Box 6.1). For example, prohibition laws in the United States were enacted primarily due to the efforts of downwardly mobile segments of the America's middle class. Similarly, theft and vagrancy laws were enacted in relation to the interests of America's ruling class (Chambliss, 1975, pp. 153–154).

Box 6.1

...the division of a society into a ruling class that owns the means of production and a subservient class that works for wages *inevitably* leads to conflict between the two classes. As those conflicts are manifested in rebellions and riots among the proletariat, the state, acting in the interests of the owners of the means of production will pass laws designed to control, through the application of the state sanctioned force, those acts of proletariat which threaten the interests of the bourgeoisie. In this way, then, acts to be defined as criminal... The criminal law is thus *not* a reflection of custom... but is a set of rules laid down by the state in the interests of the ruling class...

(Chambliss, 1975, p. 151)

More recently, Western and North American countries enacted a raft of new legislations that curbed privacy rights and other individual freedoms. The first and the most comprehensive of these was the *Uniting and Strengthening America by Providing Appropriate Tools Required to Intercept and Obstruct Terrorism Act 2001,* which was signed into law on October 26, 2001 in the U.S., just over a month after the 9/11 attacks. Subsequently, the United Kingdom passed into law the *Anti-Terrorism, Crime and Security Act* on December 15, 2001. In Canada, the *Anti-*

Terrorism Act, or *Bill C-36*, was introduced on October 15, 2001, again just a little over a month after the 9/11 attacks, and received royal assent on December 18, 2001. Other countries followed. New Zealand's *Terrorism Suppression Act* was passed in 2002, and Belgium's *Anti-Terrorism Act* was passed in 2003. Australia's *Anti-Terrorism* acts were passed in 2002 and 2005, and France's *Anti-Terrorism Law* was passed in 2005. These new laws and policies included more intensive and intrusive government monitoring of personal communication, the relaxation of *habeas corpus* where people were suspected by police or security officials of terrorism or possessing "things" or information related to terrorism, and more preemptive capacities on the part of state authorities to criminalize intention. These laws did not represent the sentiment of the community, as they were directed against members of the community. However, they were presented as protecting the community against external enemies. The speed by which these laws were passed points to minimal community consultation or minimal incorporation of the societal values and norms.

Nevertheless, as a general rule, the level of agreement or disagreement among the public is an important indicator of what is or is not deviance or crime. Moreover, conceptualization of an act as deviant or criminal changes to the same extent as the act is perceived as harmful and actually is harmful. For example, there is little disagreement that murder is harmful and a deviant or criminal act. But there is much disagreement on whether prostitution is harmful or a criminal act. Similarly, there is substantially less agreement on whether extramarital sex or adhering to new fashion is deviant. Many do not consider them harmful either. Nevertheless, we should keep in mind that many acts, which are considered criminal are defined from the points of view of those who control a social system.

John Hagan (1977) has developed a typology of deviance and crime depending on types of deviance and the severity of social response. He argued that there are four types of deviance: consensus, conflict, social deviation, and social diversion. Consensus crime, such as murder, is perceived as very harmful. For conflict crime, such as prostitution, there is somewhat of agreement among the public that it is harmful and the severity of social response is punitive. For social deviation, such as extramarital relations, there is some uncertainty about its harmfulness and the severity of the social response is indeterminate. Finally, social diversion, such as fads and fashions, receives an apathetic level of agreement, is perceived as relatively harmless, and the severity of social response is very mild.

Crime Rate

There are many ways that crime and deviance can be measured. Police reports, court data, correctional institutions, and mental health centres constitute the official data on crime and deviance. For example, the Uniform Crime Report (UCR) data has been collected since 1962 by over 400 municipal police departments about over 90 types of crime. The UCR figures are only those crime incidences that are reported. It is estimated that over half of all crimes are either not reported or have not come to police attention. Even among those that come to the criminal justice attention, less than 4 percent result in custody sentences. This means that over 95 percent of crimes that come to police attention are either not charged or not convicted.

Criminal incidences are measured by crime rate. **Crime rate** standardizes criminal incidences to the population of an area in terms of age, sex, or some other population attributes. The general crime rate measure takes the number of criminal incidences in a year and divides it to the population, then multiplies it with 100,000 (see Box 6.2).

Box 6.2 Crime Rate

Number of criminal incidences per year

*Population * 100,000*

Once criminal incidences are standardized to a given population, they can be compared across countries or population groups. For example, based on admission to the Canadian Jurisdiction programs, the crime rate in 1983 was 8,867 per 100,000 people and declined to 7,778 in 2008. Similarly the homicide rate declined from 2.67 per 100,000 to 1.83 in the same period. Likewise, the incarceration rates and average sentence lengths have been decreasing (see Table 6.1).

Figure 6.1 compares the crime rates between Canada and the U.S. from 1984 to 2000. As can be seen the U.S. has a higher rate of aggravated assault and robbery than Canada and that crime rates have been declining in recent years in both countries.

Table 6.1 Admission to Custodial Programs in Canada (1982–2008)

	2008	2003	1998	1993	1988	1983
Admission to Federal Programs						
Sentence Length						
2 years and less than 3 years (percent)	53.57	51.26	36.93	37.9	37	37.5
3 years and less than 4 years (percent)	18.97	19.85	21.8	22.4	22.4	23.7
4 years and less than 5 years (percent)	9.44	8.85	13.29	11.7	11.6	11.4
more than 5 years and less than life (percent)	13.68	16.12	23.64	18.4	20.8	20.1
Life sentence (percent)	3.5	3.36	4.17	3.1	3.8	4.1
Incarceration rate per 100,000 adults		52	61	58	53	53
Admission to Provincial and Territorial programs						
Incarceration rate per 100,000 adults		81	93	91	81	94
Total crime rate per 100,000	7778	8901	8983	10594	10160	8867
Homicide rate per 100,000	1.83	1.74	1.85	2.19	2.15	2.69

Source: Statistics Canada. (2008).

Figure 6.1

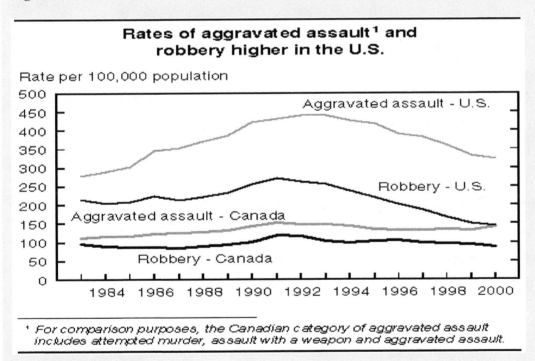

Source: Statistics Canada (2001).

C

125

orrelates of Crime and Deviance

Do some people commit more crime than others? Why? In order to answer these questions, we can look at the important correlates of crime and deviance. The best correlates of crime and deviance are age, sex, race, and social class.

Age and Crime

There is a persistent patter of age-crime relationship. Crime usually picks up among youth and adolescents and declines thereafter. Arrest rates are highest among 15- to 17-year-olds and decline afterwards. Moreover, age-crime and age-delinquency seems to have a similar pattern among various sexual or racial groups as well as in different types of crimes or countries and time in history (Gottfredson & Hirschi, 1990). Criminologists have explained the age-crime relationship by focusing on the transition from adolescence to adulthood. This period is a stressful time for youth because they are becoming independent of parental controls and negotiating new norms based on their relationships with their peers. With advancing age, individuals become mature and their behaviour changes. They acquire a job, a romantic partner, a home, and children. They become less dependent on and are influenced by their peers. Moreover, their involvement in the conventional institutions such as schools, new families, and the economy helps increase their *stake in conformity.* If they commit a crime, they may lose all that they have which they did not have when they were adolescent. They cannot live the way they did when young and among peers (Cloward & Ohlin, 1960; Matza, 1964; Zimring, 1981).

Hirschi and Gottfredson (1983) and Gottfredson and Hirschi (1990) have argued that the age-crime relationship is invariant. In fact, they provided evidence that youth with jobs or partners are more, rather than less, delinquent, and spouses or children do not account for the decline in crime with age (Gottfredson & Hirschi, 1990, pp. 138–140). They argue that since the age-crime relationship is essentially the same across time and place and by type of crime, they cannot be accounted for by the traditional criminology theories. This argument suggests that age-distribution of crime is basically the same for different types of crime.

Greenberg (1985) uses longitudinal data for seven American cities and shows that larceny arrest rates peak at 19 years of age and then decline monotonically thereafter. In contrast, the aggravated assault arrest rates rise to a peak in the 30–34 age group and then declines thereafter.

Figure 6.2 Crime Rate by Age of the Accused and Types of Offences, Selected Police Services, Canada

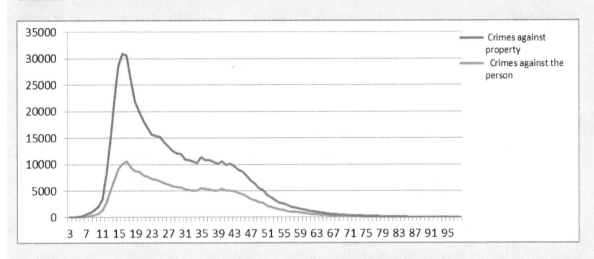

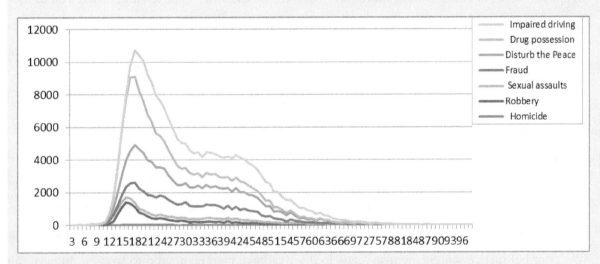

Source: Statistics Canada (2008).

As the both figures above show, property crimes peak earlier in the life course than crimes against the person, but that all types of crimes are higher among the younger age groups and decline thereafter (Figure 6.2).

Moreover, Greenberg (1985) shows that the decline in crime with age is higher among:

- higher socioeconomic status families than those in lower status families;
- city residents than among those residing outside cities;
- whites than among non-whites; and
- males.

As well, the decline is shown to be influenced by the level of social integration, moral commitment, and fear of sanction (Rowe & Tittle, 1977). Therefore, Greenberg (1985) argues that, contrary to the invariant age-crime argument, socioeconomic status, sex, race, city size, integration, and commitment are important mediators of the age-crime relationship.

Sex and Crime

Males are more likely to commit crime than females. In all categories of criminal code violations, particularly in sexual assault and use of weapon cases, males are more likely to commit and be charged with crime than females. Canadian males are 78.4 times more likely to commit sexual offences and 49 percent more likely to be found guilty for these offences than females. Males are also 7 times more likely to attempt a murder than females. After committing such acts, males are 6.14 times more likely than females to be found guilty. Overall, males are 4.7 times more likely to violate the Canadian criminal codes and 1.15 times more likely to be found guilty than females. The only case where males commit more crime but are less likely to be found guilty than females is prostitution (see Table 6.2).

There are several reasons for the higher male than female crime rate. Females are more likely to be supervised and controlled in the family upbringing process and are less likely to be defined or labelled as and thus less likely to become deviant, delinquent, and criminal. The higher guilty verdicts for males when compared to females and in relation to the total cases charged, with the exception of prostitution, impaired driving, and traffic violation, suggests that the criminal justice sentencing also tends to disadvantage men compared to women. In part, this is due to males being more viewed as dangerous and threatening to the community (Griffin & Wooldridge, 2006). Crimes committed by women tend to be viewed as an outgrowth of their victimization (Steffensmeier & Demuth, 2006). The criminal justice system may have a paternalistic view towards women, thus treating them with leniency. For example, among the 27 attempted murders committed by women in 2007, 23 were withdrawn or stayed and none were found guilty. In contrast, among attempted murders by men nearly one-quarter of men tried were found guilty.

Table 6.2 Male to Female Ratios of Arrests and Guilty Verdicts (2006/2007)

Crime Type	Offence Arrests	Guilty Percent
Sexual assault	78.44	1.49
Other sexual offences	43.13	1.09
Weapons	10.29	1.57
Homicide	8.85	1.03
Attempted murder	7	6.14
Major assault	4.41	1.17
Common assault	4.33	1.36
Crimes against the person	5.4	1.28
Uttering threats	8.19	1.31
Criminal harassment	7.42	2.09
Break and enter	9.87	1.38
Robbery	8.9	1.16
Theft	2.32	1.32
Crimes against property	3.25	1.27
Possess stolen property	3.91	1.66
Fraud	2.34	1.09
Drug possession	6.74	1.07
Drug trafficking	3.89	1.62
Prostitution	1.96	0.38
Impaired driving	6.02	0.95
Criminal Code traffic	6.54	0.97
Criminal Code total (without traffic)	4.46	1.18
Disturbing the peace	5.45	1.11
Mischief	6.7	1.18
Total Criminal Code	4.7	1.15
Total offences	4.84	1.16

Source: Statistics Canada (2008).

Despite a significant overrepresentation of males in arrest and guilty cases, the gap has been declining. For example, the female percent of cases in provincial and territorial custodies has doubled and that of federal custodies has tripled from 1983 to 2008 (see Table 6.3).

Table 6.3 Admission to Custodial Programs in Canada, Percent Females (1982–2008)

	2008	2003	1998	1993	1988	1983
Admission to federal programs	6	5	5	3	2	2
Admission to provincial and territorial programs	12	10	9	5	7	6

Source: Statistics Canada (2008).

Data Source, Age, Sex, and Conjugal Violence

The type of data used for research often dictates the results of a research question. For example, research using evidence from courts, police, women's shelters, divorce records, emergency room patients, and hospitals all tend to support the view that the perpetrators of conjugal violence are mostly if not all men. This is known as the **asymmetry** *of conjugal violence* (Dobash & Dobash, 1978; Dobash et al., 1992). In contrast, research measuring conjugal violence through the **conflict tactic scale** in surveys point to the **symmetry** *of conjugal violence* where men and women are about equally involved in violent behaviours in the home (Straus, 1979; Straus & Gelles, 1990). Not only do both sides of the argument use different data, but they also frequently ignore the importance of age. As we discussed above, all types of crime have a tendency to decline with age. Therefore, there is reason to believe that conjugal violence also declines with age. This decline may be due to the inexorable aging of the organism. As the organism ages, its criminal and/or violent behaviour diminishes.

In the process of negotiating order, young males, frequently being older than their partner, lacking alternative resources, and having been subject to a lower level of social control than females (Hagan et al., 1987), may take advantage of their physical strength and age-related experiences and establish dominance through violence. In these early years, males are better capable of inflicting violent suffering on their younger and physically weaker partners than females are on their older and stronger partners. Males, on average, are three inches taller, weigh 28 pounds more, and have better developed muscles than females. In later years, males' physical strength deteriorates faster than their partners', both because of their differences in the age of marriage (about four years) and that of a lower life expectancy (about four years) for males compared to females. This deterioration results in a lower capability for violence against the wife (particularly where the wife is younger, healthier, and physically stronger in older age), a higher need for care, and a higher degree of physical and mental impairment. In old age, female partners are more capable of inflicting violent suffering on their male partners than males are on their female partners. Consistent with this argument, Nakhaie's (1998) study of the All Alberta Survey in 1987 showed an asymmetry of conjugal violence among younger and symmetry among older partners.

Race and Crime

There is consistent evidence that minority ethno-racial groups are more likely to be in contact with the criminal justice system than are the majority white group. Among minorities in Canada, Aboriginal and black people are significantly overrepresented in prisons.

Some scholars explain such differences by the genetic differences among groups. For example, Rushton's (1995) gene-based explanation suggests that in the human evolutionary process, a group of genetic traits evolved that was important to group's survival. He called them r-strategies and k-strategies. R-strategies include high fertility, low investment in parenting, fast maturation, and low intelligence. He stated that Negroids (blacks) exemplify this group. K-strategies include low fertility, high investment in parenting, slow maturation, and high intelligence. For him, Caucasoids (whites) exemplify this group. Mongoloids (Chinese) are an in-between group but tend closer toward the k end of the r–k gradient. Rushton hypothesizes that his evolutionary model would predict higher crime rates among blacks when compared to whites and Chinese. His cross-national evidence is consistent with this hypothesis. However, Neapolitan's (1998) study of 118 countries showed that once income inequality, percent of young people, and ethnic heterogeneity of these countries are taken into account, racial differences in homicide become unimportant. Neapolitan's research suggests that the cross-national differences

Table 6.4 Admission to Custodial Program in Canada (1982–2008)

	2008	2003	1998	1993	1988	1983
Admission to federal programs						
Percent Aboriginal persons	18	18	18	13	11	9
Admission to provincial and territorial programs						
Percent Aboriginal persons	25	19	13	11	20	13

Source: Statistics Canada (2008).

131

in inequality, age, and racial compositions and not race per se are the causes of crime. Finally, the genetic explanation cannot account for the increasing overrepresentation of Aboriginal peoples in federal, provincial, and territorial programs. Genetic strategies are generally constant and cannot explain the change in crime rates in a short period of time as seen in Table 6.4.

Other scholars pay attention to the discrimination within the criminal justice system with respect to higher arrests and convictions of minorities. For example, police may concentrate their surveillance activities on poor neighbourhoods and neighbourhoods with ethno-racial minorities, which could result in higher detection and arrest of minority groups. As an example, Wortley (2002) showed that black people were more likely to be stopped and searched by police than white people. Similarly, blacks, as a group, are more likely to be discriminated in the labour market (Henry & Ginzberg, 1985), which in turn results in higher frustration and offending.

Moreover, such discrimination may result in lower occupation and income, which may prevent them from hiring a good lawyer to defend them and/or paying bail when charged. Similar patterns and explanations can apply to Aboriginal peoples (Dobb, 1997). Table 6.5, consistent with the discrimination model, shows the level of hate crime directed at ethno-racial minorities in Canada.

Table 6.5 Experience of Hate Crime by Ethno-Racial Groups

Race/ethnicity	N	%
Black	238	47.41
South Asian	66	13.15
Arab/ West Asian	61	12.15
East and Southeast Asian	25	4.98
Caucasian	24	4.78
Aboriginal	16	3.19
Multiple races/ ethnicities	37	7.37
Other	29	5.78
Unknown	6	1.20
Total	502	100

Source: Statistics Canada (2008).

Social Class and Crime

Official data show that lower classes are more likely to come to the attention of the criminal justice system and/or be convicted than the middle or upper classes. Homicide is higher in areas with a greater concentration of poor people (Parker, 1989). Similarly, self-report studies show that the youth from the lower social classes are more violent than those from middle or upper classes (Farnworth et al., 1994). There are several explanations for such class differences. Child-rearing differences between the social classes can account for deviance/crime differences in that lower-class parents are more likely to stress obedience and use coercive discipline strategies. Such child-rearing strategies in turn may increase aggressive tendencies among children (Sampson & Laub, 1993). Similarly, concentration of social classes in class-related neighbourhoods increases the potential for deviant learning behaviours through *differential association* (Sutherland, 1947). Child rearing and learning through differential association focuses on the characteristics of individuals for criminal tendencies. In contrast, others view class differences as due to the differences in the power structure of the social classes. For example, the poor are more likely to be brought in front of the law because they lack power to create *organizational strain* (Turk, 1969). If middle-class individuals are arrested, their use of lawyers and connections decreases their conviction rate. But if lower-class individuals are arrested, lack of connections or money to hire a good lawyer increases their conviction rate. Similarly, police officers may consider the poor and lower classes to be criminals and thus are more likely to patrol their neighbourhoods than to patrol the neighbourhoods of the middle or upper classes. Such attitudes and behaviour by definition may result in more arrests of the poor and lower classes than their counterparts (Taylor et al., 1975).

Theories of Crime and Deviance

Genetic Explanations

Early explanations of crime focused on the physical attributes of individuals and suggested that criminal tendencies can be predicted by looking at the individual physiques. For example, Cesare Lombroso (1835–1909), a physician in the Italian penal system, evaluated prison inmates and suggested that criminals are a throwback to an earlier stage of evolution in that criminals have low foreheads, long arms, prominent jaws, and excessive body hair (Lombroso, 1918). Similarly, Sheldon (1949) suggested that criminals are muscular types of people. Goring (1919, p. 183) focused on English criminals and showed that the most significant correlates of crime are "defective physiques, extreme forms of alcoholism, epilepsy, insanity, sexual profligacy, and weak-mindedness." At the end, he emphasized mental defectiveness as the main cause because he considered it to be the common antecedent of other correlates of criminal behaviour.

The problems with these explanations are that they were simplistic and unscientific. Attention to the visible physical appearance (the phenotype) ignores that they are not indications of the genetic blueprint (genotype) of a person. As an example, an individual may have the genetic blueprint for brown or blue eyes, but the final observable eye colour ends up to be brown. Moreover, inmates are a selective group of people. Many people may commit crime but are not detected doing so. Therefore, studies based on incarcerated individuals cannot be generalized to the other population. In this regard, Goring's explanation of the main cause of crime as being "weak-mindedness" or low intelligence has a fundamental problem. Those who are detected as criminals may not be intelligent enough to evade the justice system. Many intelligent criminals are undetected. Finally, one can observe many individuals who are muscular, have long arms and excessive hair, are weak-minded, and so on, but who are not criminals. This is because criminal behaviour cannot be explained simply with some phenotypical or even genotypical attributes. In fact, when Lombroso (1918) studied multiple correlates of crime, he came to the conclusion that biological factors account for a minority of crimes.

Other researchers focusing on the genetic explanation of crime studied animals such as monkeys. Research showed that by stimulating certain areas of the brain, monkeys displayed aggressive behaviours. The display of aggressive behaviours also depended on the structure of monkey colonies. In the presence of submissive monkeys, monkeys that are electrically stimulated exhibited aggressive behaviours. The same monkeys suppressed their aggressive behaviours in the presence of dominant monkeys (Carlson, 1977).

Another method of testing the importance of "nature" or genetic factors is to study identical (monozygotic or MZ) and fraternal (dizygotic or DZ) twins. MZ twins are genetically identical and the DZ twins are 50 percent genetically alike. Twin studies of criminal behaviours are mixed, and no consistent pattern of genetic effect on criminality has emerged. Some studies have not shown differences in criminal behaviours between MZ and DZ twins (Dalgard & Kringler, 1976; Plomin et al., 1981, 1990). Others did find significant differences of criminality (Rowe, 1986; Rowe & Osgood, 1984; Tellegen et al., 1988). Even if the evidence shows significant criminal behaviour similarity among MZ twins, one should be careful, as these twins also share significantly similar developmental environments when compared to DZ twins. Moreover, many twin studies are based on small and selective samples that suffer regarding generalizability.

Overall, many of these studies have concluded that social and biological conditions act together in order to produce criminality. Biological forces tend to influence emotional and cognitive abilities of individuals, which then interact with unique, group experiences and that of the environment thus helping to produce antisocial behaviours.

Sociological Theories

Functionalism

Functionalist theories focus on how social forces can control one's behaviour that could result in higher or lower levels of crime. They explain crime and deviance in terms of lack of individual's social integration and inability of the socialization agencies to instill values and beliefs that ensure conformity and integration. We can start with Emile Durkheim's explanation of suicide and evaluate the importance of social integration for deviant acts. Durkheim, in *Suicide* (1951), noted that individuals are not satisfied by their lot in modern society as shown by an increase in the suicide rate. He defined suicide as "every case of death resulting directly or indirectly from a positive or negative act performed by the victim himself." To shoot oneself is a positive act that entails some expenditure of energy. Going on a hunger strike is a negative act that entails a conscious refusal to take action necessary for survival. Poisoning oneself is a direct act, and refusing to leave a burning house is an indirect act.

Durkheim noticed that suicide is higher among Protestants than Catholics; higher among older people than younger people; higher among the single, the divorced, and the separated than the married; and higher among men than women. Durkheim argued that suicide is higher among Protestants than Catholics because Catholics are more integrated to the church than are Protestants. A similar argument applies to groups that have lower suicide rates. Women, married people, and younger people are more integrated into society than are their counterparts. Therefore, the reason for higher suicide rates among certain groups of people has to do with their lower degree of integration in and involvement with the society and its social organizations. Durkheim distinguished four types of suicide:

1. **Anomic suicide** entails a breakdown in social regulations that control and influence individuals. Under these circumstances individuals are left to themselves to manage their own

life. Such a state of affairs is called **anomie**: conditions of relative **normlessness** in society or a part of society. Anomie is not a state of mind but is a property of the social structure. It characterizes a condition in which an individual's desires are no longer regulated by common norms and individuals are left without moral guidance in pursuit of their goal. This type of suicide tends to increase during drastic economic depression or social disorders (e.g., the Great Depression).

2. **Egotistic suicide** varies in inverse ratio to the degree of integration of the individual to the social groups or society. Here, individuals feel little connection to the larger society and are not affected by social constraints against self-destructive behaviour. This may include suicide by an individual without friends and family who is perhaps living in an isolated environment.

3. **Altruistic suicide,** opposite to egotistic suicide, is mostly characteristic of traditional societies. In this case, in contrast to egotistic suicide, individuals are substantially integrated into society and its social organizations. One kills oneself because one is obliged to do so. Kamikaze and "suicide bombers" commit suicide for the larger good of society. This type of suicide rests upon a strong collective conscience.

4. **Fatalistic suicide** occurs when individuals feel powerless to regulate their own life. For example, a prisoner may see suicide as a way out.

You may have noticed that Durkheim was interested in finding out how social control influences individuals' self-destructive behaviour. Robert K. Merton (1938) extended Durkheim's argument on anomie or normlessness and argued that deviance and crime are due to the lack of correspondence or the strain between "culturally defined *goals*" and the institutionally defined "acceptable *means* of achieving these goals" (see Box 6.3). For example, becoming economically successful, inheriting wealth, acquiring a well-paying occupation, or accessing profitable business are some of the societal goals in Western societies. Means of achieving them

Box 6.3

In societies such as our own, then, the pressure of prestige-bearing success tends to eliminate the effective social constraint over means employed to this end. "The-end-justifies-the-means" doctrine becomes a guiding tenet for action when the socials structure unduly exalts the end and the social organization unduly limits possible recourse to approved means. Otherwise put, this notion and associated behaviour reflect a lack of cultural coordination.

(Merton, 1938, p. 681)

include acquiring higher education, hard work, and business investment. Most people are **conformists.** They use the accepted means to achieve their goals. But if opportunities are not available, individuals may choose alternative routes for success. Individuals may innovate by cheating in school, robbing a store or a bank, or committing business fraud. Merton calls these individuals as **innovationists.** He suggests that inadequate socialization help produce innovationists. On the other hand, an extreme assimilation of institutional demands may result in **ritualists.** Ritualists may think that their goals are beyond their reach but conform to the means, such as hard working individuals who lower their goals. Others are called **retreatists** because they tend to retreat from social goals and thus do not use the institutionally acceptable means. Examples include outcasts, vagabonds, chronic drunkards, and drug addicts. Finally, some individuals may **rebel** against both the means and goals, establishing other goals and means, such as joining a revolution. Merton's typology is presented in Table 6.6.

Table 6.6 Merton's Typology of Deviance

	Culture Goals	Institutionalized Means
Innovationist	+	--
Ritualism	--	+
Retreatism	--	--
Rebellion	--/+	--/+
+ = Acceptance		
-- = Rejection, --/+ Reject/accept		

Merton's strain theory seems to suggest that middle-class people do not commit crime because they are socialized to accept the cultural goals and achieve them through the institutional means. Furthermore, lower-class people are poorly socialized so that they reject either the cultural goals, institutional means, or both. He does not account for the poorly socialized middle class who do not commit crime or the white-collar crimes mostly committed by the "properly socialized" middle and upper classes.

Generally, **control theories** explain criminal behaviour in terms of a weak internal control mechanism developed in early childhood, in combination with weak or absent social rules. Social control can be external or internal. **External control** or social bonds (Hirschi, 1969) includes attachment to significant others (peers or parents), commitment or investment in conventional society (such as education), involvement in conventional behaviours (such as

Box 6.4

The major "cause" of low self-control …[is] ineffective child rearing… In order to teach the child self-control, someone must (1) monitor the child's behaviour; (2) recognize deviant behaviour when it occurs; (3) punish such behaviour. This seems simple and obvious enough. All that is required to activate the system is affection for or investment in the child. The person who cares for the child will watch his behaviour, see him doing things he should not do, and correct him.

(Gottfredson & Hurschi, 1990, p. 97)

participation in recreational activities), and belief in society's values (respect for law and authorities).

Internal control or self-control refers to early parental child rearing and school practices that can help inhibit a child's undesirable immediate act and ensure internalization of values and lessons that prevent future deviance. According to Gottfredson and Hirschi (1990), parents need to monitor a child's behaviour, recognize deviant behaviour, and punish it. Similarly, children need to learn to delay gratification, be sensitive to the desires of others, become more independent, be more willing to accept restraints in their activities, and be less likely to use force or violence to attain their goals. If children do these things properly, they internalize self-control so that when given the opportunity, they will resist deviant and criminal behaviours (see Box 6.4).

Symbolic Interactionist Perspectives

According to Edwin Sutherland's **differential association theory**, criminal behaviour is learned through interactions with other people, primarily through interactions with the intimate primary groups who help the internalization of positive or negative definitions of an act. Such interactions foster favourable or unfavourable definitions of an act, and if the definition is favourable, the motivation to commit it is encouraged. The more individuals are exposed to and are associated with deviance and criminal values, the more they will be involved in criminal activities. As such, Sutherland's theory postulates that the root of crime is in the organization of society and primarily encouraged within intimate relationships among friends and close peers.

Labelling theory suggests that deviant behaviour can be the result of the labelling of individuals (Becker, 1953). It may be that certain deviant actions, if ignored, will not be repeated. But if people bring attention to those deviant acts by labelling the individual as deviant or a criminal, the person may internalize the label and commit more deviant acts or crimes. For example, if a boy is involved in an altercation in the school yard, the principal may call him in and ask him to stop "bullying" the other students. He is suspended from school for the day. Once at home, the parents remind their son that "bullying" is not tolerated. They may punish him further. The next day at school, the boy's peers may call him a "bully" and exclude him from their social circle. Consequently, it is possible that the child will internalize the bullying self-concept and further repeat such actions. In this example, the first act, or **primary deviance**, resulted in a response to the others and consequently produced more unacceptable actions, or **secondary deviance**. Eventually, this child could grow up to become a violent criminal. In other words, negative labelling could substantially change a person's self-concept and identity.

Another mechanism that may produce secondary deviance through labelling is the involvement of the labelled individual in deviant social groups. Such groups represent a source of social support in which deviant activities are rationalized, accepted, encouraged, and facilitated. As an example of the relationship between primary and secondary deviance through labelling, Bernburg et al. (2006) studied seventh and eighth grade public school students in Rochester, New York. They showed that official labelling triggers processes that increase involvement in deviant groups. Consistent with Sutherland's (1947) differential association theory, this involvement increases the probability of serious delinquency in a subsequent period.

Deviants and criminals are also involved in an active definition of their deeds. Sykes and Matza (1957) asked "why men violate the laws in which they believe" (1957, p. 666). They theorized that the deviant individual often qualifies the normative imperatives in such a way that violations become acceptable (see Box 6.5). In doing so, individuals can avoid moral culpability for their criminal actions and argue that criminal intent was lacking. Such justification and rationalization of deviant behaviour is referred to as *techniques of neutralization.* In this process, the offenders develop specific vocabulary of motives designed to rationalize their behaviour. They may "deny responsibility" and attribute the act to forces outside their control (e.g., "I stole the money because I was hungry"). Similarly, the offenders may "deny the victim" by neutralizing the moral indignation of themselves and others (e.g., "I kicked my wife because she was abusing me"). Other obvious types of neutralization include "the condemnation of condemner" (e.g., "the judge was racist"); "appeal to higher loyalties" (e.g., "suicide bombing was in response to subjugation of our people"); and "blaming the victim." For example, Scully and Marolla's (1985) study of convicted rapists' vocabulary of motives showed that these rapists often undergo a process of justification by blaming the victim. Women are seen as seductresses or as "not nice girls," since "nice girls do not get raped."

Box 6.5

It is our argument that much delinquency is based on what is essentially an unrecognized extension of defenses to crimes, in the form of justifications for deviance that are seen as valid by the delinquent but not by the legal system or society at large.

These justifications are commonly described as rationalizations. They are viewed as following deviant behaviour and as protecting the individual from self-blame and the blame of others after the act.

(Sykes & Matza, 1957, pp. 664–670)

Conflict Theories

What roles do power and inequality play in explaining crime? Is there a tendency to define some activity and individuals as more criminal than others, depending on who is in the position of power and authority? Are lower classes more likely to be criminalized and prosecuted? See Box 6.6. Are the crimes of the powerful left undetected? ***Conflict theorists*** (Turk, 1969) believe that societies are hierarchically organized and people in different social statuses expose different values consistent with their social and power positions. Peoples' values are stable over time and are in conflict with values of people in different power positions. Moreover, laws are enacted based on the conflict and compromise between people of different positions. Nevertheless, those with more power and social statuses are more likely to enact laws that favour their values and interests. This also means that law enforcement agencies will have more difficulties processing and convicting people of upper statuses who violate the law. The result will be that people with less power and in the lower social statuses are more likely to come into contact with the criminal justice system, be charged with a criminal offence, and be convicted of a crime. In a test of conflict criminology, Kirk et al. (1980) showed that social inequality measured by Gini coefficient in metropolitan areas is significantly related to the official statistics on homicide,

Box 6.6

The lower-class is (1) more likely to be scrutinized and therefore to be observed in any violation of the law, (2) more likely to be arrested if discovered under the suspicious circumstances, (3) more likely to spend the time between arrest and trial in jail, (4) more likely to come to trial, (5) more likely to be found guilty, and (6) if found guilty, more likely to receive harsh punishment than his middle or upper-class counterparts.

(Chambliss, 1969, p. 86)

rape, assault, robbery, burglary, and larceny theft. Interestingly, as expected, the relationship between victimization and these measures of crime were all negative and/or insignificant. This means that people in lower socioeconomic positions were less likely to be victimized but more likely to be found in contact with the criminal justice system in the U.S.

Marxist theory of crime (Quinney, 1977) is a more radical version of the conflict theory. Marxists believe that social conditions, not individuals, cause crime. They argue that there exists no consensus of values and interests in society, but that there is some consensus of values among members of each social class within the society. There are two important classes, the working class and the capitalist class, with opposite interests and conflicting values. The capitalist or the ruling class owns the means of production (corporations, factories, financial institutions), and means of communication (media) and is instrumental in shaping laws based on its own values and interests. In doing so, it has a tendency to view "street crimes" as true crimes and ignore "white collar" or "corporate crimes." For example, a prostitute who may be making more money than if she was working as a waitress is criminalized and viewed as a 'sick' person who takes risks, while an executive who helps pollutes the environment is viewed as involved in normal risky and competitive business activities. In general, Marxists argue that laws help victimize lower classes through unemployment, poor working conditions, pollution, low wages, and exploitation. Finally, they argue that the contradictions in the capitalist system are responsible for crime definition and creation. Capitalism is based on the contradiction of collective production (almost all people work to produce social needs) and private appropriation (only some benefit from the work of all people) which help produce unemployment, low wages, and crime.

Therefore, for the Marxists, the crime problem cannot be solved through incarcerations and corrections but through the overthrow of the capitalist system. We should remember that the idea that the capitalist class perpetuates its values and interests may be somewhat exaggerated, because in modern times, even the working class has some ownership of the means of production through stock ownership, either directly or through their pension plans indirectly. In this sense, the working class may not wish to overthrow capitalism.

In general, conflict criminologists remind us that the definition of crime and criminals affects the identification of who is categorized as deviant or criminal. For example, there may be a perception that the poor, unemployed, and some visible minorities are more criminal than the rich, employed, and white, respectively. If such a perception is prevalent, particularly among police officers and criminal justice officials, then areas where minorities and the poor are concentrated would be targeted for crime control. Consequently, police officers may find a higher number of criminals in these areas, not so much because minorities and the poor are more deviant or criminal, but because police officers have failed to look for such individuals in the middle- or upper-class neighbourhoods or among the white population.

Similarly, they remind us that we tend to see crime as **street crime** while ignoring much of **corporate (or white-collar) crime,** which may be significantly more harmful. A business that pollutes the environment can slowly kill large numbers of people by decreasing peoples' longevity and life expectancy. Similarly, capitalists owning the means of production tend to exploit those who have nothing to sell in the market but their labour power. If they could, capitalists would pay lower wages to people in general and to women and visible minorities in particular. The workers have no choice but to work for whatever is the "going rate" in the market. Therefore, capitalists tend to get relatively rich whereas workers remain poor. Capitalists can take advantages of all social amenities. Workers and lower strata of the society, in contrast, tend to live in an unhealthy environment and poor housing with minimal access to health care, and thus they are prone to all kinds of illnesses. Therefore, the misery of workers and the prosperity of capitalists tend to be intertwined. But these differences are legitimated and accepted. There is no law on overexploitation and far less in controlling the expanding appetite of the business class to take advantage of the unpropertied multitude. The point is that capitalist society tends to define certain acts as acceptable and others as criminal and thus punishable. A corporation that evades taxes and pollutes the environment (corporate crime) is not seen as criminal. In contrast, drug users and prostitutes (street crime) who primarily harm themselves are criminalized. We tend to have more severe punishments for the latter (i.e., street crime) than the former (i.e., corporate or white-collar crime).

In a more forceful way, Frank Pearce (1976) argued that crime is the central component of the ruling political elites. He provided evidence that the ruling elites have used professional and organized criminals to sabotage competitors and control unions. In exchange, the organized criminals have converted their illegal profits into legitimate corporations, have underpinned political parties, and have frequently syndicated crime at an international level with impunity.

Marxist criminologists are also interested in crimes of the state and the use of crime across the globe as an instrument of silencing dissent and threats to the capitalist domination or expansion of capitalist control over scarce resources at the global level. Recent drone attacks that have killed hundreds of people in Afghanistan, Yemen, and other Middle Eastern countries, without the use of due process may exemplify further criminal activities of the state at international levels, as may be the illegal invasion of Iraq and the support of terrorists to kill or sabotage the "enemy" without a declaration of war or in contravention of the international justice system.

Feminist Theory

Feminist theory uses both symbolic interactionist (e.g., Greaves, 1996) and conflict theories (e.g., Smart, 1976) in order to account and explain for gender differences and similarities in deviance and delinquency. For instance, gender differences in socialization may contribute to the differences in deviance in crime due to male and female differences in association, labelling, control, and power relations. Take the example of sexual activity. A female involved in sexual activity is more likely to be labelled as "slut" while a male doing the same is labelled as "stud." In other words, females are more likely to be labelled promiscuous than are males. Similarly, a female prostitute is more likely to be criminalized than her "john" or pimp. Hence, the social definition and construction of crime and deviance is applied differently to males and females.

Boswell and Spade (1996) studied fraternity parties and showed that the normative aspects of a college campus as they relate to attitudes about and relations between men and women help produce a rape culture. Their observation of fraternities revealed that women were degraded and a double standard of sexual behaviour was prevalent. Moreover, the potential for rape was higher among "high-risk" fraternities. High-risk fraternities included those in which men and women were segregated, often drinking as groups at different sides of the bar or room;

in which men treated women less respectfully and were engaged in jokes and conversations that degraded women; in which individuals were primarily concerned with women's bodies; and in which the interaction between men and women was mainly flirtatious. The authors concluded that rape is part of the social construction of gender.

Males and females are socialized to develop different symbolic structure. Parents have a tendency to control and supervise females more than males. Such supervision and control may help increase or decrease females' association with deviant and criminal groups and thus affect their criminal tendencies. To the extent that deviant and criminal association differ by gender then males and females would differ in criminal activities. Returning to Sutherland's theory on the internalization of definitions that either favour or turn from deviance and crime, the more individuals are exposed and or are associated with deviance and criminal values, the more they will be involved in criminal activities. For instance, Kiuru et al.'s (2010) study of youth showed that the effect of peer socialization on alcohol use was stronger on females than males. This suggests that female adolescents are more susceptible to peer pressure for alcohol use than are males.

Feminists also believe that there is a systemic tendency in the criminal justice system that favours men over women. This tendency is based on patriarchy as a social system where males dominate females. It is represented in the economy, the legal system, and religious, educational, and family institutions. All of these institutions perpetuate the importance of masculinity over femininity and have a tendency to oppress women. For instance, feminists note that laws are primarily codified by male legislators, enforced by male police officers, and interpreted by male judges. The control of the criminal justice system by males may create a tendency of criminalizing some female behaviours while paying less attention to many crimes committed against women such as sexual harassment, wife battering, incest, and rape.

Consequently, feminists have developed a critique of criminology based on notions of gender and power. They argue that not all laws are class-based and some are class-neutral such as rape. They define rape as a universal sexual domination of women by men (Brownmiller, 1975). They view power not totally as encapsulated in class terms but as something that can exist outside the class structure, such as the power of men over women (White and Haines, 1996). However, within the Marxist tradition, feminists argue that the inegalitarian gender traditions of the capitalist societies tend to result in higher rape rates and provide evidence to this effect (Schwendinger & Schwendinger, 1983).

Summary

Deviance is deviation from norms and crime is institutionalization of these norms and their enforcements by legal agencies. Functionalist theory sees crime as being due to lack of integration of individuals into the society due to lack of internalization of the appropriate beliefs and ideas, and lack of attachment to and involvement in the basic institutions. Symbolic interactionists view such attachment and involvements as being due to interpersonal relationships, differential associations and social definitions of acts as acceptable or unacceptable. Conflict theories point to the importance of the powerful in defining deviance and crime and therefore making deviants and criminals the powerless who have little say in what is deviance or crime. They argue the powerful individuals' control of crime definition and their control of other social institutions result in differential crime enforcement, judgment, and imprisonment based on one's position in the system of inequality. This view is further developed by feminists who explain that men's control of crime definition and enforcement has resulted in certain crimes committed by men against women going unnoticed or not well enforced.

Key Terms

Altruistic suicide: suicide due to too much integration of the individual into the society.

Anomic suicide: suicide due to too little integration of the individual into the society.

Anomie: a condition in which society provides little or no moral guidance for individual actions; a state of normlessness. According to Merton, anomie refers to the discrepancy between culturally accepted goals and institutional means to reach those goals.

Asymmetry: an unbalanced arrangement or distribution.

Conflict tactic scale: a scale that measures frequency and intensity of family violence.

Conformist: Merton's term for the individual who accepts both cultural goals and institutional means to achieve those goals

Control theory: a criminological theory that explains crime in terms of weak internal control mechanisms developed in childhood in combination with weak or absent social rules.

Corporate (or white-collar) crime: crime committed by a corporation or people in high status positions in the course of their occupations.

Crime: violation of enacted laws.

Crime rate: number of crimes per 100,000 people in a given place.

Deviance: deviation from norms.

Differential association: a term used to explain crime based on people that individuals associate with.

Egotistic suicide: Durkheim's classification of suicide that occurs when individuals are least integrated to the society or community.

External control: type of social control that includes attachment to significant others, commitment or investment in conventional society, involvement in conventional behaviours, and belief in society's values.

Fatalistic suicide: Durkheim's classification of suicide occurring when individuals have no way out of the undesirable situation they are in.

Innovationist: Merton's classification of individuals who accept societal goals but not means. They pursue less acceptable means of acquiring societal goals.

Internal control: type of social control that refers to early parental child rearing and school practices that can help inhibit a child's undesirable immediate act and ensure internalization of values and lessons that prevent future deviances.

Labelling theory: a theory that views crime as being due to how others respond to and label certain acts as criminal.

Law: a set of formally codified legal rules or norms that either forbid or permit specific behaviours or relationships among people.

Normlessness: an anomic state where there is no or little norm to guide one's behaviour.

Primary deviance: the first deviant act before the labelling process.

Rebel: Merton's classification of deviance where individuals reject both societal goals and means and substitute their own new goals and means.

Retreatist: Merton's classification of deviance where individuals reject both societal goals and means and withdraw from the society.

Ritualist: Merton's term for the individual who lowers cultural goals and accepts the institutional means.

Secondary deviance: the extent of deviance which is due to labelling of individual as deviant.

Street crime: crime committed by ordinary individuals.

Symmetry: balanced proportion or distribution; equal correspondence between the opposite halves of a figure or pattern.

Critical Thinking Questions

1. In your view, does Durkheim's explanation of suicide make sense? Why? Do you find any problem with his explanation?

2. Among the various theories of deviance and crime, which one(s) makes more sense to you? Why?

3. More broadly, why do people commit crime?

4. What role does biology play in crime? Why?

5. Discuss the role of culture in explaining people's attitude toward terrorism.

6. Do you think that racial minorities are subject to racial profiling? Why or why not?

7. Do you think police officers and security forces should be involved in racial profiling? Why or why not?

8. Which theories of crime focus on individual characteristics and/or structural forces in explaining crime? Why?

9. Have you committed a deviant act? Use the theoretical views of crime and explain why you committed the deviant act.

10. What role does power play in crime definition? Why?

11. Do you think that if children were properly socialized crime would cease to exist? Why?

Sociological Example: Role of Self and Social Control for Crime*

Introduction: Research Purpose

What is crime and why do people commit crime? Social scientists define deviance as departure from the social norms and crime as deviation from the legislated norms. In this sense, crime is an act that is committed by an individual who violates laws decreed by the state to regulate the relations between citizens. Laws do not necessarily represent a consensus of values and norms. Nevertheless, as a general rule, level of agreement and the severity of social response by and perception of harmfulness among the public are important indicators of what is or is not deviance or crime (Hagan, 1994).

Why do some people commit crime while others do not? In order to answer this question, we focus on a sample of Canadian high school students and evaluate various theories that sociologists use to explain crime.

Theoretical Explanation

There are many explanations of why people commit crime. Early explanations focused on the individual predispositions and genetic forces. For example, Lombroso (1918) studied prison inmates and suggested that criminals are a throwback to an earlier stage of evolution in that criminals have low foreheads, long arms, prominent jaws, and excessive body hair (Lombroso, 1918). Recent theories have moved away from such explanations and instead focus on social forces. These forces can be structural or the internalization of social bonds and social control mechanisms. Some theorists focus on the structural forces such as the differences in **power** relationships among individuals, which affect their ability to define what crime is or to escape prosecution when they do commit crime. Other theorists focus on the role of family, friends, and institutions in controlling criminal behaviours as well as instituting predispositions among individuals that help them to control themselves so that they will not commit crime even if there are opportunities to do so.

---

* Based on Nakhaie, Silverman, and LaGrange (2000, pp. 35–59).

In the late 1960s, Hirschi (1969) argued that socialization processes (in the family and other societal institutions) foster an individual's bond to society. These bonds are called external or

148

social control and include attachment to significant others (peers or parents), commitment or investment in conventional society (such as education), involvement in conventional behaviours (such as participation in recreational activities), and belief in society's values (respect for law and authorities). Therefore, those individuals who have higher attachment and commitment to, involvement with, and belief in conventional institutions are expected to have lower criminal tendencies. In a more recent work, Gottfredson and Hirschi (1990) argued that although external control is important, what is needed is early parental child rearing and school practices, which would help inhibit a child's undesirable immediate actions and would ensure internalization of these values and lessons. That is, normal everyday social interaction and socialization promote more self control, which has bearing on crime control.

Gottfredson and Hirschi (1990) argue that all actors are rational and thus equally motivated to pursue their own self-interest, which may include the commission of crime. However, the degree of self control and opportunities for crime vary among individuals. Ineffective childhood socialization in the family tends to produce an enduring criminal predisposition they call low (or lack of) self control. *Internal control* or **self control** refers to early parental child rearing and school practices that can help inhibit a child's undesirable immediate act and ensure internalization of values and norms that prevent future deviance. All that is required for adequate child rearing is a social investment in the child, such as monitoring, recognizing, and punishing bad behaviour. "The result may be a child more capable of delaying gratification, more sensitive to the interests and desires of others, more independent, more willing to accept restraints in his activity, and more unlikely to use force or violence to attain his ends" (1990, p. 97).

Further, Gottfredson and Hirschi (1990) argued that this is a general theory in that it can account for other explanations of crime. For example, they argued that the reason that males, Aboriginal peoples, and members of the lower classes commit more crime is that these groups have lower levels of self control than their counterparts. They point to the research that shows that lower-class children are more often risk-takers, impulsive and physical, less diligent and persistent, and easily excitable. It has been argued that lower-class culture reduces the ability to control. The tendency to be cautious, cognitive, and verbal is higher among girls than boys. Females are less impulsive and less disposed to act on the spur of the moment than males. They are less often risk-takers than boys. According to Nagler (1975), Aboriginal peoples are more present-oriented, do not have a work ethic, and have a different conception of time than non-Aboriginal peoples. These ascribed class, ethnic, and gender personality characteristics correspond closely to attributes of self control as conceptualized by Gottfredson and Hirschi (1990, p. 89).

Previous Research

Previous research on the importance of self control and crime shows the following:

- A measure of self control based on 24 questions showed a modest but significant relationship with imprudent behaviours (drinking, smoking, and gambling) (Arneklev et al., 1993) and with fraud and force (Grasmick et al., 1993).
- Using seatbelts when driving (risk-taking), not being discouraged by those who ask them not to drive under the influence (impulsiveness), and numbers of drinks consumed (self control) are related to driving under the influence of alcohol (Keane et al., 1993).

Therefore, previous research has substantiated the importance of self control for crime. Nevertheless, it is not clear if self control affects crime independent of social control as well as independent of other traditional predictors of crime such as age, gender, class, and **ethnicity.**

Research Importance and Questions

For effective policies, we need to isolate the most important sources of crime. If it were found that crime is primarily due to self control, the focus should be on early socialization. On the other hand, the importance of social control suggests that attention should be focused on social institutions during the individual life course. Similarly, the importance of age requires policies directed at youth; class and ethno-racial effects on crime may require intervention on issues such as poverty, unemployment, and poor living environment; while gender effects may direct us on issues such patriarchy and socialization.

Research Questions

1. Does self control affect crime?
2. Is social control related to crime?
3. Are the effects of self and social control independent of age, gender, and social class?
4. Do gender, class, and ethnic effects disappear when self control's effect is accounted for?

Based on the aforementioned theory suggested by Hirschi and by Gottfredson and Hirschi, we expect individuals with higher self and social control to commit less crime and that such effect should remain independent of class, age, and gender. Finally, it is expected that the effects of age, gender, and class disappear when the effect of self control is accounted for. This is due to the expectation that more crimes are committed by males, Aboriginal peoples, and lower social classes compared to others due to the lower self control by the formers.

Requirements for Testing the Relationship

Data for this research was generated by the University of Alberta Study of Juvenile and Adolescent Behaviour. The Alberta survey was completed in 1994 and involved a cross-section of students from grades 10 to 12 in 15 secondary schools in Edmonton, Alberta: five public high schools, six public junior high schools, two Catholic high schools, and two Catholic junior high schools.

Delinquency was measured by 20 questions that identified how frequently participants committed violent crimes, property crimes, and drug offences in the previous year. Participants were also assessed on characteristics pertaining to internal self control, such as risk-seeking, temper, carelessness, impulsivity, restlessness, and present orientation, as well as characteristics pertaining to external social control, such as peer attachment, parental involvement, and school commitment. Additional variables included neighbourhood income, gender, age, and ethnicity.

Do the Findings Support the Hypotheses?

Table 6.1.1 shows the **t-tests** for the differences between means for both self control and social control as well as for sum of all delinquency measures and for specific property, drug, and violent offence measures. There is a consistent pattern of lower self and social control and higher delinquency among boys compared to girls in general and in specific terms. These differences are all statistically significant, meaning that these are real differences that we will also find in the general population. Similarly, older boys have significantly lower levels of self and social control than younger adolescents and thus higher delinquency. Self-report violence is an exception—the difference is not significant.

Table 6.1.1 Means for Self and Social Control and Delinquency Measures by Predictors

	Self Control	Social Control	Delinquency	Property	Violent	Drug
Gender						
Male	14.17*	14.15*	7.44*	4.09*	2.09*	1.10*
Female	15.48	14.76	4.18	2.21	0.99	0.76
Age						
15 years –	15.53*	15.44*	4.12*	2.19*	1.46	0.84*
15 year +	14.47	13.92	6.68	3.64	1.54	1.29
Ethnicity						
Aboriginal	12.85*	13.96*	9.26*	4.75*	2.63*	1.60*
Racialized minorities	15.48*	14.56*	4.11*	2.35*	1.23*	0.40*
White	14.80	14.47	5.94	3.21	1.51	1.10
Household Income						
High	14.51	14.16	6.38	3.42	1.45	1.34
Upper middle	14.76	14.67*	5.17*	2.94*	1.30*	0.79*
Lower middle	15.15	14.58*	5.57*	2.97*	1.56	0.82*
Low	14.70	14.19*	6.87	3.60	1.76	1.28
Mean	14.83	14.46	5.77	3.13	1.52	0.93
N	2218	2272	2414	2414	2404	2406

* $P < .05$

Source: Nakhaie, Silverman, and LaGrange (2000, pp. 35–59).

Aboriginal peoples exhibit significantly lower levels of self control, while **racialized minorities** have higher self control than the white population. This pattern of high and low levels of self control corresponds to the pattern of delinquency among these ethnic groups. The multivariate analysis that takes into account all other relevant variables revealed that ethnic differences in social control (the institutions of family, school, and peers) are not statistically significant. This may suggest that the relationship between control and delinquency among ethnic groups is due to differences in self control rather than differences in social control. Early childhood differences are more important than the type of social control established by various institutions. The relationship of household income with self and social control mechanisms and with crime is curvilinear, with middle-income groups having significantly more social (but not self) control and thus having a lower level of delinquency than other groups. In sum, Table 6.1.1 generally supports the expectation that observed relationships between age, gender, and ethnicity with delinquency could be a function of both self and social control. The same cannot be said about social class as measured by income.

In order to test if the relationships between each predictor of delinquency persists independent of other variables, we need multivariate tests. This means that we need to test the effect of each variable while holding the effect of others constant. In other words, we are interested, for example, to know whether or not self control is related to delinquency if individuals have similar age, ethnic, and class backgrounds. Such a test revealed that both self control (measured by risk-taking, impulsivity, temperament, carelessness, and restlessness) and social control (measured by attachment to peers, involvement of parents, and commitment to school) were strongly related to all three types of delinquency. But more importantly, when self and social control operated together, the delinquent propensities were significantly lower. The findings suggested that early socialization in parental values is very important for conformity development. However, the early internalization of parental control needs to continue even in adolescence, and it needs to be augmented with individuals' commitment, attachment, and belief in social institutions in order to ensure that the youth do not commit crime, or if they do, they do less than would be expected without such control mechanisms.

Multivariate results also showed that the effect of age, gender, and ethnicity persisted even after taking into account the effect of self and social control. This means that these variables affect crime and delinquency independently of self or social control. These findings are not clearly consistent with the tenets of Gottfredson and Hirschi's General Theory, which predicts that the effects of sex, ethnicity, age, and class in crime are mainly due to the differences in self (and social) control mechanisms. It seems that there are other mechanisms at work that may account for the relationship between these variables and delinquency.

A final test showed that among the six indices of self control, risk-taking is indeed the best predictor of all types of delinquency, while impulsivity is the second best predictor of delinquency. In contrast, present orientation, restlessness, and carelessness are unrelated to any of the measures of delinquency. With respect to the social control construct, involvement with parents has the strongest predictive power for all types of delinquency, followed by commitment to school. Attachment to peers is related to delinquency, property crimes, and violent behaviours, but not to drug use.

153

What Can Be Concluded from the Findings?

The results of this study point to a strong effect of self control followed by social control in diminishing delinquency. These results lend strong support to Gottfredson and Hirschi's General Theory of Crime and control theories. However, it was shown that risk-taking is the strongest and impulsivity the second strongest self-control predictor of all kinds of delinquency. This finding, diminishes the novelty of the General Theory, as earlier criminological theories also pointed to the importance of risk-taking in explaining crime. More importantly, risk-taking is also an important attribute of non-criminal behaviour. When we talk about investment strategies or leadership qualities, risk-taking can be used in a very positive sense. To some extent, socialization can explain the internalization of one concept of risk-taking as opposed to another. One type of socialization results in people becoming risk-takers as a necessary ingredient of success and social respectability, while another line of socialization results in people viewing risk-taking as unacceptable. Risk-taking tendencies are culturally and historically specific and may be channelled toward either of these behaviours depending on opportunities.

We also showed that the relationship between age, gender, and ethnicity is to some extent a function of both self and social control. However, the importance of these variables for delinquency remains even after accounting for self and social control. That is, self and social control traits could not eliminate the sex, ethnicity, and age-crime relationships. It seems that factors other than self and social control contribute to the class, ethnic, and gender differences in crime. For example, Aboriginal peoples may commit more crime because they have historically been marginalized, experienced more poverty, and received more negative messages in school than other groups.

What Are the Possible Policy Implications?

Overall, this study points to the importance of early socialization process as well as the role of various institutions in instituting the necessary social bond in order to diminish crime and delinquency. As well, policies need to be also directed to reducing inequalities and improving the Aboriginal socioeconomic environment and addressing the needs and aspiration of adolescents.

Key Terms

Ethnicity: a group of people with common ethnic descent and cultural identification.

Power: refers to one's ability to influence others and reach a goal even against opposition from those who are subject to power.

Racialized minorities: a large group of people who have little power and are lumped into a racial grouping despite their differences in culture, identification, and background.

Self control: internalization of social control, usually at a young age.

Social control: the extent to which individuals are influenced by their social attachment, involvement, and beliefs.

T-test: a statistical test of difference between groups.

Critical Thinking Questions

1. Why do people commit crime? Explain.
2. What are the strengths and weaknesses of the General Theory of Crime?
3. How is self or social control developed? Explain.
4. To what extent are class differences in crime due to the upper classes' ability to escape being charged or going to prison?
5. To what extent is gender difference in crime due to the criminal justice's leniency toward women?
6. What are possible policy implications of the findings in this research?

Chapter 7

Gender Relations

What is sex? What about gender? How are they different? Are males and females different or the same? Why? What role does biology or society play in their differences and/or similarities? Are there cross-cultural differences between the two? What accounts for gender inequality? Why are women paid less than men and are segregated in low-paying and low-status occupations? Why are men and not women often in positions of power and wealth? Why are women responsible for most household tasks? Why are they subject to abuse and violence in and outside of the home? In other words, why are most of the institutions of society controlled by men and not women? Are the social institutions responsible for the gender differences or similarities? Why? These are some of the questions that we will discuss in this chapter.

Sex and Gender

Sex refers to biological and physical characteristics of maleness and femaleness. It is the biological body into which one is born. Sex distinguishes chromosomes (XX for females and XY for males), hormones (estrogen for female and testosterone for males), genitalia (clitoris, vagina, and uterus for females and penis and scrotum for males), and reproductive organs of males and females. A *sex role* is the pattern of behaviour that is expected of the sexes, such as women as child bearers and men as sperm donors. Therefore, sex is a designation based on male and female biology. However, these distinctions are somewhat simplistic. Recent research has shown that there are more than two sexes. For example, Hird (2000) argued that both sex and gender are social constructions, not just gender. By focusing on **intersexuality** and **transsexuality**, she identified varieties of sexes (e.g., XXY, XXXY, XXXXY, XXYY, XXXYY). In fact, all fetuses spend their first six weeks as an XX (female) in the amniotic fluid, until the release of testosterone for most XY (male) fetuses.

Gender refers to an individual's social characteristics. It refers to feminine or masculine traits, interests, or behaviours that society ascribes to each sex. These traits are cultural labels for males and females. They are the system of expectations with respect to masculine and feminine roles. Rubin (1975) has argued that gender is the social divisions that are imposed on sexes. *Gender roles* are expected attitudes and behaviours based on expression of one's sexual/gender identity (see Box 7.1).

Box 7.1 Sex Role and Gender Role

	Sex Role	Gender Role
Women	Child bearer	Mother, wife
Men	Sperm donor	Father, husband

In sum, sex is women's ability to give birth, while gender is women's socially expected behaviour of caring for the children. This does not mean that men can't care for children. Social taboos in the past have limited men's opportunity to do so. Rubin (1975, p. 183) has argued that such gendered divisions function in order to maintain obligatory heterosexuality. We should keep in mind that these sex and gender distinction are not cast in stone. For example, Hird (2000) has pointed out that, historically, physicians and surgeons have at times decided whether or not one is to be a male by looking at penile growth at an early age. Physicians reasoned that if there was little or no penile growth, then the male sex should be replaced by female genitals. That is, physicians determined the male sex by size of the penis rather than by chromosomes or the ability to produce sperm. In this regard, an infant with an XY chromosome is "constructed" as male, both in terms of the body and how "he" should be raised. In other words, societies may help create categories of sex—sex is socially constructed.

We can look at the well-known example of a male infant (John) whose penis was accidentally destroyed during the circumcision process when he was a baby. A plastic surgeon advised his parent to surgically reconstruct his genitals as female and to raise him as a female (Joan). According to Money and Ehrhardt (1972), gender reassignment was successful so that Joan at first liked dolls and female toys and was adjusting successfully as a girl (i.e., she became feminine). Nevertheless, she later asked doctors to reconstruct a penis for her. He identified himself as male (David) and later married a woman and adopted three children (Diamond & Sigmundson, 1997). John/Joan/David's case points to how the category of sex is socially constructed and how sex and gender are distinguishable from each other.

Similarly, Hird (2000) has pointed out that there has been an increase in the number of intersexual individuals, which points to the variability of sexual identification beyond the male/female binaries. The increase of intersexuals and transsexuals also raises the question of whether one can experience the world authentically as female or male. This problem thus challenges feminist and male movements. Hird (2000) asked: is male or female identity sexed or gendered? She argued that we cannot use "nature" to define the constitution of sex or how individuals know their gender. As Mead said long ago, self cannot exist without society. Hird similarly argued that sex itself is a construction.

Almost all societies are stratified along sex or gender lines. Even though there have been some changes in recent times, there is a general tendency for females to be viewed as sentimental, emotional, and subjective, whereas males are viewed as independent, logical, and objective. If a male is weak, he is called a sissy, and if a girl is tough, she is called a tomboy. Males tend to become physicians, engineers, and firefighters, and females tend to become nurses, secretaries, and kindergarten teachers. Why are there such differences in perceptions, attitudes, behaviours, and outcomes? There are various explanations for these differences.

Importance of Gender

Although there was a great deal of women participation in abolitionist and prohibition movements, gender became more of an important topic of interest in society and among social scientist after World War II. Before World War II, although working class women were generally participating in the labour force, middle-class women mostly stayed home and did not participate in the paid force. In general, women were isolated in the private sphere and relied on male breadwinners for their subsistence and livelihood. Their sense of satisfaction was based on the prestige of their husband/father's job (Friedan, 1963). After World War II, women's labour force participation increased, as did their organizational activities and consciousness. They began to question their dependency on men as natural and inevitable. Moreover, they started to question the educational curricula that were designed to make them docile and passive. They started to transform the educational system and develop a sociological imagination that saw institutional discrimination as the source of their oppression and subjugation.

Three important factors have contributed to the importance of gender since World War II:

- Feminist ideology and the women's liberation movement have highlighted the struggle for women's interests.
- Female labour force participation has increased substantially.
- There has been more role strain between males and females.

Gender is an important social ordering component. Males and females are hierarchically ordered in most societies and human periods. Division of labour is historically based on gender roles.

As Table 7.1 shows females are more likely to do unpaid work of looking after children and the elderly and doing housework than are males.

Table 7.1 Average Hours of Unpaid Work by Gender

Unpaid Tasks	Female	Male
Hours spent doing unpaid housework	3.37	2.78
Hours spent looking after children	2.22	1.82
Hours spent providing care or assistance to seniors	1.36	1.24

Source: Adapted from Statistics Canada (2006).

Table 7.2 Percent of Males and Females in Sex-typed Occupations

	Males	Females
Male Occupations		
Heavy equipment operators	97.8	2.2
Construction	96.8	3.2
Forestry, mining and oil	93.1	6.9
Primary production labourers	82.9	17.1
Protective services	81.6	18.4
Professional occupations	61.5	38.5
Senior management	75.3	24.7
Machine operators	70.7	29.3
Female Occupations		
Secretaries	2.1	97.9
Registered nurses and supervisors	5.9	94.1
Child care and home support	6.4	93.6
Assistant occupations in health	13.3	86.7
Cashiers	14.1	85.9
Food and beverage services	22.6	77.4
Clerical	27.3	72.7
Administrative and regulatory	27.4	72.6
Retail sales and clerks	39.9	60.1

Source: Adapted from Statistics Canada (2001).

When women work for pay, they are less likely to be in managerial occupations and more likely to work in lower paid clerical and service occupations than are males. Moreover, males and females tend to occupy **sex-segregated occupations.** *Sex-typed* occupations are those occupations that are seen as appropriate for males and females. Men are perceived to be strong and authoritarian and best to perform construction, manufacturing and managerial occupations. Women are perceived as nurturers and supportive and best to fill nurturing or service occupations (see Table 7.2).

Such sex-typing and the resulting *sexual segregation* of the labour force would also result in pay differences. For example, in Canada, for every dollar that males earn, females earn about 70 cents (see Table 7.3). Generally, in all societies past and present, males are advantaged in terms of wealth, power, authority, and status.

Table 7.3 Average Earnings by Gender, 1995–2004 (Constant Dollars, 2004)

	Full-Time, Full-Year Workers		
Year	**Women**	**Men**	**Ratio W/M**
1995	35,500	49,100	72.4
1996	34,900	48,300	72.3
1997	34,600	50,700	68.3
1998	37,100	51,700	71.9
1999	35,700	52,200	68.4
2000	36,900	52,200	70.6
2001	37,200	53,300	69.9
2002	37,500	53,400	70.2
2003	37,300	53,200	70.2
2004	38,400	54,900	69.9

Source: Adapted from Statistics Canada (2011).

Gender and Violence

Women not only occupy lower status and occupations and are paid less than men but also are subject to significant violence at home, school, and work. That is to say, patriarchal relations persist both in the public and private domains. Dobash et al. (1992) reviewed the evidence from courts, police, women's shelters, divorce records, emergency room patients, hospitals, victimization, and self-report surveys and concluded that there is a clear sexual asymmetry in conjugal violence. Males are significantly more likely to engage in violent activity in conjugal relationships than females.

This evidence clearly supports the feminist argument that males use violence to establish their patriarchal power within the family (i.e., sexual asymmetry of violence). Other research relying on self-report surveys, have pointed to a sexual symmetry in conjugal violence. They suggest that men and women equally engage in violent activity in conjugal violence. This evidence moves away from a single cause explanation and searches for the root of conjugal violence in such factors as education, income, occupation, employment status, class, culture, age, and alcohol. For example, Nakhaie (1998) showed that conjugal violence is age-graded. It is asymmetrical among the younger couples and more symmetrical among the older couples. In the early years of marriage, males are better capable of inflicting violent suffering on their younger and physically weaker partner than females are on their older and stronger partners. In the later years, males' physical strength deteriorates faster than their partners', both because of the differences in the age of marriage and that of a lower life expectancy for males compared to females. This deterioration results in a lower capability for violence against the wife, a higher need for care, and a higher degree of physical and mental impairment. It is, therefore, important to understand that there are many reasons for sexual violence and its dynamic is not well explained.

Biological Explanation of Gender Differences

Evolutionary theorists have argued that much of gender differences in attitudes and behaviours can be explained by differences in survival and reproductive adaptation. Biological explanation of gender tends to promote sexism. **Sexism** is the belief that women are inferior to men, often based on their biology.

Evolutionary theorists argue that the human brain is developed to solve problems that are important to the survival and reproduction of human beings. Trivers (1972), for example, argued that gender differences in attitudes and behaviours are due to historically developed and biologically adapted gender differences in sexual selection. Accordingly, men and women faced different adaptive challenges. Women's challenges included their increased need for resources such as food and their diminishing ability to provide for themselves during pregnancy and child rearing. Men's challenge was to ensure that the child that they provided for and reared was 100 percent their own child. This meant that males and females developed different sexual strategies, such as male competitiveness towards other males in order to have sexual access to many females, while females preferred sexual encounters with a limited number of males who had high quality resources. Consequently, females developed a strategy of choosing long-term partners while males were satisfied with short-term partners.

Evolutionary theorists believe that these sexual selection practices in turn explain gender differences in behaviours such as in aggression, risk-taking, adventurousness, emotionality, and desire for and care of babies. Evidence does not seem to support the theory. A review of research by Smiler (2011) has shown that, in fact, there are more male-female similarities in sexual behaviours than differences. Critiques have also argued that by paying attention to between-gender differences we cannot account for within-gender differences—differences between males or between females in sexual strategies are substantial.

Other researchers have focused on hormonal differences between males and females. Ross et al. (2006) have shown that X chromosomes tend to influence aspects of cognition. Doreen Kimura (2002) has argued that men and women display different cognitive and behavioural patterns because of differences in hormonal influences on brain development. Similarly, more male-typed interests and behaviours such as aggressiveness and preference in participation in male activities are shown to be related to prenatal androgen excess (Pasterski et al., 2005). Research has also shown that human biology is not static. For example, the environment helps change the brain. As an example, studies have shown a large difference in the spatial ability of males and females. Spatial ability is also related to gender differences in math and science performance. Nevertheless, studies have shown that computer and action games increase mental rotation and spatial attention. More importantly, females gained more than males in these abilities when playing these games (see Cherney, 2008; Feng et al., 2007).

Generally, we tend to have a misleading view of the difference between males and females. For example, there is a perception that men are aggressive and women are passive. The evidence does not exactly support this perception. Both men and women are found to be aggressive. The only difference is that on the average males are more aggressive than are females. But, it does not mean that males are aggressive and females are passive. A substantial number of females would be more aggressive than a substantial number of males. As the graph in Box 7.2 shows, a large number of male are less aggressive than average females (the blue area) and a large number of females are more aggressive than the average males (the pink area).

Box 7.2*

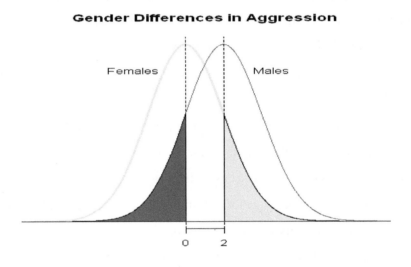

Gender Differences in Aggression

* The graph was drawn by Robert Arnold

Moreover, the research on the difference in aggressive behaviours between males and females has increasingly come under scrutiny and been questioned. Tieger (1980) reviewed the previous research and argued that existence of sex differences in aggression among adults does not justify the conclusion that males are more aggressive than females, because adults have been subject to socialization and influenced by sex-role stereotypes. Therefore, it is appropriate to study children since they are less likely to be subject to social development. His re-evaluation of previous research among children below six years of age showed a number of contradicting results. First, cross-cultural evidence is inconsistent and even does not show that males are more aggressive than females. When gender differences in aggression are observed in a community, it

164

is often due to the extent to which that community has a dominance structure. As an example, boys are more aggressive when in the presence of peers and less aggressive when parents are present. Second, among animals, many species show no clear sex differences in aggressive behaviour, and male aggressiveness depends on type of animal selected. Baboons are highly aggressive while our closest cousins—chimpanzees, gorillas, and orangutans—are relatively nonaggressive. Even among baboons, savannah-dwelling baboons are more aggressive than those inhabiting a forested region.

Anthropological Explanations of Gender Differences

Another explanation searches for the sources of gender inequality in early human history. For example, Marvin Harris (1977) argued that gender inequality and the tendency for males to be aggressive and females passive can be traced to early societies where males were the principle combatants. He argues that early combat was extremely dangerous and that many men did not want to fight despite the fact that the existence of the whole community could depend on it. In order to motivate and psychologically prepare males' involvement in warfare, a system of reward was developed where victorious warriors were awarded wives and concubines. In fact, military alliance in some societies was solidified by exchanging women. These practices, Harris argues, may have been the source of male aggression and dominating characteristics.

Others suggest that women's involvement in childbearing and child rearing resulted in a sexual division of labour in the early history of humanity. Accordingly, bearing and rearing children prevented women's geographical mobility. Instead, they developed domestic skills. Men, not being limited to their immediate domestic environment, became hunters, were involved in warfare and religion, and controlled cultural ideas. This division of labour resulted in the development of two types of personalities. Women were socialized to focus on feelings, communion, and nurture and men to develop task mastery, competition, and a strong ego. This differentiation resulted in men's acquisition of privileges, power, and resources that put them in dominant positions. They utilized this position to rule subordinate groups such as women by defining norms and rules. As can be seen, the real source of males' dominant personality is their early historical control of power and resources, which resulted in further production of cultural meanings and privileges compared to females.

Functionalist Theory

Functionalists believe that the social system is made of interdependent parts. Each part performs a function that is necessary to the social system. In hunting and agricultural societies, social roles were assigned based on male and female role specialization. Men were involved in hunting and agricultural production and were responsible for bringing food and protecting the family. They were designated as the 'breadwinners.' Women, due to pregnancy, childbirth, and nursing were assigned the home responsibility tasks. They gathered food and took care of children and family members. These historical responsibilities ensured task specializations based on expressive and instrumental roles and helped maintain social equilibrium. **Instrumental roles** involve occupations external to the house and include achievement and task orientation. When husbands/fathers take these roles, they are expected to maintain the physical integrity of the family by providing food and shelter. **Expressive roles** are emotionally oriented types of roles and involve tasks related to the house that are suited for women's biological ties to childbirth and nursing. In performing specific roles, husbands/wives/fathers/mothers ensure that the household runs smoothly. Basic needs are provided and children have a positive and warm growth environment. This equilibrium and the family's survival are threatened when there is too much deviation from these roles, such as when tasks are overlapped. For example, if both partners work outside and become 'breadwinners,' conflict between them could arise, thus increasing family instability and divorce. Therefore, for functionalists, it is functional for the survival of the family if husbands work outside and wives work inside the house.

Symbolic Interactionism

Recall that socialization is defined as the process by which one learns to become a member of the society. That is, one acquires selfhood, knowledge, and skills, which would link him or her to the wider social world. Gender socialization refers to the process by which the society teaches masculine or feminine characteristics. Each society has its own **gender scripts** or emotions, thoughts and behaviours, shaping femininity and masculinity. A gender stereotype is a gender script. A **stereotype** is an exaggerated view of a group of people where there is substantial agreement among the public on the attributing characteristics of the group. Stereotypes could be true or false. Either way, stereotypes tend to both represent and distort reality (see Box 7.3). For example, there is a prevailing gender stereotypes that women are emotional while men are objective. Cross-cultural research shows that people in many countries tend to have stereotypes of males and females as instrumental and expressive respectively (see Box 7.4).

Box 7.4 Cross-cultural Stereotypes about Males and Females

Male	Females
independent	sentimental
adventurous	submissive
dominant	affectionate
aggressive	passive
not emotional	emotional
objective	subjective
never cries	cries often
ambitious	not ambitious

Source: Based on research by Broverman et al. (1972, pp. 59–78).

Stereotypes tend to help gender socialization which in turn helps further development of masculinity and femininity. Parents give masculine and feminine names to their children and they tend to use blue and pink clothing to distinguish them. When interacting with their children parents often use phrases such as 'my big boy' and 'my sweet little girl.' Language has a tendency to ensure gender identity development. We often use terms such 'mankind,' 'man the social animal,' 'men of good will,' and 'gentleman.' A girl behaving like a boy is called 'tomboy,' and a boy behaving like a girl is called 'sissy.' Other terms such 'slut,' and 'whore' are used to denigrate women. The term 'bitch' is used to insult a woman while there is no such term for men. Instead, the phrase 'son of a bitch' still references and devalues women. These patterns of devaluation and creation of gender hierarchy is then produced and reproduced by media and other social institutions. In general, the socialization process tends to reaffirm and justify the pattern of segregation, inequality, and role differentiation by the creation of a psychic structure wherein women are socialized to be passive and subservient while men to be active and dominant. The socialization process is therefore very important for the development of **gender identity** where males and females develop a sense of belonging to and identify with their specific sex.

Gender identity is shaped in interaction with 'significant others,' 'generalized others,' 'role taking,' and 'the looking-glass self.' Symbolic interactionists believe also that gender differences in identity and roles emerge due to interactions with others in the family, school, and religious institutions. The socialization of boys and girls in the family differs by giving them either a boy's name or a girl's name, blue or pink clothing, and different curfew times, among other things, all of which helps to shape different types of gender identities. For example, parents were asked to rate their infant children on a variety of terms. The girls were often rated by their parents as softer, more delicate, pretty, cute, while boys were rated as big (Rubin et al., 1974). Although many of these gender-typing stereotypes remain, nevertheless, they are in decline (Hildebrandt et al., 1995). Most parents still tend to stimulate boys more than girls in "gross motor behaviours." They handle girls as if "they are more fragile than boys." They encourage gendered toy choices for their male and female children and are more physically punitive toward boys than girls. These gender differences in stimulation help with gender role socialization during infancy and greater or lesser aggressive behaviours later in life (Maccoby & Jacklin, 1974; Tieger, 1980).

Eagly and Steffen (1986) review of 63 different studies on sex differences in aggression revealed a relatively small difference and inconsistent results. Bjorkqvist's (1994) review of the research concluded that sex differences in aggression are most likely developed through learning processes.

Moreover, Tieger (1980) reviewed the research that showed that girls acquire language earlier than boys and are more likely to involve themselves in interpersonal language use than boys are. Therefore, girls are more likely to use their language skills as a conflict resolution strategy than boys. This may be a rational female survival strategy since they are physically weaker, on average, than males. Boys instead use their physical strength. Similarly, females are discouraged from being aggressive as it is "unladylike," while boys are encouraged to be aggressive because "boys will be boys."

Boys and girls may rely on the same-sex parent as a role model. Since traditionally fathers tend to have more authority than mothers at home, boys and girls might develop different authority personalities. As well, the types of games boys and girls play differ. Boys tend to be involved in games with larger numbers of individuals, which fosters competitiveness and aggressiveness. Females tend to play in small groups, which allows development of emotional attachment to playmates.

Other agents of socialization also play important roles in shaping differential gender identities. School officials may direct boys and girls toward different subject matters based on sex. For example, teachers may play a key role in promoting gender stereotype attitudes and behaviours among pupils. Fennema et al. (1990) showed that first-grade teachers view their male students to be more logical, independent, competitive, and interested in math than female students. Teachers with such gender-stereotype views of their students also have gender-stereotypes view of their students' math ability (Tiedemann, 2002). Such attitudes may result in students having gender-stereotyped math abilities themselves. Therefore, teachers' views and attitudes towards students' ability and students' incorporation of those views may explain why female students have more negative math (or other abilities) attitudes when compared to male students (Gunderson et al., 2012).

Television and movies are also somewhat responsible for development of gender stereotypes. In a study of nine Disney Princess movies from 1937 to 2009, England et al. (2011) showed that these movies, though declining, portrayed some stereotypical representations of gender. The findings are consistent with Thompson and Zerbino's (1995) study of 175 episodes of 41 different American television cartoons, which presented gender stereotype messages where males were presented more as assertive and independent while females were presented more as sensitive and affectionate. Similar findings are observed in over 50 years of magazine product advertisements (Mager & Helgson, 2011).

Religion also may help shape male and female perceptions of authority along gender lines. In most religions fathers are viewed as the head of the family. Most religious authority figures both in the past or present are males. There are also verses in holy books that encourage female subordination. For example, we can find statements such as wives be in subjection to your own husband (Peter 3:1), women are commanded to be under obedience (I Corinthians 14:34), and the head of the woman is the man (I Corinthians 11:3) in the Bible.

Overall, these agents of socialization tend to portray males and females in stereotypical ways (see Box 7.5, page 171). To the extent that boys and girls internalize these stereotypes, their personality is shaped along masculine and feminine divides. Males learn to be strong, tough, competitive, aggressive, and violent, and girls learn to be affectionate, caring, and passive. However, these attitudes and behaviours are not consistent across time and place. Societies that emphasise gender-egalitarian attitudes are less likely to promote gender-stereotype behaviours and attitudes. Moreover, the tendency for gender stereotypical attitudes and behaviours has declined in families, in schools, in media, and among males and females.

Marxist Theory

According to Marxists the development of private property facilitated control of women's labour and body by men in the past. In more recent times, under capitalism, Marxists view women as workers who are involved in reproduction of labour power in the house by performing housework tasks and by rearing and nurturing future workers. In this sense, women's work in the house is seen as necessary for capitalist production and reproduction. First, their labour ensures availability of future workers, and second, it ensures that their husbands' needs, as workers, are satisfied, making available a fresh and relaxed worker for capitalist exploitation on a daily basis.

Friedrich Engels, Karl Marx's close friend and collaborator, argued that the development of private property in agricultural society was an important source of gender inequality. In modern days, Marxists argue that society tends to value commodities produced for exchange and undervalue commodities produced for use at home. For example, people in the capitalist system tend not to consider household labour (such as childbearing, cooking, and cleaning) to be real work and do not pay women for this work. Since women generally work inside the house and their work has only **use value** (produced for using at home), their work is undervalued. On the other hand, because men generally work outside the house and produce **exchange value** (produced for exchange in the market), their work is valued more than that of women. Consequently, despite the fact that the work women do is essential for perpetuation of capitalist society (e.g., producing and socializing future labourers and ensuring that existing labourers—husbands or working family members—are properly rested and taken care of, thus ready for another day of work), women's work has lower status, and women get paid less (refer back to Table 7.3).

Box 7.5 Agents of Socialization and Gender

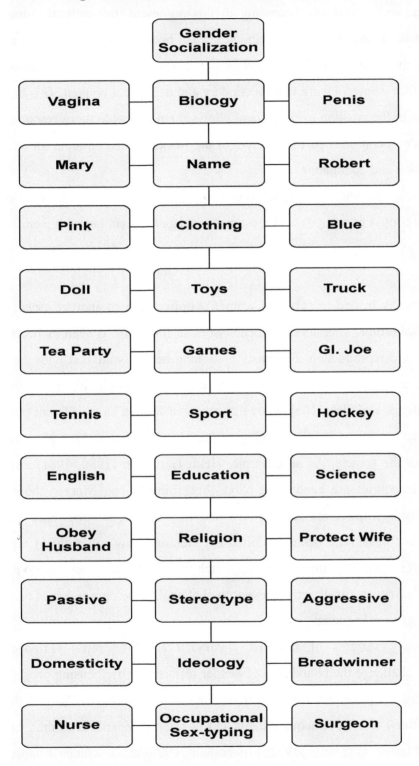

Similarly, Marxists argue that capitalists use women's labour as a **"reserve army of labour."** Women are called into the labour force when they are needed and sent back to the home when there are extra workers. According to this argument, the cultural value that "a woman's place is in the home" helps the capitalist system because it gives just cause to send women home when they are no longer needed in the labour force. Therefore, the capitalist system tends to consider women's work to be secondary and dependent on men. This differential treatment places men in the position of power and allows them access to more resources. Thus, for Marxists, women's liberation is part and parcel of the working-class struggle for elimination of capitalist exploitation and domination.

A Marxist's solution, short of a revolution for communism, is for women to enter the labour force and take control of property and resources, not against men, but with men.

Feminist Theory

Marxists have historically tended to subsume women's **oppression** as another aspect of class **exploitation** and **domination**. Therefore, women's work in the house is seen as necessary for capitalist production and reproduction. Feminists have long been dissatisfied with the Marxist explanation of women's oppression that tends to subsume women's liberation under the working-class struggle for socialism. They argue that men and women have different positions in society that are crucially significant in explaining women's oppression as long as sex structure remains significant in the society. As an example, Heidi Hartmann (1980, 1981) argued that Marxist theory and categories are gender/sex blind. According to her, Marxist theories have failed to deal with feminist questions such as how and why women are oppressed as women perform unpaid labour for, and are being exploited by, men and how patriarchy is reproduced within capitalism. Not surprisingly, the feminist approach has insisted that they should produce a theory about women's lives that is directly relevant to challenging the oppression of women and improving women's position in society.

There are many variants of **feminist theory**. *Liberal* feminists (Frieden, 1963; Wollstoncraft, 1971) challenge the boundaries of gender differences by focusing on gender role socialization. Their main solution is for women to educate themselves as well as join the labour force, which would allow women to acquire status and position independent of their husbands' or partners.' *Marxist* feminists (Engles, 1972; Rowbotham, 1973) relate women's oppression to that of capitalism, as discussed above (see also Box 7.6). *Radical* feminists (Brownmiller, 1975;

Firestone, 1970) focus on the biological source of women's oppression and the use of violence by men to control women. For these feminists, the most important social division is not based on class, as Marxists would suggest; rather, the main division is based on sex where men strive for power over women. This form of domination is called **patriarchy**: a male-dominated social system that ensures female subordination and oppression. Sexism is rooted in patriarchy. *Socialist* feminists (Hartmann, 1980; Mitchell, 1971, 1974) agree with Marxists on the importance of class relations for understanding women's oppression but focus on the interconnection between sexual oppression and class oppression. For them, *both* patriarchal and capitalist oppression needs to be eradicated. *Psychoanalyst* feminists focus on how women are made and girl infants are gendered through guilt and anxiety and experiences such as lack of penis or phallus (Barrett, 1992; Lacan, 1968). *Post-structural* feminists (Parr, 1990), rooted in the work of the French post-structuralist Jacques Derrida (1967), try to unmask binary

Box 7.6

Men and women are brought up for a different position in the labor force: the men for the world of work, the women for her family. This difference in the sexual division of labor in society means that the relationship of men as a group to production is different from that of women... Female production in the family means that the commodity producer, the husband, and the future producers, the children, survive to produce commodities which are exchanged. The separation of male/female roles is thus materially as well as ideologically part of the way in which capitalism is maintained.

(Rowbotham, 1973, p. 61)

oppositions such as masculine/feminine, public/private, paid/unpaid work, which have made women invisible, and ignore differences between women by race, ethnicity, and class. From this, anti-racist feminists or feminists of people of colour emerged. In general, all feminists agree that gender inequality is a pervasive feature of most (if not all) societies and that gender inequality requires a distinct theoretical framework because women's oppression is distinct from other oppressions.

Summary

Gender is a social construction distinguishable from sex or biological differences between males and females. Various social institutions historically have been responsible for helping socialization of males and females with different aspiration and their differences in access to scarce resources. Gender differences in socialization start with parents and caretakers and continue with peers and other agents of socialization such as religion, education, media, politics, and economy. Not only these microlevel forces but also macrostructural forces such as capitalism and patriarchy are responsible for the inequality between males and females. Sociological theories such as functionalism see gender differences as functional to the survival of the society while conflict and feminist theories view these differences as resulting in gender inequality and oppression of women in a class-divided and/or male-dominant society.

Key Terms

Domination: institutionalization of control of one group by another.

Exchange value: value or product created for exchange in the market.

Exploitation: the process by which members of one class (e.g., capitalists) extract surplus value or surplus labour from members of another class (e.g., workers).

Expressive roles: emotionally oriented roles involving tasks related to household such as child rearing, childbearing.

Feminist theory: the evaluation and explanation of why women have less power and resources than men and how to challenge and transform such imbalance.

Gender: personal traits and social positions that are attached to males and females.

Gender identity: culturally appropriate male and female traits and personalities.

Gender script: emotions, thoughts, and behaviours shaping femininity and masculinity.

Instrumental roles: achievement and task-oriented roles involving occupations external to the household.

Intersexuality: an individual showing biological characteristics of both sexes.

Oppression: the act of keeping individuals or groups in subjugation through the unjust use of force or authority; the state of being in subjugation.

Patriarchy: social organization where males dominate females.

Reserve army of labour: a part of the labour force that is drawn into the labour market when needed by capitalists and is pushed out of that market when no longer needed. Women and minority ethno-racial groups are said to constitute such a flexible labour supply.

Sexism: a belief that one's own sex is innately superior to the other.

Sex-segregated occupations: the extent to which any occupation is concentrated by males or females. The higher the concentration of one of the sexes in one occupation, the more that occupation is sex-segregated.

Stereotype: a simplified belief about characteristics of a social group. Such belief minimizes a group's differences and maximizes its similarities. It exaggerates based on too little information.

Transexuality: people who feel they are one sex though biologically they are the other.

Use value: value of things created for self-consumption.

Critical Thinking Questions

1. In your mind, what is the best explanation of gender differences in personality development?
2. What is the best explanation of gender inequality? Why?
3. Pay attention to the negative terms used to refer to males and females by you and your friends. Do these terms place males or females in an inferior position? Why do you think these terms are used?
4. What are your views on the various schools of feminism? Explain your views on those that you agree with and also those that you disagree with.
5. Do you think that sex is biological or a social construction?
6. Are men and women fundamentally different from each other? Why or why not?
7. To what extent do you think men's and women's career choices are based on gender socialization and gender stereotypes?
8. Why is gender an important sociological topic? Was gender always an important topic of research?

Sociological Example: Housework Contribution of Professors*

Introduction: Research Purpose

Gender is an important social ordering component. Males and females are hierarchically ordered where, in most if not all societies and human periods, males are advantaged in terms of wealth, power, authority, and status. Division of labour is historically based on gender roles and on norms that guide human actions. Women are allocated roles that include nurturing and taking care of the home, while men are allocated roles that include breadwinning and decision making.

These roles have been recently under attack with the advent of industrialization, the increasing economic independence and labour force participation of women, and a significant increase in women's aspirations and entry into professional careers. These occupations require greater time commitments, motivation, responsibility, and competency. If individuals focus on work at the expense of family, they will likely experience work–family conflict by neglecting one domain for the other. The balance between paid and domestic work for women may require husbands who are willing to share family responsibilities. A supporting husband reduces family-to-work conflict (i.e., he helps decrease work distraction, work irritability, and the efforts needed to devote to the job). Nevertheless, almost all studies show that women, even those who work full-time outside the house, are doing the lion's share of the housework.

Why do women do more share of the housework? In order to answer this question, we focus on a sample of Canadian university professors and evaluate various theories that sociologists use to explain housework.

Theoretical Explanation

There are several explanations for the housework contribution of partners. These theories can be divided into *instrumental* and *symbolic* approaches. The instrumental or pragmatic approach includes rational/practical and resource/power considerations. The *rational/practical* approach focuses on time availability. That is, the contribution to housework is said to depend on free time after involvement in paid work. It is argued that as individuals' free time increases, their participation in housework will increase. The *power/resource* approach suggests that resources

---

* Based on Nakhaie (2009, pp. 399–411).

176

such as income are instrumental in the family structure. Those with greater income are better able to exercise their will or bargain in order to achieve desired goals, such as doing less housework. This explanation is derived from the notion of fair exchange, which is negotiated on the basis of each spouse's earnings.

While the time availability and power/resource hypotheses are useful in explaining how partners negotiate housework, these models fail to explain why, for example, men who earn less than their partners or are unemployed do not share housework.

One reason for these models' shortcoming is that they do not pay attention to cognitive and ideological strategies used by men in order to avoid housework or used by women to justify doing more housework than their partner. For this reason, the *symbolic/relational* approach pays attention to the importance of gender-based ideology or gender identity in the performance of housework. Although this approach has different names (gender socialization, gender-role attitudes, or orientation), the fundamental argument is that the principle of sexual equality and men's and women's gender attitudes, beliefs, and ideas, are instrumental in the division of housework. Therefore, this model suggests that as the support for gender equality increases, the housework performed by men increases and that of women decreases.

The rational/symbolic approach highlights the importance of ideas and beliefs about fairness and justice within the context of the household and in relation to gender alone. This approach can be extended to include the ideas about justice in a broader societal context. Another important ideology is rooted in dominant *class relations* under *capitalism*. The dominant groups in each society adhere to and promote a type of ideology that legitimizes their position. This "dominant" ideology tends to legitimize social inequalities by assigning worldly success or failure to personal rather than structural causes. It encourages individual choice as opposed to social responsibility. To the extent that this ideology is embedded in every aspect of society, it also provides the framework for validating other social inequities such as patriarchy. Thus, men's powerful economic position in society can be used to legitimatize their dominance at home and elsewhere in society. Yet those who question this ideology may be more likely to view all inequities as unacceptable. In other words, cognitive congruency in adherence to various types of ideology may exist. Egalitarian attitudes in one area (e.g., class-based egalitarianism) help shape, or at least may be correlated with, egalitarian attitudes in another area (e.g., gender equality). Therefore, it can be expected that not only does class-based ideology affect housework, but that it may even diminish the potential effect of gender-based ideology on housework.

Previous Research

Previous research generally supports the rational/practical and power/resource approaches, but its support for the symbolic/relational support is not consistent. Previous research has shown the following:

- The number of hours of paid work is negatively related to housework for both men and women (Estes et al., 2007). However, a study of Canadian data showed that men's hours of paid work decrease their share of housework more than the same hours do for women (Nakhaie, 1995).

- Some researchers have shown that as income increases, one's share of housework decreases (Nakhaie, 1995). Others have been unable to support this relationship (see Harpster & Monk-Turner, 1998). Similarly, it has been shown that men's higher income compared to their wives tends to decrease their share of housework (Kamo, 1988). But, women's higher income compared to their husbands does not result in the same effect (Brines, 1994).

- Religious individuals have more traditional gender attitudes and husbands seem to structure their contribution to housework dependent on their adherence to a gender-based ideology (Nakhaie, 2002). The effect of gender-related attitudes on housework tends to be stronger for men than for women (Estes et al., 2007).

Therefore, previous research though at times inconsistent has substantiated the importance of time availability, power/resources, and ideology for contribution to housework. It is not clear if the importance of ideology can be extended to include the ideas about justice in other contexts, such as class-based views.

Research Importance and Questions

There has been a significant increase in women's entry into professional careers, including academic work. For these women, traditional gender roles, which require that women do most if not all of the housework, act as a barrier to success in academia. Although research has substantiated the importance of the traditional explanation for division of housework, its effect has not been substantial. All studies have shown that gender plays the most important role in explaining housework contribution of partners. Therefore, it is important to scrutinize other forces that may explain housework and thus help women diminish the burden of the **"double shift."** For this purpose, we focus on the role of a class-based **egalitarian ideology.**

Research Questions

The research question that guides this study is the following: How does class-based ideology help explain the housework of male and female professors?

Based on various theories discussed above, we hypothesize the following:

1. The higher the time availability of men or women, the higher their share of housework.

2. The higher the relative income of men or women compared to their partner, the lower their share of housework.

3. The more support for gender and egalitarian ideology, the more equal will be the share of housework.

Requirements for Testing the Relationship

The data source is Nakhaie's survey of the *Academic Profession in Canada: Political and Ethnic Culture of Canadian Universities*. It was administered to a stratified random sample of full-time faculty members. The present study focuses on married and cohabiting male and female professors, consisting of 72.3 and 9.1 percent, respectively. Housework is measured by a question asking professors to indicate the percentage of general household tasks (cleaning, cooking, child care, etc.) done by them and by their partner. Support for gender equality is measured by asking whether respondents agree/disagree on a four-point scale with two statements: 1) "It is important to guarantee equal opportunities between men and women in all aspects of life," and 2) "One of Canada's goals should be to guarantee equal rights for men and women." Similarly, measurement of class-based egalitarianism also asks respondents to indicate on a four-point scale whether they agree or disagree with the following two statements: 1) "People of high income should pay a greater share of the taxes than they do now," and 2) "One of Canada's goals should be to even out differences in wealth between people." The relative income is measured by subtracting the respondent's income from the total reported household income, which would imply that what is left is their partner's income. Time availability is measured by the number of hours spent doing university work per week.

Other variables that were included in this study are the discipline of employment such as liberal arts (humanities, social sciences) and sciences (engineering, health sciences), religiosity (religious or not), and presence of pre-school children.

Do the Findings Support the Hypotheses?

Table 7.1.1 shows that female professors are significantly more likely than male professors to do housework (58.7 versus 37.8 percent). Female professors' relative contribution to housework is about 21 percent more than that of male professors. As well, men and women of academia do less share of the housework if their contribution to the family income is higher than their partners and if they are in the liberal arts disciplines. Female professors who have more available time (i.e., they work fewer hours in the university) contribute more to housework when compared to their counterparts, while the more religious male professors do less housework. Although gender ideology does not affect the share of housework (i.e., the relationship is not significant), class-based ideology strongly affects male professors' share of housework. In fact, after gender, class-based ideology and working in liberal arts disciplines have the strongest effect in decreasing the share of housework performed by female and increasing that of male professors. For example, the difference between male and female professors' share of housework is 16.9 percent ($57.7 - 40.8 = 16.9$) among those with a high level of class-based egalitarianism, and 14.5 percent ($57.2 - 42.7 = 14.5$) among professors working in the liberal arts disciplines. Similarly, the difference in housework between male professors in liberal arts and sciences is 7.7 percent, while for females, it is only 2.6 percent. The difference in share of housework between male professors with a supportive attitude toward egalitarianism and those who do not have such supportive views is 5.8 percent. This type of ideology also reduces women's share of housework but not significantly (i.e., only 2.6 percent). In other words, ideology and discipline affect male professor's share of housework more than that of female professors.

Multivariate results generally confirmed these findings. That is, when we evaluated all professors with similar characteristics, males with higher relative incomes, those who were more religious, those in the science disciplines, and those with a lower support for class-based egalitarianism tended to perform less share of the housework. An egalitarian attitude, more hours spent on university work, and a higher relative income resulted in lower housework performance by female professors.

Table 7.1.1 Canadian University Professor's Average Share of Housework by Predictors

	Males			Females		
	Mean	Sig	N	Mean	Sig	N
Share of housework	37.8	*	1779	58.7		613
Lower or equal to partner's income	43.5		61	62.2		153
Higher income than partner	37.5	*	1809	57.6	*	502
Less than 35 hours of university work	35.6		406	62.4		147
More than 35 hours of university work	38.5	*	1212	57.7	*	423
Religious	36.9		777	59.2		280
Not religious	38.4	*	1077	57.9		368
Science disciplines	35.0		1208	59.8		360
Liberal Arts disciplines	42.7	*	674	57.2	*	298
Low support for gender equality	35.0		113	57.8		13
High support for gender equality	37.9		1718	58.6		632
Low support for class egalitarianism	35.0	*	928	60.3		228
High support for class egalitarianism	40.8		850	57.7		385

* P < .05
Source: Nakhaie (2009, pp. 399–411).

What Can Be Concluded from the Findings?

Overall, gender, followed by class-based ideology, is the best predictor of housework in academia. Moreover, the study finds support for the hypothesis that time availability and relative income are important predictors of housework, supporting rational/practical and power/resource approaches. However, the results from this study indicate that support for gender equality does not necessarily reduce women's or increase men's contribution to housework among the academics. This is consistent with a qualitative study by Hochschild (1989). As an example, Hochschild highlights the case of a **"feminist"** (p. 42) who justified doing more of the housework compared to her husband. Nancy Holt (an educated and paid working female) stated that she was doing substantially more housework compared to her husband, but her attitude was that of "benign resignation." Nancy evaluated her share of housework and then negotiated with her husband on the basis of comparison to the so-called "going rate" of housework performed by other men and women. Thus, even some professional women tend to comply with traditional gender roles by comparing their own contribution to housework to others. This within-gender comparison is consistent with Thompson's (1991) theory of distributive justice and perception of fairness. The comparison acts as an ideological cloak producing a myth of marital equality. In the process, women feel better and protect themselves from the contradictions in their marriage and the cultural and economic forces that press on them. What seems to help academic women is men and women supporting class-based equality. This finding seems to support the argument that reduction of class inequalities and their ideological ramifications have important bearings on the reduction of gender inequalities.

The findings show that, on average, significantly more housework is performed by female than male academics, even after we account for gender and class-based ideology or other variables, may point to the historical forces that have gradually helped institutionalize a **"gender factory"** (Berk, 1985) in the house. This gender factory is one wherein each generation of sons learned to do less housework and each generation of daughters continued to be trained in the best social cement of all: the patterns of daily life, the relationship between parents and children, and the normative constraints of wife as mother or homemaker and husband as breadwinner. The "gendering" of the household, learned through socialization and the pattern of everyday activities, tends to produce "normative constraints on who *should* do what," which "may well affect who *does* do what" (Berk, 1985, p. 72, italics in original). The gender factory ensures that women and men construct and perceive that it is the mother's job to take care of the house and young children.

The "socialization factory" is not as powerful as implied above. Men and women are not blank canvases that can be inscribed upon at will and, if inscribed on, are unable to change. Connell (2005) cites the Nordic "experiment," which showed that the majority of men can change their practices when circumstances are favourable. For example, when reform policies were well-designed and targeted towards an ongoing cultural process of change, men's active support for gender equality increased.

What Are the Possible Policy Implications?

The implication of the evidence presented here is that women's oppression is systematically interwoven into the fabric of capitalist social relations, particularly at the level of class subjectivity. The other side of this argument is that class struggle and women's liberation are intertwined. This means that we need to move toward gender equality by promoting profound changes in economic, political, and ideological arenas. The increased participation of women in the labour force, and their aspirations and mobility into higher status and pay jobs, tends to erode men's "patriarchal dividend" and, optimistically, perhaps will bring an end to gender inequalities (Connell, 2002, p. 10). This outcome is more feasible if the recent **neoliberalist** trend, which promotes the unfettered action of the market and aims to minimize state intervention, is prevented through the government's involvement in the public domain.

Key Terms

Double shift: a term often used to refer to women doing both paid work and housework.

Egalitarian: believing in political or social equality.

Feminism: a worldview intended to challenge and transform the economic, social, and political imbalances between men and women.

Gender factory: a system of socialization that reproduces unequal gender relations.

Neoliberalism: a philosophy or set of economic policies and views that desires to intensify and expand the market by increasing the frequency of transactions and minimizing the role of governments.

Critical Thinking Questions

1. Why do women perform more housework than men, even among academics?
2. What are some of the implications of female professors doing more housework than male professors?
3. How does the gender factory help produce and reproduce gender inequality in the house?
4. Why do women with higher incomes than their partners contribute less to housework than women with lower incomes than their partners?
5. Should the government get involved in helping to reduce the burden of double shift on wives? Why or why not?
6. Why do you think professors' belief in gender equality did not influence the amount of housework they performed?

Chapter 8

Social Inequality

What is social inequality? Why are there large differences among people in rank, status, education, occupation, income, wealth and property? Are these differences achieved or ascribed, acquired or born into? Are rich people born rich or is their wealth due to their motivation and hard work. What accounts for success and failure in wealth, power and prestige? What are the consequences of unequal distribution of scarce resources? Answers to these questions are part and parcel of understanding the nature, causes, and consequences of unequal distribution of education, wealth, power, and prestige. In sum, the study of social inequality tries to answer the questions of who gets what, when, and how? *Social inequality* exists where an individual or a group in a social system is excluded from behaviour that is open to others. Social inequality refers to structured and patterned inequality which is regular and recurring and that allows one group to control rights and opportunities more than other groups. Those who control these rights, privileges, opportunities, and benefits often reproduce themselves across time and place. That is, inequality is a form of structured violence and not just unequal reward for one's achievements or contributions.

Paul Farmer in his book the *Pathologies of Power* argues that inequality is a form of **structured violence.** It is structured because it is a form of stable patterns of social relationships that bring the society into the individual where the individual experiences the results of state policies, economic crisis, war, racism, sexism and other forms of degradations. It is violent because the consequences include accumulated vulnerabilities and the nullification of capacity in both individuals and communities, frequently sanctioned by government. For example, the experience of poverty for a young boy means that he may become a child beggar, die in some cruel environment, such as a landmine in no man's land, and is the first to go to a war, the first to be in the front of that war, and the first to be killed, far from home. Such a young boy may live in a freezing shelter, be suffocated in cramped and confined damped space, suffer malnutrition, starve, and be subject to physical and sexual abuse. A young poor girl will experience many of the same vulnerabilities and degradations as well as being forced into prostitution and unwanted marriage.

Social inequality can best be seen in hierarchies of power, prestige and privileges. **Power** refers to individual's ability to influence other people in spite of their opposition. It refers to differential capacities to command resources and thereby to control social situations. There are three basic sources of power: economical, political and ideological. **Economic power** refers to the control of production of means of subsistence and productive resources (e.g., ownership of

185

means of production). **Political power** refers to the control of laws and government and means of legitimization of inequalities (e.g., domination of political offices). **Ideological power** refers to the control of ideas, knowledge, and information (e.g., control of media, religion, education).

Power should be distinguished from **authority.** Authority allows individuals to influence other people's behaviours, attitudes, and beliefs, but it needs their concession or agreement. Thus in schools and universities, teachers have authority as do clerical and managerial officials in bureaucracies and organizations. Their authority is based on norms and regulations that are legally sanctioned. The institutional bases of authority are rational-legal arrangements (as in private and public bureaucracies), tradition (as in parents and elders), and charisma (as in persons whom are seen with extraordinary and/or supernatural power).

Another dimension of inequality is *prestige*. Prestige is based on evaluation of the social standings of a position. It is assigned in one of the three grounds: taste (fashion, education), birth (age, sex, race), or resources (education, occupation, ownership, wealth, income and power). People often judge a social position in terms of their preferences. For examples, in most societies, parents may wish to have a boy more than a girl as their first or only child. In some societies, white skin is valued over other types of phenotypes. Most people value high education and prefer to have managerial, professional, or administrative well-paid occupations. And people may prefer a specific style of housing, clothing, or furniture.

Empirical Evidence of Inequality in Canada

According to the 2006 Census, 15.6 percent of Canadians are poor or in low-income groups. This figure was slightly higher in 2001 at 16.8 percent and the same as in 1991 at 15.6 percent. Table 8.1 shows distribution of Canadians in different occupations as well as their average yearly and investment income. As can be seen, there is a clear **hierarchy** of occupations and income groups in Canada. Those with higher occupations have higher income and have more disposable income for investment. Thus, managers as a group earned about $78,000 in 2006 and earned another $38,000 from their investment. In contrast, manual workers eared about $2,400 and only earned $321 from their investment.

Table 8.1 Distribution of Canadians by Occupation and Incomes

Occupations	Percent	Average income	Average investment income
Managers	9.3	78,022	3,833
Professionals	16.1	65,086	2,013
Semi-professionals and technicians	8.2	35,724	758
Supervisors	3.8	42,552	1,774
Administrative and senior clerical personnel	5.1	40,630	2,036
Skilled sales and service personnel	4.1	37,331	1,139
Skilled crafts and trades workers	8.0	43,090	763
Clerical personnel	10.0	30,705	565
Intermediate sales and service personnel	11.7	24,639	580
Semi-skilled manual workers	10.0	32,951	483
Other sales and service personnel	9.7	16,174	306
Other manual workers	3.9	24,308	321
Total	100.0	41,155	1,239

Source: Adapted from Statistics Canada (2006).

Table 8.2 shows the median net worth of Canadians. Median is the middle point. It is the point at which half of people have a net worth above it and the other half below it. The table reveals that the poorer 10 percent of the population have a negative net worth and that their situation has deteriorated—they are more in debt. In contrast, the top 10 percent of people own over 50 percent of the wealth, and this has increased between 1984 and 1999. To put it differently, over 94 percent of the wealth in Canada is owned by the top 50 percent of the population, and less than 6 percent of the wealth is owned by the bottom 50 percent of the population. Why are some people wealthy and others not?

There are three theoretical explanations of inequality: Functionalism, Marxism, and Weberian approach.

Functionalist Theory of Inequality

Recall that functionalism believes that societies are integrated and organized systems in which every component fulfills some functions. Each part is contributing to the survival of the system and thus we can understand parts only in relation to the whole. Kingsley Davis and Wilbert

Table 8.2 Median and Share of Total Net Worth

| All Family Units | Median Net Worth | | | Share of Total Net Worth | | |
	1984	1999	% change	1984	1999	Difference
Deciles						
1st	-1,824	-5,700	-85	-0.5	-0.06	-0.1
2nd	674	101	-12.2	0.1	0	-0.1
3rd	6,743	5,920	6.2	0.5	0.4	-0.2
4th	21,380	22,700	9	1.7	1.3	-0.4
5th	45,365	49,580	3	3.5	2.8	-0.7
6th	72,155	81,466	12.9	5.6	4.7	-1
7th	104,764	129,000	23.1	8.2	7.4	-0.8
8th	147,751	192,500	30.3	11.5	11	-0.6
9th	222,861	299,373	34.3	17.5	17.4	-0.2
10th	464,376	628,100	35.3	51.8	55.7	3.9

Source: Statistics Canada (2006).

Moore (1945) have provided a comprehensive theory of inequality that is rooted in functionalism. According to them, the main functional necessity for every society is to place and motivate individuals in the social structure. That is to say that a society must induce its member to perform the duties of various positions in the social structure. A society must concern itself with motivation at two different levels:

- to instill in the individuals the proper desire to fill certain positions; and

- once in these positions, they should have the desire to perform the duties attached to them.

However, some positions are more desirable, others require special talents or training, and finally some are functionally more important than others. Therefore, the question is that of how society can ensure that various important social duties are performed with diligence. Davis and Moore's answer is **differential rewards.** A society must have some types of rewards that help to induce members performing important jobs and must have some way of distributing these rewards according to importance of various positions. Of course, there are various rewards that a society can use in order to ensure that essential services are performed. These include:

- *material rewards:* the things that contribute to sustenance and comfort;

- *recreational rewards:* the things that contribute to humour and diversion; and

- *symbolic rewards:* the things that contribute to self- respect and ego expansion.

Therefore, according to Davis and Moore "social inequality is an unconsciously evolved device by which societies insure that the most important positions are conscientiously filled by the most qualified persons who are in turn rewarded according to their contribution to society." Accordingly, every society, no matter how simple or complex, must differentiate people in terms of wealth, prestige, and esteem and must therefore possess a certain amount of institutionalized inequality. But how should the rewards be distributed? What positions should get more rewards, and hence have the highest rank in the system of inequality? Davis and Moore respond that most rewards should be given to positions that:

- have greatest functional importance for the society,

- require the greatest training or talent, and

- are most scarce in term of finding people who can fill these positions.

According to Davis and Moore, a person's qualifications to fill such positions can come about through inherent capacity, talent, and training. Therefore, if the required skills are scarce (rarity of talent or the costliness of training), the position must have an attractive reward attached to it so that it will draw the necessary skills in competition with other positions. This means, in effect, that the position must be high in the social scale—must command great prestige, high salary, ample leisure, and the like.

Many critiques have questioned this explanation of inequality. Among these, Melvin Tumin (1953) is well known. Tumin agrees that social inequality is present everywhere in society. But, he questions that it is inevitable and positively functional to society. He asks what does it means to be "functionally important?" Does it mean something that has "survival value" for the social structure? If so, we have to identify and calculate functionality and know what is the minimum vs. maximum survival requirement of a society. For example, while an engineer is functionally important to society, so too is the unskilled worker without which the engineer can't do the work. Is a mother less functional than a doctor? Can a society survive without production and socialization of children? It is also questionable that only a limited number of individuals in any society have the talents that can be trained into the skills appropriate to these positions (i.e., the more functionally important positions). The problem here is that not all talents are recognized in a society. In fact, inequality may make it more difficult to recognize and realize such talents. For example, access to education depends upon the wealth of one's parents, and when wealth is differentially distributed, large segments of the population are likely to be deprived of the chance even to *discover* their talents. Moreover, the unequal distribution of rewards in one generation tends to result in the unequal distribution of motivation in the succeeding generation. Parents pass their wealth and knowledge to their children who in turn benefit from such resources. Finally, there is some noticeable tendency for upper **class** elites to restrict further access to their privileged positions, once they have sufficient power to enforce such restrictions. They may limit access to upper-class clubs, which are sources of job networks and intra-class marriages, restricting marriage among members of different classes, thus limiting the opportunity for upward mobility of individuals from lower to upper classes. In these senses, **stratification** systems are *inherently antagonistic* and not functional to the development of equality of opportunity and realization of talent.

Tumin also questions whether the allocation of differential rewards in scarce and desired goods and services is the only or the most efficient way of recruiting the appropriate talent to these positions. There are other motivational schemes that may be more efficient and adequate. People may work for "the joy in work," "an instinct for workmanship," "intrinsic work satisfaction" or "social duty." Finally, the argument that higher rewards should be given to those who sacrifice money and time in order to train themselves is more of a justification of inequality by the powerful than its explanation. As an example, in Canada, children of the privileged class sacrifice little since the education system is largely subsidized by the taxpayers. Even if we accept that there is such a sacrifice, it is not often the individuals who undergo the sacrifice but their parents. There is ample evidence that shows that privileged parents are better able to help their children attain higher education than the less privileged (see Nakhaie, 1996; Nakhaie & Curtis, 1998).

Marxist Theory of Inequality

The Marxian approach distinguishes the distributive and relational aspects of inequality. The functionalist approach is based on a distributional approach in that it focuses on how the individual is placed in various status levels or status groups such as who is more educated, who has more income and wealth, and who has less. The Marxist approach, in contrast, focuses on a relational approach to inequality in that it pay attention to the interaction and activity of social groups. These groups are understood in relation to each other. The emphasis is in the actions and characteristics of the group rather than individuals. Marxists try to understand how and why one social group or a class has superior material, cultural, and ideological resources to another, which would allow it to be placed in position of advantage and benefit from the disadvantage of another group or to receive more than to give.

According to Marx, those who control the production process also control other aspects of life such as the distribution of rewards. For example, capitalists own the means of production such as factories, technology and land. They decide who to hire, for how long, and in what capacity, as well as what to produce, how to produce it, and in what quantity. In contrast, workers, not having any ownership of means of production, are forced to sell their labour power to the capitalists for wages that allow them to maintain a minimum level of subsistence. The difference in wages paid to the workers and the income received by the capitalist from selling the products produced by the workers constitutes **surplus labour.** Therefore, the more the workers produce, the richer the capitalists become, while the workers remain at the subsistence level. That is to say, for Marx, the difference in income or rewards among people is a function of class relations and has less to do with motivation and/or hard work.

One can argue that there is nothing unfair about capitalists being able to use their property ownership, employ propertyless individuals, and in the process become rich by extracting what Marxists call **surplus value** from these workers. But is it also fair that individuals from different backgrounds do not have equal access to the positions of power and wealth? In a classic Canadian study, Wallace Clement (1975) shows that there exists a persistent pattern of upper-class selection into the corporate elites. The Canadian corporate elites are significantly more likely to have come from the (economic) elite background, that is, to have had fathers (or other family members) among the corporate CEOs, to have had private schooling and postsecondary education, and to have been members of private clubs, as well as to have used engineering, science, finance, and law to accomplish an elite career.

For Marxists social classes are common structural positions within social organization or relation of production. That is:

1. Classes are common positions—there are 'empty places' in the social structures which are filled by individuals.

2. Classes are common positions within social relations of production—classes must be seen in their relations with other classes.

3. They are rooted in social organization of production.

Classes designate social relations between actors. Ownership of the means of production, purchase of the labour power of others, and sale of one's labour power are the basic ingredient of

Marxist class definition through which three social classes can be identified (e.g., bourgeoisie, petite-bourgeoisie, and workers). Classes are related to occupations but at the same time are distinct from it. Occupations designate positions within technical divisions of labour. Classes are positions in social divisions of labour.

Social classes are not just objective categories of people who are placed in the system of inequality based on their ownership of means of production (e.g., bourgeoisie) or lack of it (e.g., workers). Social classes can also be groups of people who are aware and conscious of their class position, and unite and organize to achieve their collective interests. **Class awareness** is when members of a class recognize that they are tied to membership in a given class. **Class consciousness** is when members of one class recognize the existence of other classes whose members share different attitudes, beliefs, and lifestyles. Class consciousness requires an awareness of common class membership, a perception of common class interests, and a capacity for class action in pursuit of these interests.

Marx distinguished between **class-in-itself** and **class-for-itself:**

- A class is in itself when individuals have common position in relation to the organization of production with no or little consciousness about that position. They do not see each other as conflict groups.

- A class for itself exists when those who are in a class are aware of their position and view their interest as opposite to the interest of other class and therefore view their relationship as conflictual. They tend to take collective action to promote their interests.

Therefore, class consciousness exists at three levels:

1. One recognizes that he/she is a member of a class and this class is distinguishable from the other classes.

2. One recognizes that interests of one class are in opposition to the interests of the other classes.

3. The belief that action by members of one class results in revolutionary reorganization of power arrangement.

Therefore, class consciousness refers to the common interests, beliefs, and values among the members of an objective class. This implies the recognition that objective material interests of one class are different from those of other classes and the subjective awareness that those common interests, beliefs and, values result in the attainment and defence of the objective class interests.

How class conscious are Canadians? Table 8.3 shows that less than 30 percent of Canadians believe that they are members of the working class and about 60 percent believe that they belong to the middle class. In contrast, Table 8.4 shows that close to 90 percent of Canadians are actually workers in the sense that they don't own the means of production while selling their labour power by working for others. In this sense, the level of Canadian class consciousness is low.

Table 8.3 Subjective Class Placement of Canadians

	Percent
Upper class	0.9
Middle class	64.9
Working class	30.2
Lower class	4.0
Total	100.0

Source: Adapted from World Values Survey (2009).

Table 8.4 Class Distribution of Canadians

Social Classes	Class of Worker in the Census	Percent
Bourgeoisie	Self-employed with paid workers	3.9
Petite-bourgeoisie	Self-employed without paid worker	7.5
Workers	Paid worker	88.6
Total		100

Source: Adapted from Statistics Canada (2006).

Why do the majority of Canadians believe that they belong to the middle class while actually the majority are workers? There may be two explanations of this difference in class-in-itself versus for-itself:

1. It may be that the dominant ideology in Canada provides no analysis of society in terms of social classes. There is no clear structure in Canada where people see each other and in relation to one another.

2. People in general often compare each other in terms of income or other valued resources. This means that they can always see some people having more and others less income or valued resources than they. Therefore, they tend to see themselves in the middle of others.

Marx used the example of religion and suggested that "religion is the opium of the masses" because it tends to make people accept their lower position in the system of inequality as "God's will," in exchange for the hope of finding a better place after life. It is not that people live in an illusion. Rather, their minds are subject to contradictory types of awareness that may confuse and fragment their judgment about the nature of the world they inhabit. In other words, the dominant groups are able to control the production of ideas and therefore subject the masses to such cultural and ideological production. In controlling the production and reproduction of ideas, the dominant groups tend to perpetuate their own cultural ideas as that of the society and thus have a tendency to legitimize inequality. As such, most people may not be aware of class distinctions and may accept the dominant view of Canada as a middle-class society.

Marxist theory of inequality has been criticized for ignoring recent structural changes in the process of production such as the decrease of manual and industrial workers and increase of white collar and service sectors. Moreover, it has been argued that the real wages of the working class and the proportion of the middle class have both increased, thus suggesting that Marx's theory of class polarization and **class conflict** is inapplicable in the post-industrial societies.

Weberian Approach

Marx's view has also been challenged by Max Weber. He objected to Marx's emphasis on property relations as the only axis of class relations. Weber defined class as numbers of people who share similar opportunities for acquiring material goods in the market. For him, marketable skills in addition to property relations are important determinants of class. Weber distinguished three types of classes: property classes, commercial classes, and social classes.

Property classes are determined by the differences of property ownership among the owners resulting in positively and negatively privileged classes. They are not communities and might not become class-for-itself or class conscious. There are two types of property classes:

- Positively privileged classes are those with monopoly over high-priced goods, wealth accumulation, executive positions, costly education, and the policy of sale of economic goods.

- Negatively privileged classes are 'unfree' individuals who are objects of ownership such as outcasts, declassed (proletariats), debtors, and paupers.

Commercial classes are occupational gateways in life chances. Again they can be positively or negatively privileged. There are two types of commercial classes:

- Positively privileged commercial classes have monopolization of entrepreneurial management of productive enterprises and are responsible for security and safeguarding of the business interests. Examples of positively privileged commercial classes are merchants, ship owners, bankers, financial, industrial and agricultural entrepreneurs, and highly skilled labourers.

- Negatively privileged commercial classes don't have any monopoly on life chances and include low-level skilled labourers.

Social classes are composed of the plurality of class statuses between which an interchange of individuals on a personal basis is possible and observable. They are communities with the same honour and prestige, conventions, laws, rituals, and styles of living. There are four social classes:

1. privileged classes through property and education
2. intelligentsia and specialists without property
3. petite-bourgeoisie
4. working class.

Weber also distinguished status from class as another basis of hierarchy. **Status** refers to the relative *prestige* of an individual and the negative and positive perception by others. That is, the dimension of social status is prestige. Statuses consist of sets of rules (statements of rights and obligations) specifying how the interaction is to take place: how people should respond towards a person with specific status and how that person should behave when in a particular position such as a teacher. Status can be ascribed or achieved. **Achieved status** depends on one's accomplishments such as education, occupation, and income statuses. **Ascribed status** is assigned irrespective of one's accomplishments and usually ascribed at birth such as race, sex, and ethnicity. Social status is based on:

1. a mode of living
2. a formal process of education
3. prestige at birth
4. prestige of an occupation.

Weber also identified power as another dimension of inequality. According to Weber, power refers to the chance that a person or a number of them are able to realize their own will in a common action, even against the resistance of others participating in it. Power does not need legal sanctions but can also be based on such sanctions. Therefore, power can be defined as the capacity to influence a common action irrespective of what its content may be. The more power one has, the more one is able to put his or her wishes into practice at the expense of others.

The last dimension of inequality for Weber is called the *party*. Parties are groups organized to acquire power. Parties may or may not represent the interests of one class. For Weber, classes, statuses and parties are all important in the acquisition of power. Weber's analysis of power has not gone unchallenged (see Box 8.1).

Box 8.1

Dahl (1957, 1958) specifies three properties which are essential to existence of power.
1. there must be a time lag between an action by A and response of a
2. there must be a connection between A and a
3. the behaviour of a after incidence of power must differ in an observable way from the behaviour she or he would have shown without.

However, power can exist without any of the above essential properties. For example, there is no direct interaction between religious beliefs and an individual's God, but God has power over that individual and the individual does not resist that power. That is, Weber's definition of power ignores structured relationships. As another example, those with wealth and property have power over the poor. There is not direct relationship (interaction) here and there is no resistance. But power of the rich is socially structured through state policies and laws where the poor rely on rich for employment and are therefore subject of their power. In this case, workers produce surplus value for the owners of capital, factories or other organizations due to the economic pressure that they must work in order to live. In this case, power can be exerted with no direct relationship or resistance.
(Based on Baldus, 1975)

Weber also criticized Marx for his understanding of **alienation** in being rooted in the economic process. Weber argued that modern bureaucracies are responsible for development of alienation because in bureaucracies, individuals are alienated from the means of administration and decision making. Marx argued that capitalism is an irrational system because of the contradiction of the **collective production** and **private appropriation.** That is, all people are involved in the production, but only a small segment of the society benefits from most of the collective production. Therefore, he suggested that because of its internal irrational contradictions and its oppressive system, capitalism will be destroyed. Weber, on the other hand, emphasized the rationality of capitalism in the bureaucratic administration (legal rational relations) and argued that this bureaucracy would persist in both capitalism and socialism or communism.

Comparison of Marx's and Weber's views of inequality shows that both emphasize economic relations. However, for Marx, economic relations are fundamental, while for Weber, that is one among many dimensions of inequality. For Marx, the key factor in assessment of a person's position in the overall social hierarchy is that of ownership and non-ownership. Therefore, Marxists see classes in terms of individuals' relation to the organization of production, with two dichotomous and opposing classes of proletariats and capitalists and a disappearing petite-bourgeoisie. Weber adhered to a multidimensional view of social classes. For him, inequality is based on the degree to which an individual is able to enjoy life in the distribution process, which could be determined by income as well as other economic, social, and political factors. For Weber, classes are not just rooted in the economic organization of production, though that is important, but also in the social institutions and organizations of society. Overall, functionalists emphasize the role of individual responsibility for inequality, Marxists pay attention to the structural forces, and Weberians see inequality as rooted in the institutions of the society.

Health Consequence of Inequality: The Case of Aboriginal Canadians

A fundamental source of identity and pride in Canada is its unique healthcare system. Canadians cherish their healthcare system and use it as a source of demarcation between themselves and the United States. The Canadian healthcare system is based on government's responsibility in providing comprehensive, accessible, and universal healthcare for all Canadians. Does this mean that there is no health inequality in Canada? Do all Canadians benefit from the healthcare system equally? If we were to look at Aboriginal Canadians' health situation, our immediate answer would be negative. Aboriginal Canadians have more than twice the **infant mortality rate** and death rate of the general population. Their **life expectancy** is about 30 years lower and their suicide rate is about three times higher (six times higher for the 15–24 age group) than the general population. Their major causes of death, in addition to motor vehicle accidents, drowning, and fire, are diseases of the circulatory and respiratory system, cancer, suicide, and chronic conditions (e.g., tuberculosis and diabetes) (see Frideres, 1996).

Why do Aboriginal Canadians have more health conditions than others? Four possible explanations of health conditions are lifestyle, environment, healthcare system, and biological makeup. Lack of a proper diet, heavy smoking, and alcohol consumption, as well as lack of physical activity are examples of lifestyles that are related to an individual's health and well-being. According to the lifestyle explanation, Aboriginal Canadians are responsible for their own health conditions. They need to exercise, change their diet, not smoke, and moderate their drinking level. We should also remember that Aboriginal Canadians are more likely to live in areas that are a substantial distance from the major metropolitans, and they have the lowest **socioeconomic status** in the country. This means that they have limited access to health services, prescription drugs, and the barest of material necessities (e.g., heat, food, and clothing). They also have less knowledge about healthy lifestyles, such as nutritious diets. Aboriginal Canadians living in rural areas are also exposed to hazardous environments. Various industrial and resource development projects have polluted water and disrupted fish and game stock, resulting in environmental pollution in Native communities. For example, the amount of mercury in the blood of Aboriginal residents of the White Dog and Grassy Narrows Reserves in Ontario is 40 to 150 times higher than among average Canadians. Native communities in Cluff Lake and St. Regis in Saskatchewan and Serpent River in Ontario have been subject to uranium pollution, acid discharge, and fluoride pollution, respectively (Frideres, 1996).

Summary

Social inequality is concerned with cause and consequences of access to scarce resources among different groups of people. Inequality can be produced during one's lifetime or inherited from the past through parents. Functionalists generally view inequality as due to what people deserve. Accordingly, those with higher motivation, hard work, and skill end up getting higher education, occupation, and income while those who lack such characteristics end up in poverty. Conflict theories emphasize structural forces such as inheritance, economic crisis, and unequal ownership of means of production, which results in some people being disadvantaged at the get-go even if they are highly motivated and work hard while others become successful even without motivation and hard work. Weberians emphasize institutional forces that help a group control ideas, rules, and regulations benefiting them at the expense of those who can't control the basic institutions of the society. Feminists agree with both conflict and Weberian approaches but see the source of inequality in patriarchy, which favours men over women.

Key Terms

Achieved status: a social position that one assumes as a result of personal choice, by learning skills or gaining credentials. It reflects personal ability and effort.

Alienation: the term, as originally used by Karl Marx, refers to loss of control over one's work and product. It is a feeling of powerlessness from other people and from oneself.

Ascribed status: a social position that one assumes at birth or receives involuntarily later in life.

Authority: power that people perceive as legitimate rather than coercive.

Class: generally, it means an individual's relative location in a society based on wealth, power, prestige, or other valued resources. Marxists view class as individuals' relationship to the organization of production. Weberians refer to class in terms of an individuals' access to life chances.

Class awareness: awareness of being tied to a specific social class.

Class conflict: antagonism between social classes in a society. Marx used this term to refer to the struggle between capitalists and workers because of their clash of interests.

Class consciousness: awareness of being tied to a social class, having common interests with members of that class, and acting to realize common class goals.

Class-for-itself: Marx's term to refer to an objective category of people belonging to a social class but not being aware of their class position or interest.

Class-in-itself: Marx's term to refer to an objective category of people belonging to a social class who are aware of their class position and interest and act to realize common class goals.

Collective production: Production performed by members of a society.

Differential rewards: various types and amounts of rewards that help induce individuals to become qualified and perform socially necessary and important jobs.

Economic power: control of wealth, property, and means of production.

Hierarchy: ranked positions within a society or social system.

Ideological power: control of ideas and knowledge.

Infant mortality rate: the number of deaths in the first year of life for each thousand live births in a year.

Life expectancy: the average length of time that a person can expect to live.

Political power: control of laws, government, and political apparatus.

Power: one's ability to influence others and reach a goal even against opposition from those who are subject to power.

Private appropriation: confiscation and ownership of the collective production of members of the society.

Socioeconomic status: one's social status in the stratification hierarchy based on education, occupation, and income.

Status: the relative prestige or position of an individual and its negative and positive perception by others.

Stratification: the existence of inequality between groups of people in a society based on their access to material and nonmaterial resources.

Structured violence: a type of violence that is sanctioned by a stable pattern of social relationships.

Surplus labour: used to produce products over and above what is needed for subsistence.

Surplus value: according to Marx, it is the difference between wages paid to the worker and the value created by the worker in the act of producing commodities.

Critical Thinking Questions

1. List some of the factors that motivated you to attend university and identify the main reason for you to study, write assignments, and attend classes.

2. What do you think are reasons for those who do not attend university or your classmates who do not study as much as you? How do your and their motivations differ? To what extent do these reasons correspond with Davis and Moore's conceptualization of inequality?

3. Trace the sources of your father's or mother's occupational attainment. What factors do you think helped them to achieve their present occupational position? What are the factors that prevented them to move further up in the occupational ladder? Do you think lack of motivation on your parent's part is responsible for not moving higher in the occupational ladder? How does their situation differ from your classmates' parent?

4. List 10 very functionally important and 10 not very functionally important occupations. Also list the approximate levels of education and skill required by each occupation. Finally, list the approximate level of income attributed to these occupations. Do you think that there is a close correspondence between education, skill, and income of these occupations? How does this experiment support or reject Davis and Moore's theory?

5. Compare and contrast Marx's and Weber's views of class. In what way do they differ and/or

are similar? How do they explain the relationship between class position and class consciousness?

6. How do we know if someone is exploited? What would happen to the income/profit of the capitalists if workers withdraw their labour? Can capitalists produce commodities and/or acquire profit if workers stop working?

7. Imagine two factories. These factories are the same in every aspect except one is owned collectively by workers and the other is owned by a capitalist. In which of these factories can workers have a higher income? Why?

8. What is the difference between equality of opportunity and equality of condition? Which of these views are more supported in the Canadian popular views? Why is it important that there should be equality of opportunity? What about equality of condition?

9. Based on your own personal experiences, what is most important for landing a good job: who you know or what you know?

10. List the 10 most powerful and/or rich people in your city. Trace their class background. Are they more likely to be "self-made people"? How easy is it for an ordinary person to acquire a job like theirs?

11. Based on your own experience do you think Canada's class system is becoming more open or closed? Why?

Sociological Example: Class Background and Educational Attainment*

Introduction: Research Purpose

What do we mean when we say that some social classes are better able to reproduce themselves than others? Are upper social class people wealthy because they are born into money or is their wealth due to their own motivation and hard work? As we know, one of the main reasons that students continue with their education past high school is because they want to get a degree relevant to a well-paying job. Is entry into higher education a matter of students' choice, motivation, or talent, or is it prescribed through their class or origin? Do children of the upper classes have a higher likelihood than those of the lower classes of enrolling in colleges and universities, acquiring a degree, and obtaining a good job? These are the types of questions that we will answer in this chapter. In order to find out whether the social standing of parents is important for their children's access to scarce resources such as high educational attainment, we will study the relationship between parents' social class and offspring's education.

Theoretical Explanation

According to Marx, capitalists own the means of production, such as factories, technology, and land. They decide who to hire, for how long, and in what capacity, as well as what to produce, how to produce it, and in what quantity. In contrast, workers, not having any ownership of means of production, are forced to sell their only marketable skill (i.e., their labour **power**) in exchange for wages that allow them to maintain a minimum level of subsistence. Marxists argue that the difference in wages paid to the workers and the income received by the buyer of the labour power (i.e., capitalists) through selling the products produced by the workers constitutes **surplus value** and is called **exploitation.** Therefore, the more the workers produce, the richer capitalists become, while the workers remain at the subsistence level. That is to say, for Marxists, the difference in income or rewards among people is a function of class relations and has little to do with motivation and hard work. For Marxists, individuals are not placed in the social or occupational structure primarily by their level of motivation and what they know, but rather by their existing position in the system of inequality, such as their parents' social class, as well as

---

* Based on Nakhaie (2000, pp. 577–609) and Nakhaie and Curtis (1998, pp. 483–515).

sex, race, ethnicity, and whom they know (e.g., Tumin, 1953). These scholars, following Marx, believe that the social system is more open to the dominant groups and more closed to the lower classes.

Other scholars believe that social inequality is a device by which societies ensure that the most important positions are filled by the most motivated and qualified persons, who are in turn rewarded according to their contribution to society (e.g., Davis & Moore, 1945). According to this understanding, every society, no matter how simple or complex, must differentiate people in terms of both prestige and esteem and must therefore possess a certain amount of institutionalized inequality. These scholars have a *pluralist* perception of modern society (e.g., Erikson & Goldthrope, 1992). They argue that inequalities still exist, but that these inequalities tend to decrease because of industrialization. Industrialization entails technological advancement, more differentiation of division of labour, and more rational organization of social selection. Traditional ascriptive norms are replaced by new norms based on universalism and equality of opportunity. Therefore, this view suggests that individuals are not placed in various **socioeconomic** positions based on class background, gender, race, or what is directly inherited, but instead earn these positions through their hard work, merit, and achievements. This theory suggests that educational attainment is now more open and independent of class background.

New Marxists incorporate some of the insight developed by Weber and account for changes due to industrialization. Accordingly, they argue that capitalists do not just exploit workers and pass their wealth to their offspring. They are also able to provide better educational opportunities for their children, both because of their possession of more economic resources and because of their advantaged access to better education and their greater appreciation of the importance of higher education for their children. Parents in dominant classes are better able to a) provide expensive higher education and enroll their children in private schools; b) ensure contact with children of similar background, and in similar curricula; and c) foster personality traits, values, expectations, cognitive skills, and attitudes in the family that are congruent with the educational curriculum. Each of these factors is believed to pay off in better educational attainment for children (e.g., see Bourdieu, 1977). This view is known as the **cultural capital** theory.

Included in the cultural capital of a class is what Bourdieu calls "causality of the probable." Accordingly, the propensity for a student from a given class to abandon his or her studies increases as the probability of access to higher levels of the educational system, calculated for the average number of this class, decreases (Brubaker, 1985, p. 737). For Bourdieu, this negative predisposition toward school, self-depreciation, and a resigned attitude to failure (or what is generally known as aspiration and achievement orientation) must be understood as the unconscious estimation of the objective probabilities of success or failure for the whole class (see Bourdieu, 1977, p. 495). Thus, the tendency for members of dominant classes to reproduce themselves is determined, among other things, by their evaluation and perception of the present and future position of their class in the social structure.

In other words, although wealth and economic resources are important for the success of the offspring, their success also depends on their cultural capital. Cultural capital refers to the ensemble of high-status culture and cultivated dispositions that manifest themselves in such things as appreciation of higher education and the best schools; attendance at museums, art galleries, theatres, and concerts; appreciation of classical music and knowledge of composers; and strong language and literary skills. To the extent that the dominant classes have at their disposal a much larger share of cultural capital than other classes, they are better able to cultivate this type of capital in their children. The greater cultural capital of the dominant classes makes a high level of educational attainment on the part of the offspring more likely because possession of cultural capital makes it easier to do well in the school curriculum. In other words, by its own internal logic, the educational system ensures the perpetuation of privilege. This explanation is known as the *reproduction theory* because it believes that social classes reproduce themselves in their offspring through transfer of wealth and/or cultural capital.

The reproduction theory also notes that the widespread increase in the numbers of managers who do most of the work previously performed by the capitalists (e.g., hiring and firing of workers, control of what needs to be produced and how), established rules of recruitment, and the demands for more equality of opportunity means that upper classes have modified their strategy of reproduction. Nowadays, they transfer their position of power through inculcation of cultural capital among their offspring.

Either way, most sociologists believe that parents' social class is an important predictor of children's success. The difference is in whether or not the social system is more open to lower classes, and if not, how do the upper classes reproduce themselves: economically or culturally?

Previous Research

Previous research has shown the importance of parents' social class for educational attainment of their offspring. They have shown the following:

- In France, individuals with a capitalist/manger father rather than a working-class father were provided a modest advantage in achieving a higher education, whether sons or daughters, while having a petite-bourgeois father had little advantage for getting an education (Robinson & Garnier, 1985).
- In a five-nation study, it was shown that having either a capitalist father or one in a managerial position produces an educational advantage for sons in comparison to those with a working-class father. This analysis did not explore the effects on daughters or the impact of the mother's education (Robinson, 1984).
- A study in the United States found that dominant class secondary school students have higher levels of cultural capital than other students, and this positively affects their grades and educational obtainment (DiMaggio, 1982).
- A Toronto study showed that obtainment of cultural capital is higher among the dominant class, and that this type of capital positively affects education level (Erickson, 1991).

Research Importance and Questions

While there has been some research on the relationship between a parent's class and offspring's education at the international level, rarely has the research focused on the Canadian setting, which has a more open and accessible educational system. Moreover, previous studies have primarily focused on the effects of the father's class while neglecting the effects of the mother's class. Finally, research has been inattentive to the multidimensional conceptualization and measurement of social classes. In this study, we will use three different measure of class for both mothers and fathers in order to evaluate their importance for educational attainment of male and female Canadians.

Research Questions

We are interested to know if parents' class, variously measured, affects offspring's education and whether this effect is same-sex directed. Our research questions are as follows:

1. What is the effect of parental class background on offspring's educational attainment?
2. To what extent is this effect amenable to change?

   Based on various theories discussed above, we hypothesize:
- The higher the parents' class, the higher the offspring's education.
- The effect of fathers' class would be higher on sons and that of mothers' would be higher on daughters.

- The importance of class background on educational attainment of offspring has declined in the recent years.

Requirements for Testing the Relationship

We use two data sets. First, we use the 1986 General Social Survey conducted by Statistics Canada to evaluate the effect of various dimensions of parents' class on their offspring's education. This survey is a nationally representative sample of Canadians based on telephone interviews with 16,390 adults. Second, we include the 1995 General Social Survey in order to evaluate the changes on the role of parents' class, measured by occupation, on their offspring's education from 1986 to 1995. The 1995 survey is also a nationally representative sample of Canadians based on telephone interviews with 11,876 adults. For the purposes of this study, a sub-sample was selected composed of males and females who were born in Canada and who were 25 years of age or older (respondents this age had likely completed their education).

Table 8.1.1 Typology of the Post-Industrial Class Structure

Classes	Control over Productive Assets				Forms of Appropriation of Social Surplus
	Capital	Organization	Skill	Labour	
Bourgeoisie	Yes	Yes	Yes	Yes	Profit
Managers	No	Yes	Yes	Yes	Loyalty-Dividends
Experts	No	No	Yes	Yes	Rent-Component
Workers	No	No	No	Yes	None

Source: Compiled from Wright (1985).

Before proceeding further, we need to conceptualize a *neo-Marxian* notion of social classes. As we discussed above, Marxists are interested in exploitation and **domination**. For them, the organization of production is hierarchical and exploitative, where those who own the means of production (e.g., capitalists owning economic capital, land, machineries, etc.) have an advantage in the market because they are able to hire those who don't own such means and make a profit through the labour of the workers. In addition, there are people who have control over organizational assets (i.e., managers) and receive loyalty dividends as well as those who have skill assets and are able to benefit by renting their skills (i.e., experts). Finally, there is a fourth group who do not own the means of production but who sell their own labour power (i.e., workers). This conceptualization results in a four-class model as shown in Table 8.1.1.

Of course, as we discussed above, there are other ways to conceptualize class. For example, we can place people in various position based on their level of education (i.e., educational classes) or based on their occupation (i.e., occupational classes). Therefore, we measured three dimensions of the social classes of mothers and fathers in addition to the offspring's number of years of educational attainment. Other relevant variables included age, ethnicity, and region of residence, which were included in multivariate analysis.

Do the Findings Support the Hypotheses?

Table 8.1.2 presents average years of education and numbers of cases for the respondents' years of education by categories of parents' social classes. The table shows an educational advantage of having fathers and mothers in the bourgeoisie, expert, and managerial classes, for both male and female respondents. The one exception to this pattern is that female respondents with mothers in the working class are not particularly disadvantaged compared to others. Further, there are linear relationships between maternal and paternal years of schooling and occupational **status** on the one hand and levels of education, for both male and female respondents, on the other. Fathers' years of schooling appeared to be more beneficial for sons than for daughters. More specifically, on average, males and females with bourgeois (i.e., capitalist) fathers accumulated over 13 years of education, and males and females with expert or managerial fathers had more than 14 years of education when compared to under 12 years for males and females with working-class fathers.

The educational gap of males and females was comparatively higher depending on parents' education. For example, males who had fathers with a university degree had 15.4 years of education compared to 11.1 years of education for males with fathers who only had an elementary school education. In general, evidence shows that parental class positions and other parental class measures influence their offspring's education attainment. As well, the fathers' education has a slightly stronger relationship with sons' education, and mothers' education has a stronger relationship with daughters' education. Nevertheless, fathers' education has a stronger relationship than mothers' education with both male and female offspring's education attainment.

Overall, the results indicate that there is an educational advantage for both male and female children with fathers and mothers in the bourgeoisie, expert, and managerial classes. This means that children from these classes receive more education than children from other classes.

Table 8.1.2 Mean Years of Education by Various Measures of Social Classes
(Native-Born Canadians, 25 Years of Age and Higher)

	Males		Females	
	Mean	N	Mean	N
Father's Class				
Bourgeoisie	13.08	192	13.62	257
Petite-bourgeoisie	10.48	1557	11.10	1979
Expert	14.45	260	14.24	264
Manager	14.11	280	14.07	312
Worker	11.85	2187	11.64	2633
Not working	10.66	114	10.77	177
Mother's Class				
Bourgeoisie	13.23	35	13.63	54
Petite-bourgeoisie	12.16	88	11.97	144
Expert	14.83	133	14.61	186
Manager	13.80	42	13.12	50
Worker	13.17	439	12.75	836
Not working	11.38	4248	11.49	5121
Father's Education				
University degree	15.43	195	14.97	223
Postsecondary	14.42	285	14.05	312
Secondary	13.62	899	13.51	1099
Elementary	11.10	2064	11.25	2629
Mother's Education				
University degree	14.50	152	14.84	195
Postsecondary	14.07	313	14.38	439
Secondary	13.27	1257	13.28	1570
Elementary	11.00	1865	10.94	2544
Father's Occupation				
Upper white collar	14.95	314	14.63	341
Middle white collar	13.61	329	13.69	382
Lower white collar	12.73	782	12.84	967
Blue collar	10.87	3029	11.06	3720
Other	11.07	638	10.97	980
Mother's Occupation				
Upper white collar	15.21	70	14.65	110
Middle white collar	14.06	107	14.32	131
Lower white collar	13.49	369	13.16	534
Blue collar	11.95	189	11.60	288
Other	11.32	4357	11.39	5327

Source: Adapted from Statistics Canada (1986).

This is understandable, since the bourgeoisie can provide economic resources for their children's educational success, while managerial and expert classes are themselves well-educated, helping them to transfer their knowledge and skills to their children.

Table 8.1.3 focuses on the pattern of change in the effect of parents' occupation on offspring's education from 1986 to 1995. It shows the percentage of fathers and mothers in different occupational categories, cross-sectioned with the level of education of the offspring. This applied to both males and females in 1986 and 1995. This table, as well as Table 8.1.2, shows an educational advantage for having fathers and mothers in white-collar occupations for both men and women respondents in both 1986 and 1995. The table also shows that parents in higher occupational positions were more likely to ensure a university degree for their offspring in 1995 than in 1986 when compared to parents in lower occupational positions. As an example, in 1986, 43.0 percent of professional and managerial fathers had sons and 30.5 percent had daughters who possessed a university degree. By 1995, these figures had increased to 52.3 percent and 43.9 percent respectively. The comparative figures for offspring of blue- collar fathers were 8.5 percent, 6.5 percent, 12.6 percent, and 8.3 percent respectively. Moreover, having a father or a mother in a higher occupation has become more important in recent years for females' than males' chances of university attainment, but less important for postsecondary (non–university degree) attainments of females than males. As an example, 43 percent of sons with professional or managerial fathers had a university degree in 1986, which increased to 52.3 percent in 1996, an increase of 9.3 percent. For sons with mothers in professional or managerial occupations, these figures increased for 42.9 percent to 53.6 percent, an increase of 10.7 percent. Overall, this table shows that not only has the effect of parental class on offspring's education not decreased, it in fact has increased.

What Can Be Concluded from the Findings?

Results indicate that the class background of parents, variously measured, has a strong impact on children's educational attainment. This lends support to the contention that parents try to pass on their class position through their wealth, which may grant their children access to dominant positions in society. However, the effect of parents' class seems to also operate through parental

Table 8.1.3 Percentage of Respondents in Three Educational Categories by Father's and Mother's Occupation

	1986			1995		
	Diploma or less	Post. Sec.	Univ.	Diploma or less	Post.Sec.	Univ.
Males						
Father's Occupation						
Professional/managerial	29.6	27.4	43.0	21.4	26.3	52.3
White collar	51.0	29.2	19.7	40.1	32.2	27.7
Blue collar	67.0	24.5	8.5	57.1	30.3	12.6
Farm	79.0	13.9	7.1	68.2	21.6	10.1
Other	72.3	19.6	8.0	57.5	30.8	11.7
Mother's Occupation						
Professional/managerial	22.9	34.3	42.9	13.0	33.3	53.6
White collar	42.9	38.9	18.3	36.7	36.9	26.3
Blue collar	57.1	33.5	9.3	53.4	35.1	11.5
Farm	85.7	14.3	___	50.0	40.9	9.1
Other	65.9	21.7	12.4	56.0	26.5	17.5
Females						
Father's Occupation						
Professional/managerial	29.0	40.5	30.5	20.7	35.4	43.9
White collar	49.6	35.2	15.2	38.6	39.4	22.0
Blue collar	68.8	24.8	6.5	60.1	29.0	10.9
Farm	72.3	20.1	7.6	64.6	27.1	8.3
Other	72.3	23.7	4.0	54.9	35.3	9.8
Mother's Occupation						
Professional/managerial	28.2	46.4	25.5	23.1	35.9	41.0
White collar	46.9	38.8	14.3	36.6	37.5	25.9
Blue collar	67.9	28.9	3.3	61.0	27.4	11.6
Farm	66.7	25.1	9.3	59.6	31.6	8.8
Other	65.6	25.1	9.3	57.1	30.6	12.3

Source: Adapted from Statistics Canada (1986, 1995)

differences in education attainment. This means that parents can influence their offspring's educational attainment not just because of their ownership of assets, but because of the accumulation and transmission of cultural capital. Thus, parents that obtain more "certified cultural capital" (education) are better positioned to reproduce this status to their offspring than parents with less such capital.

Moreover, the findings do not lend support to pluralist theory. They are more consistent with neo-Marxists and reproduction theorists. Although educational attainment of lower classes has increased, it has increased more for the offspring of higher social classes. It seems that lower social class children have to run faster and harder than ever to just keep from falling behind. Results also provide support for the same-sex and role-modelling hypothesis as a father's education has a stronger effect on a son's education than a daughter's, and a mother's education has a stronger effect on a daughter's education than a son's. In addition, a father's class position was a better predictor than a mother's class for the educational attainment of either sex of offspring.

What Are the Possible Policy Implications?

This study showed that educational success is not just due to individuals' hard work or motivation. Rather, such traits are themselves class-based, and the upper classes are better able to reproduce themselves even more now than in the past. Policies that address inequalities among social classes with regard to education access need to be developed. Traits that are important for educational success such as self-direction, self-reliance, independence, curiosity, and style of speech are learnt in the family, and it seems that upper classes possess more of such traits and are better able to pass them to their offspring than the lower classes are. If so, the idea of equal opportunity without equality of conditions becomes problematic. Canadian policy-makers should give serious consideration to widespread inequalities in Canada.

Moreover, the government should provide more grants for students who are willing to continue in the educational system but do not have access to economic resources. Finally, given the importance of cultural capital as exemplified by the powerful effects of the managerial and expert class as well as parents' education on educational attainment of offspring, it is important that values related to educational success are taught to children early on in elementary schools. Students need to be inculcated with an ensemble of elements of high-status culture, such as appreciation of higher education and the best schools; attendance at museums, art galleries, theatres, and concerts; appreciation of classical music and knowledge of composers; and strong language and literary skills. Finally, it is important that the school curriculum be revised so that their dominant class biases are minimized.

Key Terms

Cultural capital: a term used by Pierre Bourdieu to refer to people's assets, including their values, beliefs, attitudes, and competence in language and culture.

Domination: institutionalization of control of one group by another.

Exploitation: the process by which members of one class (e.g., capitalists) extract surplus value or surplus labour from members of another class (e.g., workers).

Power: one's ability to influence others and reach a goal even against opposition from those who are subject to power.

Socioeconomic status: one's social status in the stratification hierarchy based on education, occupation, and income.

Status: the relative prestige or position of an individual and its negative and positive perception by others.

Surplus value: according to Marx, the difference between wages paid to the worker and the value created by the worker in the act of producing commodities.

Critical Thinking Questions

1. How does cultural capital influence educational attainment?
2. Are school curriculums closer to the values and beliefs of the upper or lower social classes? Why?
3. What are the strengths and weaknesses of the Neo-Marxism theory?
4. How is surplus value created? Who benefits from surplus value? Why?
5. What are the strengths or weaknesses of reproduction theory?
6. What factors have been important in your educational achievement? Explain.
7. What would you recommend as a policy to promote equality in education?

Chapter 9

Race and Ethnic Relations

Canada is a society composed of diverse ethnic and racial groups. Some of these groups have more power, privilege, and access to resources than others. For example, Canada is built on conquest and immigration. The conqueror, perhaps understandably, established rules of conduct, avenues of mobility, and laws and regulations based on their own white, English, Protestant preferred cultural and institutional values. The conquered and the new arrivals are left out of this process. John Porter (1965), one of the most famous Canadian sociologists in his famous book *Vertical Mosaic*, identified three broad groups in terms of power and privileges in Canada. First are the **charter groups** (English and French) whose rights are enshrined in the Canadian Constitution. Among the charter groups, the British have more power and privilege than the French. The British control key economic and political institutions in Canada. They have also implemented policies that aim at assimilation of French into the Anglo-Saxon way of life and culture (i.e., assimilate them to the dominant culture). When we look at Canadian history, we notice that from the time of the conquest of New France to the present, the French have been subject to various policies of conformity to Anglo-Saxon domination. However, in the past and recent times, Quebeckers have been able to resist British domination. For example, Quebeckers enacted Bill 101 (the language bill), thus limiting and even reversing previous language loss (i.e., reversing the process whereby the proportion of people speaking French was decreasing and those speaking English was increasing). In addition, the **Quiet Revolution** (i.e., the process of increasing urbanization, industrialization, and bureaucratization in Quebec) resulted in an improvement in the standard of living in Quebec. This "revolution" was important in that it helped expand a new Francophone middle class and organized labour whose political loyalty and economic interests rested with Quebec and not with Canada. Therefore, it is not surprising that, in recent times, French earnings have become more comparable to those of the British. Together, the British and French constitute more than half of the Canadian population Table 9.1 shows the distribution of ethnic groups in Canada. It reveals that the British and French are not as numerically dominant in Canada as they were in the past. This is due to the fact that in recent censuses, Canadians were allowed and encouraged to select "Canadian" as their ethnic group. Most British and French respondents choose this option. The "Canadian" group amounts to 36.8 percent of the single origin population. The table also shows that visible minorities are now a major numerical group, with 18.6 percent of single origin response category, a significant increase since the 1971 Census.

Table 9.1 Distribution of Single and Multiple Ethnoracial Origins in Canada

Ethnic Origin	Single 1971	Single 2001 %	Multiple 2001 %		Single and Multiple 2001 %
British Isles origins	46.1	14.4	30.2		23.5
French origins	29.9	5.9	15.1		11.1
Québécois		0.4	0.1		0.2
Canadian		36.8	20.4		27.6
Other North American origins		0.2	1		0.6
Western European origins	10.5	6.1	11.1		8.9
Northern European origins	1.8	0.9	3.3		2.3
Eastern European origins	5.7	4.8	6.8		5.9
Southern European origins	3.5	7.6	3.9		5.5
Other European origins		1.1	0.7		0.9
Oceania origins		0.1	0.2		0.1
Subtotal		78.3	92.8		86.6
Caribbean origins	0.1	1.8	0.7		1.2
Latin, Central and South Americans		0.8	0.4		0.6
African origins	0.2	1	0.5		0.7
Arab origins		1.3	0.5		0.8
West Asian origins		0.9	0.2		0.5
South Asian origins		4.4	0.7		2.3
East and Southeast Asian origins	0.8	8.4	1.1		4.2
Subtotal		18.6	4.1	4.1	10.3
Aboriginal origins	1.4	3.1	3.1		3.1
		3.1	3.1		3.1
Total	100	100	100		100

Source: Adapted from Statistics Canada (1971, 2001).

Porter called the second broad group the **entrance groups.** These are non-charter first, second, or third generation immigrants from Europe and elsewhere. Generally, in terms of power and privilege, Europeans are more similar to the charter groups than other entrance groups. However, some Europeans (e.g., Spanish, Greek, and most of East Europeans) have lower status and privilege than Northern and Western Europeans and charter groups. In contrast, the other entrance groups who are bioculturally different from Europeans experience significant negative stereotype, prejudice, and discrimination. These groups are broadly identified as visible minorities. On average, they have higher education but lower paying occupations, income, and status. Table 9.2 displays the average income of Canadians working the full year and full time. It shows that some of the groups identified as visible **minority** earn substantially less than others, even if they were born in Canada (e.g., Aboriginal peoples, South Asians, blacks, and Filipinos). Although the extent of ethno-racial earning inequalities is substantial in Canada, the largest of these inequalities is among immigrants, wherein visible minorities earn substantially less than nonvisible minorities. Nevertheless, some of the nonvisible minority groups are not doing very well either (e.g., Greeks).

Porter called the third group the **treaty groups.** These include Aboriginal peoples who have signed treaties with the government. Of course, some Aboriginal peoples do not have such treaties. Among all groups in Canada, Aboriginal peoples have substantially lower education, occupation, income, and status. They have poor housing and health, and higher mortality and suicide rates than all other groups in Canada.

As discussed above, according to John Porter, individuals from various ethnic groups have access to different resources and are evaluated differently. Porter's view of Canada has been the subject of substantial discussion and controversies. For example, Ogmundson and McLaughlin (1992) have provided evidence that for each category of elites (business, political, media, labour, etc.), the British proportion has declined from 1935 onward, and that the proportion of the French and other ethnic groups has increased. Therefore, according to these researchers, British domination is a thing of the past, and there is a tendency towards a decline of British power and privileges. In contrast, Nakhaie (1997) questions such generalization on the grounds that Ogmundson and McLaughlin fail to take into account the changes in the ethnic composition of the Canadian population. That is, when we take into account the declining population of the British and the increasing proportion of other ethnic groups, the evidence suggests that the British have maintained their elite domination, particularly among the directors

Table 9.2 Average Earnings of Ethno-racial Groups in Canada Working, Full Time, Full Year, Ages 25–65)

	Total Population	Native-Born	Immigrants
Aboriginals	$25,918	$25,912	$26,629
Latin American	$28,517	$35,882	$28,224
Korean	$30,609	$36,604	$30,211
South Asian	$29,251	$35,383	$29,093
Filipino	$29,832	$36,264	$29,593
Black	$31,800	$34,130	$31,495
West Asian	$34,334	$42,236	$33,887
Vietnamese	$32,466	$34,058	$32,444
Arab	$36,625	$41,819	$36,050
Chinese	$35,566	$46,941	$34,303
East Indian	$35,881	$39,675	$35,618
Southeast Asian	$39,641	$51,490	$33,367
Canadian	$37,184	$37,170	$38,816
Portuguese	$36,460	$35,952	$36,614
Polish	$40,454	$45,737	$37,558
Hungarian	$39,697	$40,822	$38,331
Balkan	$40,230	$47,146	$37,284
French	$40,891	$40,867	$41,250
Greek	$36,005	$38,749	$33,548
German	$41,667	$41,370	$42,729
Dutch	$42,787	$42,595	$43,184
Ukrainian	$41,940	$42,190	$39,500
Italian	$43,034	$43,976	$41,606
British	$45,211	$44,186	$48,827
Jewish	$61,309	$66,295	$52,597
Other European	$41,010	$41,558	$40,434
Others	$40,518	$40,351	$42,239
Total	$39,568	$40,031	$37,884

Source: Adapted from Statistics Canada (2001).

of the largest economic corporations. Nevertheless, there has been a modest increase in French and other ethnic group representation among the elites. However, this increase has not been at the expense of the British; it is more likely that the French and other groups have established parallel institutions of upward mobility.

The charter and entrance groups are each composed of more than one ethnic or racial group. An ethnic group is made of people with

- common ancestry, and
- common sense of belonging to that ancestry.

Line of descent can be evaluated based on mother's line of descent (matrilineally), father's line of descent (patrilineally), or both.

An ethnic group can be a minority or dominant in terms of number or status or both. Minority ethnic groups have little power when compared to the dominant ethnic group.

The common aspects of being a minority are:

- being a subordinate group
- being perceived as having low esteem with respect to some cultural traits
- having common identity with awareness about that identity
- having the same descent
- having inter-group marriage.

Some ethnic groups have higher **ethnic identity** than others. Breton (1964) argued that a sense of identity can be formed because of a common culture, territory and religion, shared history, and charismatic leadership (e.g., French in Quebec share a Catholic religion, a shared history often defined in relation to the British and various charismatic leaders who have championed the Québécois cause). Possession of key institutions (e.g., economy and education) is also important for ethnic identity formation.

Ethnic groups can be differentiated by their orientation, though their orientation might change over time and even have multiple orientations. There are four types of orientations:

1.   **Assimilationist** ethnic groups tend to wish to eliminate their differences with other ethnic groups. They often desire to fully participate in the culture of the dominant group and melt into the society.

2.   **Pluralist** ethnic groups tend to maintain some degree of distinctiveness and at the same time, linkage to the others. Such groups have tolerance for differences but also take pride for their own group.

3.   **Secessionist** ethnic groups wish to maintain their group distinctiveness and desire cultural and political independence.

4.   **Militant** ethnic groups tend to wish to dominate other groups. They are often convinced of their own superiority.

Ethnicity is different from race. Historically, race is defined genotypically (genetic makeup) and phenotypically (physical attributes such as skin colour). However, sociologists have come to the conclusion that the term "race" is not a useful scientific concept. The reason for this has to do with the fact that:

- There are few biological differences between groups identified as "races."

- There are more similarities between "races" than differences.

- There have been significant intermarriages and immigration in human history. Interracial marriages and immigration have wiped out "pure races," if there was such a thing to begin with.

- There is no evidence that biological makeup attributed to race can explain human attitudes, knowledge, and behaviour.

As an example, scientists recently discovered a tiny genetic mutation that could explain the first appearance of white skin in humans. Their work suggests that the skin-whitening mutation occurred by chance in a single individual after the first human exodus from Africa. This person apparently became the first ancestor of the "white race." They found out that this skin-whitening mutation involved a change of just one letter of DNA code out of the 3.1 billion letters in the human genome (Weiss, 2005). This finding should make us critical of attributing any significance to "racial" differences.

The above considerations do not mean that there is no correlation between the phenotypical makeup of individuals (e.g., skin colour) and certain ideas and behaviours. But that such a correlation exists does not mean causality. Take the example of Canadian Aboriginals. Evidence suggests that they are significantly more likely to be found in prison than white people. At first we may explain this by their "race." However, ask yourself the following questions: is their rate of incarceration a function of their race or of a racist justice system that has criminalized their way of life, officers who have targeted Aboriginal people, and judges who have issued harsher sentences against Aboriginals compared to whites? Furthermore, is the higher rate of incarceration a function of their "race" or their poverty, which was produced through colonization of their way of life? Finally, if biology is a determinant, why is it that some members of a "racial" group commit crime and others do not? Do they not all have the same biological makeup? Questions such as these should make us think twice when attributing a group's higher rate of incarceration to their "race" or considering race as a useful concept in explaining human behaviours. So if it is not race, what accounts for differences and inequalities between groups? Explanations include present and past discrimination and racism, stereotypes, prejudice, cultural differences, institutional closures, and structural limitations.

Sociologists prefer to see race as a constructed social category. For example, the Canadian government instituted or constructed the term **"visible minority"** to refer to ethno-racial groups in Canada, despite the fact that it is composed of multitudes of different ethno-racial backgrounds, cultures, languages, religions, localities, and shades of colouring. The government of Canada classifies those persons who are not Caucasian in race or white in colour as visible minorities. They are also not Aboriginal Canadians. For the purpose of the Act, the following groups are included among the visible minorities: Chinese, South Asians, blacks, Arabs, Central/West Asians, Filipinos, South-East Asians, Latin Americans, Japanese, Koreans, and Pacific Islanders.

Stereotyping refers to an exaggerated and one-sided view about a group. A stereotype is basically a picture in one's head that tends to minimize internal differences of a group and maximize the group's similarities (i.e., Mini-Max principle). Therefore, stereotypes are often based on perceptions rather than factual information about a group. Stereotypes can be positive, such as when a group is seen as "hard workers" or "smart," or negative, such as when a group is seen as "drunks" or "criminal." Such perceptions may have a kernel of truth, but this does not mean that all members of a group are either smart or criminal. A stereotypical perception can result in prejudice, discrimination, and opportunity obstacles for a group.

Prejudice is often a biased attitude based on an unfavourable attitude toward a group. It is a type of rigid judgment that informs and shapes one's perception of others. Once prejudicial attitudes are formed, they result in inflexible generalizations about the group. When you see a visible minority and ask the person, "Where are you from?" you may be asking the question based on a prejudicial attitude that tends to view all visible minorities as foreigners, ignoring that many have been born in Canada. This example suggests that prejudice is based on erroneous generalizations and inaccurate information.

Table 9.3 shows the level of comfort Canadians have with four targeted ethno-racial groups. There are three ways of reading this table. First, most Canadians are comfortable with

220

Table 9.3 Canadian's Perception of Comfort with Visible Minorities

Do you feel comfortable:

if your boss is someone who is:

	Black	Aboriginal	Asian	Muslim
British	1.60	1.65	1.69	1.75
French	1.65	1.76	1.67	2.05
European	1.61	1.72	1.63	1.81
Canadian	1.89	1.91	1.91	2.12
Visible	1.79	1.64	1.64	1.82
Other	1.63	1.76	1.67	1.70
Total	1.66	1.73	1.70	1.87
N	628	628	628	628

if a teacher in your local school was someone who is:

	Black	Aboriginal	Asian	Muslim
British	1.58	1.61	1.65	1.76
French	1.62	1.62	1.63	1.94
European	1.59	1.66	1.57	1.90
Canadian	1.69	1.69	1.70	1.90
Visible	1.73	1.79	1.85	1.85
Other	1.52	1.77	1.58	1.69
Total	1.60	1.66	1.64	1.84
N	619	619	619	619

if your relative like your sister or daughter was going to marry someone who is:

	Black	Aboriginal	Asian	Muslim
British	1.71	1.79	1.73	2.06
French	1.79	1.82	1.83	2.29
European	1.86	1.79	1.82	2.23
Canadian	1.90	1.99	1.91	2.27
Visible	2.02	1.96	1.78	2.06
Other	1.86	1.84	1.76	1.97
Total	1.82	1.84	1.80	2.16
N	617	617	617	617

1 = very comfortable, 4 = very uncomfortable

Visible = Chinese, East Indian, Filipino, Aboriginal

Source: CRIC, Centre for Research and Information on Canada (2003).

Prejudice is an attitude whereas **discrimination** is a behaviour. The latter means unequal treatment of groups based on negative prejudice and stereotypes. Discrimination involves practices that limit development of full potential and opportunities for members of racial minorities. For example, discrimination occurs in the circumstance where a black and a white person with similar qualifications apply for the same job and only the white person is offered the position. In a 1985 Toronto study, Henry and Ginzberg (1985) asked job applicants with similar resumés to apply for the same job. They found that the chance of white applicants being offered the job was three times higher than that of black applicants. In some cases, a black applicant without an accent was offered an interview, but once there, he was informed that the job had been taken. Soon after, a white applicant arrived and was offered the same job. Researchers concluded that there exists substantial racial discrimination affecting the mobility of members of racial minorities. More recently, Oreopoulos (2009) showed that Toronto employers are significantly less likely to respond positively to an ethnic name applicant than other types of applicants. Oreopoulos and Dechief (2011) extended this study to the three major Canadian cities (Montreal, Toronto, and Vancouver), and results were remarkably similar. Applicants with English-sounding names were 35 percent more likely to receive callbacks than applicants with Indian or Chinese names.

The relationship between prejudice and discrimination can be summarized in Table 9.4. If a person is prejudicial and also discriminates, he may be called an active bigot such, as members of the Ku Klux Klan. Another person may have a prejudicial view but fail to act on it. This person can be called a timid bigot. An all-weather liberal is neither prejudicial nor discriminatory. Finally, a person may not be prejudicial but may still discriminate against others. For example, a restaurant owner with white clients may not be prejudicial against minorities but because he or she thinks that his or her clients don't like minorities, he or she may not hire minorities and thus discriminates by not hiring them. Some institutional types of racism may be predicated on legislation of policies by fair-weather liberals where, even though the policymakers are not prejudicial, the policy in effect results in discrimination.

When prejudice or discrimination is directed against ethnic or racial minorities, it is also called **racism.** Racism refers to the process of categorizing people on the basis of presumed physiological characteristics and their association with psychological, cultural, or social attributes. It is rooted in human history and a need for cheap slaves or labour, fuelled with

Table 9.4 The Relationship between Prejudice and Discrimination

	Discriminatory	
Prejudicial	Yes	No
Yes	Active bigot	Timid bigot
No	Fair-weather liberal	All-weather liberal

Based on Merton (1949: 99-126).

prejudice, religious justification, and mistaken "scientific discoveries" that some racial groups have smaller brain sizes than white Europeans. Racism has three interrelated aspects to it. First, there is belief that biologically distinct races exist. Second, there is a belief that races are organized hierarchically. Third, there is a belief that this hierarchy is based on the superiority of one race and the inferiority of the other race(s) (Potvin, 2000). The consequence is a belief that inferior people can't succeed without the help of the superior people and that any struggle for racial equality is doomed. This type of belief has been the rationalizing cornerstone of attempts to Christianize or bring god to the native people of Asia, America, and Africa and has helped fuel wars between nations. Table 9.5 shows the genetic assumption of racism.

Racism can occur at the individual level and includes racial slurs, jokes, name calling, and mistreatment of individuals considered biologically inferior. Racism can also occur at the institutional level. **Institutional racism** or **systemic racism** refers to rules, regulations, and policies that systematically produce and reproduce differential treatment of specific ethno-racial groups.

Table 9.5 Genetic and Human Structure of Race Assumptions

Antecedent Conditions	Intervening Conditions	Outcome
Genotype-------------->	Phenotype------------------>	Social behaviour
Genetic structure---->	Physical characteristics--->	Social behaviour

Below are a few examples of institutional racism in Canadian history (see Anderson & Frideres, 1985):

- *Cultural and physical genocides:* Aboriginal Canadians have been subject to physical and cultural annihilation. For example, blankets of the Aboriginal peoples were infected with diseases that whites had become immune to, resulting in many Aboriginal deaths. Similarly, Aboriginal Canadians' way of life has been frequently criminalized in Canada.

- *Chinese head tax:* At the turn of the 20th century, the Chinese were forced to pay $500 tax for being Chinese.

- *Oriental Exclusion Act:* From 1925 to 1947, Orientals were barred from coming to Canada.

- *Internment of the Italian and Japanese:* During World War II, Italians and Japanese were placed in internment camps for fear of collaboration with the enemy. Germans were excluded from internment.

- *Immigration policies:* Early immigration policies defined visible minorities as undesirable groups and restricted immigrants' family formation and unification. European immigrants were given preference.

In recent years, overt racism has been declining and has been replaced with a type of racism called **democratic racism** (Henry et al., 2000). This form of racism makes two conflicting sets of values congruent. On the one hand, there is a dominant view that cherishes equality and justice. On the other hand, prejudice and discrimination are tolerated by blaming the victim for not having "acceptable" credentials, "being a poor fit," or "being unable to adapt" to the Canadian ways of life. For example, people may no longer say that black people are inferior. Rather, some tend to say that black people are disadvantaged because of their lack of effort. Thus, if black people have lower status and less power than white people, this difference is perceived to be due to black people's assumed lower work ethic rather than their experiences of prejudice and discrimination. Given the assumption of equal opportunity, it is believed that if black people work hard they can succeed similar to white people in Canada. The tendency in democratic racism is to promote equality of opportunities without acknowledgment of past discrimination that has limited equality of conditions.

Multiculturalism

Canadian **multiculturalism** is built on the three pillars of social justice, civic participation, and identity (specifically, a sense of belonging to Canada). With respect to social justice, though ethno-racial minorities generally achieve higher education levels, they are less likely to appear in the upper income groups, or to work in the types of occupations to which such educational credentials usually lead. Moreover, recent immigrants experience more of these types of inequities. Those who arrived in Canada in the 1980s and later have lower incomes, on average, and work at lower-level occupations compared to those born in Canada. Finally, among recent immigrants, a clear demarcation exists between those classified as visible minority and the British or French charter groups. These differences tend to persist even after education and other social capital characteristics are accounted for.

Table 9.6 shows that visible minority immigrants earn less than white people or those born in Canada and that their income has decreased from 1986 to 2001. Analysis of the 2001 Census further confirms that foreign-born individuals arriving in Canada before 1970 earn more than those coming after and are generally better off than are the Canadian born. The most disadvantaged group are those who arrived between 1991 and 2001. Immigrants as a group, as well as new immigrants (particularly new visible immigrants), earn significantly less than British immigrants. A large number of South and East European new immigrants also earn less than British immigrants.

Table 9.6 Earnings of Visible and Non-Visible Ethno-racial Groups (Working Full-time, Ages 25–65)*

Visible	1986	1991	2001
Native-born	$36,928	$36,892	$40,065
Foreign-born	$32,310	$31,654	$32,952
Non-visible			
Native-born	$36,439	$36,541	$40,030
Foreign-born	$36,850	$39,947	$43,163
Non-visible/Visible Ratio			
Native-born	98.68	99.05	99.91
Foreign-born	114.05	126.20	130.99
Native-born /Foreign-born Ratio			
Non-visible	98.88	91.47	92.74
Visible	114.29	116.55	121.58

* Adjusted to 2001 Consumer Price Index

Findings are not as clear with respect to the second pillar of multiculturalism, civic participation, which tries to ensure the individual's ability and opportunity to participate and shape his or her community and Canadian society. Evidence does indicate that visible minorities less likely to vote in federal, provincial, and municipal elections; on average, they participate in the electoral process about 15 to 20 percent less than do charter groups or other Europeans. The voting gaps between visible minorities and the British is substantially higher among the second generation (those born inside Canada) than among the first (those born outside Canada). The gap between third generation visible minorities and the British is, however, much reduced (to about 6 percent). It seems that socioeconomic inequities account for some of the voting gap. Other evidence shows that visible minorities are somewhat less likely to be involved in voluntary associations and are less likely to mobilize themselves politically (sign petitions, boycott organizations, and/or be involved in demonstrations, for example) than other groups, though they are more involved in religiously affiliated groups. They are, nevertheless, just as attentive to political issues on television and radio and in newspapers as the other groups, except for the French, who are the most attentive of all. Although there is a tendency for a lower engagement of visible minorities in the dominant civic associations, those who are involved appear to be more politically aware than other groups. This pattern of consciousness seems to have held in the past as well, where minorities have proven very willing to mobilize. They have demanded equal participation and the right to vote, for example, and demanded an end to discrimination.

With respect to the last pillar, identity, which entails both a positive attitude toward one's own culture and a felt sense of belonging and attachment to Canada, the tendency is for ethno-racial groups to have an emotional connection to both Canada and their own ethno-racial group. Evidence shows that despite experiencing economic inequities, a very large majority express warmth for Canada and their province of residence. These feelings are higher among immigrants than French citizens, but lower than those of British ancestry report (86 percent versus 81 percent). On a scale of 1 to 5 (1 being the lowest, 5 the highest), a sense of belonging to Canada is 4.25 for visible minorities compared to 4.4 to 4.5 for the British and other Europeans, 4.3 for the Jews, and 3.9 for the French. In terms of a sense of belonging to one's ethnic or cultural groups, the British and East, West, and North Europeans have the lowest scores of 3.15, 3.03, 2.87, and 2.85, respectively, and the Jews have the highest score at 3.99. The French, South Europeans, and visible minorities score in the middle: 3.57, 3.67, and 3.70, respectively.

In sum, there is little ethno-racial difference when it comes to a felt sense of belonging and attachment to Canada; in fact, visible minorities have a strong sense of attachment. Moreover, the idea that one can be proud of one's ethnicity and at the same time have a strong sense of belonging to Canada is a pervasive feature of this country, particularly for visible minorities. What seems to be clearly demarcated among the various groups in Canada is a substantial experience of injustice in terms of socioeconomic achievement as experienced by minorities concurrent with a lower minority participation rate in the formal political arena.

In other words, despite a well-intended policy, there remain significant inequities among ethno-racial groups, most of which are experienced by the minorities. The extent of these inequities is such that some have called Canada a racist society (Lian & Mathew 1998). Such inequities also tend to be responsible for minorities' lower civic and, even more so, political participation.

Employment Equity

The implementation of Employment Equity (EE) programs was intended to combat discrimination against designated groups (women, Aboriginal peoples, visible minorities, and persons with disabilities). Such programs and their predecessor in the U.S., Affirmative Action (AA), are justified by their supporters on the grounds that they combat past discrimination and help the development of an ideal just society. For example, Abella argued that EE "is a strategy designed to obliterate the present and residual effects of discrimination" (Abella, 1984, p. 214). The Canadian Employment Equity Act (EEA) asks employers to establish achievable goals. It requires employers to institute policies and practices and make reasonable accommodations to ensure that persons in designated groups achieve a degree of representation that reflects in (i) the Canadian workforce, or (ii) those segments of the Canadian workforce that are identifiable by qualifications, eligibility, or geography and from which the employer may reasonably be expected to draw employees (EEA, 1986, Section 4; EEA, 1995, Section 5b). The purpose as stated in the Employment Equity Act (1986) is to achieve equality in the workplace, eliminate obstacles to employment opportunities, and correct disadvantageous conditions for employment of designated minority groups.

The history of Employment Equity in Canada shows that it is a contested policy. It is frequently referred to by its opponents as systemic preferential hiring. The supporters focus on hiring of qualified minorities, while the opponents focus on the "quota hiring," "preferential hiring," "reverse discrimination," and/or "undermining of merits." For example, the Canadian Manufacturers' Association, the Canadian Federation of Independent Business, and others have argued that there is no need for Employment Equity legislation and regulatory controls in Ontario. They rejected government intervention into the business activities and instead

...phasized the ethic of competition, individualism, and equality independent of race. They insisted that if there is discrimination in the workplace, the Charter of Rights or the Human Rights legislation can address it (see Bakan & Koyabashi, 2000, 2002, 2007).

The provincial Conservative government of Ontario in 1993 successfully challenged the Ontario Employment Equity Bill 79. Bill 8 (December 13, 1995) entitled *An Act to Repeal Job Quotas and Restore Merit-Based Employment Practices in Ontario* successfully repealed the Employment Equity Act (Bill 79, 1993) and other related legislation. Although the 1993 Ontario bill was overturned, the Federal Employment Equity Act (1986) became strengthened by the 1995 Employment Equity Act, which came into effect on October 24, 1996. The new Act required employers to specify "positive policies and practices" that need to be instituted for the hiring, training, promotion and retention of members of the designated groups, eliminate barriers, and correct their underrepresentation (Article 10.1.a).

Theories of Ethnic and Racial Inequality

Basically, there are two broad explanation of ethno-racial inequality. One explanation focuses on the individual and cultural characteristics that are often viewed as inherited and result in inequality. The second explanation emphasizes the characteristic of society and the fault of society such as **ethnocentrism,** prejudice, racism, and unjust economic system (see Breton in Curtis & Scott, 1979).

Cultural and Individual Attributes

Some scholars explain ethnic inequality by individual or cultural characteristics of the group. For example, Nagler (1975) argued that Aboriginal peoples are more present oriented, do not have a work ethic, and have a different conception of time than non-Aboriginal peoples. Similarly, Herrnstein (1990) argued that black people and white people have different characteristics. He suggested that black people have lower intelligence as measured by aptitude tests and are less motivated than white people. According to these researchers, these differences in attributes, traits, and cultural values tend to explain the extent of inequalities between ethno-racial groups.

This argument is rooted in functionalism, which views that the organization of work as interrelated occupations requires different kinds and levels of skill. This means that:

- the organization of work is hierarchically shaped
- the labour market is perfectly competitive

- information flow between employer and employee is free and without obstacles
- the labour market allocates individuals in the hierarchy of positions
- allocation of individuals to these positions is based on their motivations and abilities, and
- individuals are rewarded according to their productivity and contribution in meeting the societal needs.

Given the requirements of free and competitive market, individual's productivity is based on:

1. finding the best job possible
2. an ability for 'impression management' motivation, talent, energy, training, material resources, and contacts, which are important to increasing productivity.

Ethnic groups are therefore allocated into the system of inequality based on their members' personal resources and inter-ethnic attitudes and orientations.

Personal resources are important for:

- gaining access to information (network of contacts),
- bargaining with employees, and
- performing on the job.

Accordingly, due to cultural backgrounds and language differences, individuals acquire personal attributes that affect their ability to find a job, perform on the job, and reach the optimal level of output. Therefore, ethnic differences in the occupational and class structure are due to the unequal ethnic individuals' characteristics in the competitive market. It is true that the labour market is not perfectly competitive due to the:

1. difficulty of moving people around because of social attachment and ethnic ties,
2. difficulty of a systematic comparison among various employees,
3. heavy cost of making information available to all potential employees, and
4. discrimination and prejudice that prevent:

    - employers recognizing the right cues as to the true productivity of potential employees, and
    - employees recognizing the best opportunities when looking for a job.

Such obstacles, however, are temporary because in the long run, for example, the discriminating employers would lose out to the non-discriminating ones who hire the best workers at the lowest prices, irrespective of ethnic origin. Moreover, individuals from various ethnic groups tend to retain from their culture only those elements that are useful in helping them to have a better life in the new society. This means that they tend to selectively assimilate resulting in cultural homogenization and thus the destruction of ethnic differentiation.

In sum, this approach is rooted in an understanding that the industrial labour market is competitive, and individuals are allocated to the best positions based on their motivation, qualification, and skills. Therefore, either minorities are doomed to remain at the bottom of social inequality due to their traits and attributes, or they should change their cultural values and become similar to dominant white groups with respect to motivation and work ethic in order to advance in industrial societies.

Institutional Barriers

Recall that according to Porter (1965), Canadian history is rooted in immigration and conquest. Consequently, the British, as the conquerors, have institutionalized avenues of upward mobility based on their own cultural values, norms, laws, attitudes, behaviours, language, and institutions. Therefore, the conquered and the newly arrived, particularly those who are bioculturally different from the British, have been subject to their institutional power. Dominant groups possess a much larger share of cultural and social networks and thus are better able to reproduce themselves through their children. On the other hand, immigrants' and visible minorities' cultural value systems and social networks are undermined due to the ability of the British (and French) in privileging their own institutions and value system.

This approach is rooted in the Weberian model which argues that inequality is based on social closure. **Social closure** is a two-sided process wherein members of one group try to exclude others from scarce resources, and usurp the scarce resources of others. For example, in capitalist societies, the bourgeoisie who control the productive private property and/or monopolize services create and use laws in order to exclude others from scarce resources and usurp their resources by the institution of private property and professional qualifications and credentials available to it.

In Canada, the conquering British legislated laws that favoured themselves in, for example, the fur trade against the Aboriginal peoples, pharmaceutical occupations against East Indians, and a taxing system against the Chinese. Other examples include legislations against Japanese and Italians in the World War II resulting in their internment and significant loss of their property.

230

Structural Mechanisms

Marxists define classes in terms of individuals' relation to the organization of production, where a minority of non-producers control the means of production and this power allows them to extract surplus-value from the majority of producers. Although this approach sees ethnicity as secondary to class in explaining inequality, it points to the historical forces that have resulted in one class becoming overrepresented by a specific ethnic group. This coincidence of class cleavages and ethnic cleavages thus accounts for ethnic inequality, particularly within a class. Here the concept of **split labour market** is instructional. Split labour market occurs when there is a difference in the price of labour between groups of workers doing the same job.

Bonacich (1972, 1976) argued that due to certain historical events (slavery, immigration, immigrants' poor organization, etc.), the labour market has been divided based on race and ethnicity, wherein one group gets paid less than the other despite their similarity in efficiency and productivity. This division is beneficial to the capitalists who search for cheap labour but is a source of conflict among the working classes themselves. Recall that in the Marxist conceptualization of class, capitalist employers are interested in hiring cheap labour and they always look for cheaper labour.

They may use the existing prejudice, discrimination, and poverty of minority ethnic groups and hire them cheaply. Minority ethnic groups and newly arrived immigrants tend to sell their labour power cheaply because they are unfamiliar with the new labour market economy, and do not have good organization or unions to protect their labour value. Therefore, the less organized and often unfamiliar with the labour market ethno-racial minorities may strike a bad bargain and work for less pay. The hiring of cheap ethnic minority and immigrant labour tends to threaten higher paid labourers who belong to the dominant ethnic groups. The latter may have to sell their labour power cheaply too. They view these ethno-racial minorities and new immigrants who work for low pay as a source of problems because these workers tend to lower the average wages and therefore increase the working-class competition. This often gives rise to what is known as working-class racism: the better paid white working class may use minorities as a *scapegoat*, blaming them for their lower wages and directing their anger toward them through racist slurs, insults, hate crimes, and so on. In Canada, Bolaria and Li (1988) similarly have attributed ethno-racial inequalities and development of racism to capitalists' continual search for docile and cheap labour.

Colonization Process

The **colonization** model is a closely related structural model of inter-ethnic inequality. Frideres (1988) argued that white colonizers have destroyed Aboriginal social and cultural systems and have subjected Aboriginal peoples to economic and political dependence. In the process, the colonizers have ensured that Aboriginal peoples have lower education, higher poverty, and more health problems. Finally, they have used these inequities as justification of their own racial superiority and thus have further exploited Aboriginal resources.

Intersection Model

Feminists of colour, such as bell hooks (1984) and Patricia Hill Collins (1990), have brought to our attention the fact that there are simultaneous effects of racism, sexism, and class exploitation as interconnecting systems of privilege and domination. They suggest that gender is racialized, race is gendered, and both are subject to class-related domination. Therefore, they point to the intersection of race, class, and gender that produces distinct forms of oppression that are not captured by any of these individually (see Stasiulis, 1999).

Summary

Aboriginal peoples have lived in Canada for centuries. Hhistorically their land has been confiscated and they have experienced cultural and physical annihilation. Nowadays, they still live in abject poverty, experience significant health problems, high mortality, and suicide rates, and are overrepresented in the Canadian prisons. To some extent, their situation is due to their experiences of colonization by the new comers. This is because Canada is built on immigration and conquest. The conquering group has not only placed Aboriginal peoples into reserves with little amenities but also destroyed their cultural reproduction by placing Aboriginal children into residential schooling and preventing them from practising their way of life and ceremonies. The conquest of Canada by the British has also affected other ethno-racial groups. The French experienced significant inequality after their defeat on the Plains of Abraham, though they have recovered somewhat since the Quiet Revolution and have now substantial control at the provincial level and some power at the federal level. Immigrants, particularly recent racial minority immigrants, also suffered the result of conquest. The British conquerers have established rules and regulations in accordance with their own cultural ways of life, which has resulted substantial problems for those with different bio-cultural characteristics to adjust to

Canada. Experiences of prejudice, discrimination, and structural and institutional barriers have been and are key obstacles to upward mobility for ethno-racial minorities. Nevertheless, Canadian multicultural policy, built on three pillars of social justice, civic participation, and identity, has ensured tolerance of immigrants and minority ethno-racial groups, which has made it somewhat possible avenues of success for the newcomers.

Key Terms

Assimilation: the process by which minority ethno-racial groups lose their distinctive culture and adopt that of the dominant groups.

Charter groups: the two original European groups (British and French) whose rights and privileges (such as language rights) are enshrined in the Canadian Constitution.

Colonization: the process by which a country takes over another country by force of arms and governs that country without people's consent.

Democratic racism: a type of racism that results in unequal outcomes when people are treated equally, without paying attention to their differences or unequal conditions.

Discrimination: unequal treatment of various groups; actions of the dominant group that deny members of minority groups resources available to other groups.

Entrance groups: late immigrants whose group rights are not enshrined in the Canadian Constitution.

Ethnic identity: the extent to which members of an ethnic group differentiate themselves from others, consider themselves as a common people separate from others, and have a positive sense of attachment to their own group.

Ethnocentrism: the practice of judging members of another cultural group by one's own cultural standards; a belief in superiority of one's own culture.

Institutional racism: the established rules, procedures, and practices that directly and deliberately prevent full and equal involvement of the minority group members in society.

Intersection model: a theoretical framework that views humans as governed by multiple identities and life worlds.

Militant: an individual or groups who wish or act to dominate.

Minority: a category of people distinguished by physical and/or cultural traits and who are often disadvantaged.

Multiculturalism: policies designed to ensure cultural and ethnic maintenance of ethnic groups and to promote equality of opportunity for all ethnic groups in Canada. Social justice, identity, and engagement are the three pillars of multiculturalism.

Pluralist: a view of the state system suggesting that it is made of a great variety of people and interest groups which help to ensure that everyone gets a fair and representative voice in its management and decision-making process.

Prejudice: negative judgment of individuals on the basis of assumed characteristics of the group to which the individual belongs. A biased attitude based on an unfavourable attitude toward a group.

Quiet Revolution: social changes in Quebec that included educational expansion, industrialization, and urbanization.

Racism: the belief that one group sharing certain physical characteristics is innately superior to another group with different characteristics.

Secessionist: an individual or group who wishes or acts to separate from other individuals or groups.

Social closure: a Weberian term that refers to a two-sided process where one group tries to exclude other groups from important scarce resources as well as to confiscate those resources.

Split labour market: division of the economy into two sectors—primary and secondary. The primary sector is more unionized and capital intensive with high-paying jobs than the secondary sector. Often subordinate group members work in the secondary economic sector.

Stereotype: a simplified belief about characteristics of a social group. Such belief minimizes a group's differences and maximizes its similarities. It exaggerates based on too little information.

Systematic racism: practices that systematically discriminate against one or more racial groups because of their colour of skin, religion, language, or nationality.

Treaty groups: First Nations peoples with treaty rights.

Visible minority: official government classification of non-white and non-Caucasian groups.

Critical Thinking Questions

1. Do you think that minorities are portrayed negatively in the media? If yes, is there evidence that things are changing?

2. What are your views on Canadian multiculturalism?

3. Was there anything in this chapter that changed your views on visible minorities or the way they have been treated in Canada? If yes, what was it?

4. Do you think that once in Canada, minorities should abandon their way of life and assimilate into the Canadian way of society? If so, what are some aspects of this Canadian way of life?

5. Do you think that Canadian society provides opportunities for minorities to assimilate?

6. Do you think ethnic communities continue to influence the attitudes and behaviours of their members?

7. Why do you think racial and ethnic inequality persists in Canada today?

8. What do you think explains income and or occupational differences among various Canadian ethnic groups?

9. Why do you think Muslims tend to be viewed more negatively? Do you think that 9/11 is somewhat responsible for intolerance toward this group? Why?

10. How do Marxists and Weberians explain ethnic inequality?

11. Why is there discrimination and racism in Canada today?

Sociological Example: Race and Ethnic Inequality*

Introduction: Research Purpose

Canada is a society composed of diverse ethnic and racial groups. Ethnicity refers to people with common ethnic descent, culture, and language, while race refers to the genetic and physical differences in characteristics of individuals. Sociologists believe that there is no reality to race. Race is a constructed group. For example, the Aboriginal or racialized minority "races" are each made of different groups and composed of multitudes of different backgrounds, cultures, languages, religions, localities, and shades of colouring. The government of Canada, through the Indian Act, has lumped all First Nations groups into the Aboriginal "race," and through the Employment Equity Act, it has classified all persons who are not Caucasian in race or white in colour as "racialized minorities." Therefore, it is customary to refer to "racialized minorities" or Aboriginal peoples as *racialized minorities*.

Recall that Porter divided Canadian ethnic groups into **charter groups** (British and French), entrance groups (immigrants), and Aboriginal or First Nations peoples. Each of these groups has a different level of identification with Canada and their own groups. Some strongly identify with their own groups, while others have a higher tendency to be assimilated into Canadian society and identify with Canada. In addition, some of these groups have more power and privilege than others. For some, the charter groups' power and privileges are institutionalized due to conquest of Canada or because of the colour of their skin and their cultural heritage, while others entered Canada as new immigrants. Many immigrants have different physical characteristics and cultures from the well-established groups. New immigrants have less power and privileges and may experience racism in Canada or have problems integrating into the labour market. In this chapter, we will look at various dimensions of power and privileges for various groups in Canada. We are interested to know if power and privilege are due to one's own accomplishments or due to "race" and ethnicity. If they are due to "race" and ethnicity, we want to know why.

---

*Based on Nakhaie (1997, pp. 1–24; 2004, pp. 92–110; and 2006, pp. 19–46).

Theoretical Explanation

Some scholars attribute inter-ethnic inequality to the group's culture or to the individual characteristics of that group. For example, Nagler (1975) has argued that Aboriginal peoples are more present-oriented, do not have a work ethic, and have a different conception of time than non-Aboriginal peoples. Similarly, Herrnstein (1990) has suggested that blacks have lower intelligence, as measured by aptitude tests, and are less motivated than whites. According to these researchers, these differences in attributes, traits, and cultural values tend to explain the extent of inequalities between ethno-racial groups. Whether their suggestions are correct or not, their argument is rooted in an understanding that the industrial labour market is a competitive one where individuals are allocated to the best positions based on their motivation, qualifications, and skills. Therefore, either minorities are doomed to remain at the bottom of social inequality due to their traits and attributes, or they should change their cultural values and become similar to dominant white groups with respect to motivation and work ethic in order to advance in industrial societies. Perhaps one of the best measures of motivation, aptitude, and hard work is educational attainment. Therefore, according to this approach, Aboriginal peoples, blacks, and other racialized minorities have lower power and privileges because they have lower education.

Other scholars believe that inter-ethnic inequality is due to institutional barriers or structural limitations experienced by minorities. The Weberian model pays attention to the institutional barriers while the Marxist approach focuses on structural limitations (for example, see Bonacich, 1976; Porter, 1965). Bolaria and Li (1988) similarly have attributed ethno-racial inequalities and development of racism to capitalists' continual search for docile and cheap labour. This approach is called the *split labour market model*. A final approach is known as the *intersection model*. This approach focuses on the simultaneous effects of racism, sexism, and class exploitation as interconnecting systems of privilege and domination. The point is that people are placed in different subject positions based on their race, ethnicity, gender, class, and other societally based categories. The combination of subject positions cannot be captured by any of these individually (see Stasiulis, 1999).

Previous Research

Previous research has shown the following:

- Porter's (1965) study of ethnic groups in Canada showed that ethnic minorities experienced *"blocked mobility."* They were less likely to be among the powerful groups or have a high status occupation and income compared to the British and French charter groups.

- Clement (1975) showed that those of British origin represented 45 percent of the Canadian population but more than 86 percent of the economic elites.

- Ogmundson and McLaughlin (1992) showed that the proportion of British among the powerful economic, political, educational, media, and other elites has declined since 1935. They suggested that the days of British domination had come to an end and that elite status in Canada was becoming a more egalitarian concept.

- Lian and Matthews (1998), based on the 1991 Census, found that among those with a university degree, racialized minorities earned somewhere between 22 and 39 percent less than the average Canadian income. They suggested that Canada can be best characterized as a "coloured mosaic" or "a racist society" (p. 476).

- Li (2000), based on the 1996 Census, showed that native-born or immigrant Canadian racialized minorities earn less than non-racialized minorities.

Therefore, previous studies have shown that there are significant ethnic inequalities in Canada where ethno-racial minorities are disadvantaged in terms of power, occupation, and income, despite their education.

Research Importance and Questions

Canada officially initiated a multicultural policy in 1971 and instituted the Canadian Multiculturalism Act in 1988. This Act and the Employment Equity Acts passed in 1986 and 1995 are the twin pillars of social justice for the ethno-racial groups in Canada. The Employment Equity Act specifically aims to combat discrimination against the designated groups (women, Aboriginal peoples, racialized minorities, and persons with disabilities). How successful have these two policies been? If there are ethnic inequalities in Canada and these inequalities are not due to educational differences between groups, one can suggest that governmental policies have not been effective in overcoming barriers to the full economic integration of the Canadian population.

Research Questions

1. Do ethnic inequities exist in Canada?

2. If there are ethnic inequities, to what extent are these due to the differences in education (representing motivation and hard work) of different groups?

Based on the theoretical model and evidence suggested above, we hypothesize that there is little ethnic inequality in Canada, and if there are such inequalities, they are due to the ethnic groups' different level of education.

Requirements for Testing the Relationship

In order to test our hypotheses, we need information on access to education, occupation, income, and power of various groups. Census 2001, *Canadian Who's Who*, and the Parliament of Canada provide us with such information.

Do the Findings Support the Hypotheses?

Before we test the relationship between education, occupation, and income, we present historical evidence on the nature of British control of the key Canadian institutions. Table 9.1.1 shows the index of British elite representation. Each index represents the ratio of the ethnic proportion of the elite to the corresponding proportion of the Canadian population for each of the closest censuses. A figure above 1.00 denotes overrepresentation and a figure below 1.00 suggests underrepresentation. Therefore, this table shows that in each of the economic, political, and educational elites, the British are overrepresented by about twice the size of their population. For example, in 1951, 94.4 percent of the university presidents were from among the British ethnic groups, while 47.9 percent of the Canadian population consisted of the British ethnic ancestry. Therefore, in 1951 with an index of 1.97 (94.4/47.9 = 1.97), there are about twice as many British university presidents as one would expect based on their population. This table also shows a remarkable stable pattern of British dominance. Despite minor fluctuations, the British group maintained about the same level of overrepresentation in all years, among all dominant or elite categories.

How would this picture look if we were to look among all ethnic groups for the general population and not just the powerful elites? Table 9.1.2 shows the percentage of various ethnic groups in the 2001 Census who have a post-graduate degree or are in professional or managerial occupations and their earnings. This table shows that, on average, racialized minorities have higher education but lower income and are underrepresented in higher occupations. For example, 11.2 percent of racialized minorities compared to only 7.2 percent of non-racialized minorities have post-graduate education while racialized minorities have lower income.

Table 9.1.1 Index of British Elite Representation

Year	1951	1972	1977	1985
Economic elites*	1.93	1.92	1.79	1.98

Year	1951	1971	1991	2001
Education elites**	1.97	1.86	1.92	2.23

Year	1975	1985	1989
Media elites***	1.47	1.38	1.47

Year	1940–1960	1960–1973	1974–1987
Political elites****	1.6	1.79	1.48

* Director of firms with 500 and more employees
** University presidents
*** Directors of the broadcast corporations
**** Federal cabinet ministers, provincial premiers, Justices of the Supreme Court
Source: Nakhaie (1997, 2004).

Table 9.1.2 Educational, Occupational, and Income Attainment of Ethno-racial Groups, Full-time, Ages 25–65, 2001

| | Education | Occupation | Average Earning ($) | |
| | | Percent Professional | | |
	Post-Graduates	Managerial	All Canadians	Immigrants
Aboriginal	1.3	12.6	25,918	26,629
Aboriginal (multiple)	3.8	14.2	35,060	36,857
Latin American	7.3	10.9	28,517	28,224
Black	5.7	15.4	31,800	31,495
Vietnamese	5.5	15.2	32,466	32,444
Korean	14.3	21	30,609	30,211
Chinese	14.2	26.9	35,566	34,303
Filipino	6.3	13.2	29,832	29,593
South Asian	13.3	16	29,251	29,093
South-East Asian	10.3	22	39,641	33,367
East Indian	13.5	18.7	35,881	35,618
West Asian	15.1	22.3	34,334	33,887
Arab	18.6	26.4	36,625	36,050
Greek	8	16.9	36,005	33,548
Portuguese	2.1	9.2	36,460	36,614
Italian	6.5	17.6	43,034	41,606
Polish	12.9	18.5	40,454	37,558
Hungarian	7.8	17.5	39,697	38,331
Balkan	8.5	19.2	40,230	37,284
Ukrainian	7.6	19.4	41,940	39,500
German	5.6	15.8	41,667	42,729
Dutch	6.6	18.2	42,787	43,184
French	8.9	22.2	40,891	41,250
British	7.4	19.5	45,211	48,827
Jewish	30.1	42.3	61,309	52,597
Other European	13.9	21.9	41,010	40,434
Canadian	4.2	15.2	37,184	38,816
Can, Brit, Fre, Prv.	8.2	22.1	43,080	48,647
Can, Brit, Fre, Other	8.8	22.5	42,553	42,459
Multiple Others	11.4	23.5	42,460	40,157
Other	6.4	17.1	32,440	39,464
Non-racialized	7.2	19.2	40,402	43,163
Racialized	11.2	19.9	33,654	32,953
Total	7.7	19.3	39,568	37,884

Source: Statistics Canada (2001); adapted from Nakhaie (2006).

Given a significantly higher percentage of post-graduate racialized minorities, we would have expected an equally significantly higher percentage of them among the professional managerial groups. However, an approximately equal percent of both groups are among the professional and managerial occupations. More importantly, the average income of racialized minorities in 2001 was $33,625, which is significantly lower than the average income of non-racialized minorities at $40,402. This gap is even higher among the immigrant groups. Let's focus on South Asians and East Indians. They have a significantly higher percentage of post-graduate education than both charter groups of the British and French, but a lower percentage of them are among the professional and managerial groups when compared to the charter groups.

What Can Be Concluded from the Findings?

Overall, the evidence suggests that the main institutions of Canadian society (economy, politics, education, and media) are controlled by the British. Moreover, the evidence does not support the idea that the most educated people have the best jobs and highest incomes, though there is some support for this idea as well. Those of British ancestry earn substantially more than racialized minorities, and gaps are even wider among immigrants. Furthermore, the general tendency is for racialized minority immigrants, and somewhat less for European immigrants, to have a lower return on their education.

A few words on the extreme inequalities experienced by the Aboriginal peoples are in order. Frideres (1988) has argued that white colonizers have destroyed Aboriginal peoples' social and cultural systems and have subjected Aboriginal peoples to economic and political dependence. In the process, they have ensured that Aboriginal peoples have lower education, higher poverty, and more health problems. Finally, they have used these inequities as justification of their own racial superiority to Aboriginal peoples and further exploitation of Aboriginal resources. This explanation is known as the *colonization model,* and the evidence seems to be congruent with its basic argument.

What Are the Possible Policy Implications?

Although **multicultural** and **employment equity** legislations provided some protection from discrimination against racialized minorities, they have not been successful in addressing the existing ethnic inequities in Canada. Moreover, these legislations are limited in that they do not list immigrants as a designated group. This group has been, and still is, one of the most disadvantaged groups in Canada. The barriers experienced by racialized minorities and the immigrant population, particularly if they are racialized minority immigrants, tend to undermine the notions of equality of opportunity that we proudly present as part of the "Canadian way." Unless measures are taken to address these inequities, the hardships experienced by racialized minorities and the immigrant population could result in social unrest as in Europe, particularly when the population of racialized minorities in major Canadian cities surpasses those of other ethno-racial groups.

Key Terms

Charter group: the two original European groups (British and French) whose rights and privileges (such as language rights) are enshrined in the Canadian Constitution.

Employment equity: a law passed in 1986 in order to provide a level playing field for the designated groups (women, ethnic minorities, Aboriginal peoples, and people with disabilities).

Multiculturalism: policies designed to ensure cultural and ethnic maintenance of ethnic groups and to promote equality of opportunity for all ethnic groups in Canada. Social justice, identity, and engagement are the three pillars of multiculturalism.

Critical Thinking Questions

1. If sociologists believe that "race" is a constructed category and not real, why do they believe that ethno-racial minorities are subjects of racism?
2. Why do you think that the British have been able maintain the control of key Canadian institutions?
3. What other policy changes can be made to allow greater equality among immigrants (and particularly immigrants of racialized minority status)?
4. Why are the educational credentials of immigrants valued less in Canada?
5. Do you think that minorities are portrayed negatively in Canada? Why?
6. Why do you think racial and ethnic social inequalities persist in Canada today?

REFERENCES

Abella, R. S. (1984). *Equality in employment: A royal commission report.* Ottawa: Minister of Supply and Services.

Adler, C. (1995). Feminist criminology in Australia. In N. H. Rafter & F. Heidensohn (Eds.), *International feminist perspectives in criminology.* Buckingham: Open University Press.

Anderson, A., & Frideres, J. (1985). *Ethnicity in Canada: Theoretical perspectives.* Toronto: Butterworths.

Arneklev, B. J., Grasmick, H. G., & Tittle, C. R. (1993). Low self-control and imprudent behaviour. *Journal of Quantitative Criminology, 9*(3), 225–247.

Arnett, J. (1995). Adolescents' use of media for self-socialization. *Journal of Youth and Adolescence, 24*(5), 519–533.

Ashley, D., & Ornstein. D. M. (1998). *Sociological theory; classical statements.* Boston: Allyn and Bacon.

Bakan, A., & Kobayashi, A. (2000). *Employment equity policy in Canada: An interprovincial comparison.* Ottawa: Status of Women Canada.

Bakan, A., & Kobayashi, A. (2002). Employment equity legislation in Ontario: A case study in the politics of backlash. In C. Agocs (Ed.), *Workplace equality: International perspectives on legislation, policy and practice,* (pp. 91–108). New York: Kluwer Law International.

Bakan, A., & Kobayashi, A. (2007). Affirmative action and employment equity: Policy, ideology, and backlash in Canadian context. *Studies in Political Economy, 79,* 145–166.

Baldus, B. (1975). The study of power: Suggestions for an alternative. *Canadian Journal of Sociology, 1*(2), 179–201.

Bandura. A., & Walters, R. (1963). *Social learning and personality development.* New York: Holt, Rinehart and Winston.

Barrett, M. (1992). Psychoanalysis and feminism: A British sociologist's view. *Signs, 17,* 455–466.

Becker, H. (1953). On becoming a marihuana user. *American Journal of Sociology 59*(3), 235–42.

Berk, S. (1985). *The gender factory: The apportionment of work in the American household.* New York: Plenum Press.

Bernburg, J. G., Krohn, M., & Rivera, C. (2006). Official labeling, criminal embeddedness, and subsequent delinquency: A longitudinal test of labeling theory. *Journal of Crime in Research and Delinquency, 43*(1), 67–88.

Berti, A. E., Bombi, A. S., & De Beni, R. (1986). Acquiring economic notions: Profit. *International Journal of Behavioral Development, 9,* 15–29.

Bjorkqvist, K. (1994). Sex differences in physical, verbal, and indirect aggression: A review of recent research. *Sex Roles, 30,* 177–188.

Bolaria, B. S., & Li, P. (1988). *Racial oppression in Canada.* Toronto: Garamond.

Bonacich, Edna. (1972). A theory of ethnic antagonism: The split labor market. *American Sociological Review, 37*(5), 547–559.

Bonacich, E. (1976). Advanced capitalism and black/white relations in the United States: A split labor market interpretation. *American Sociological Review, 41*(1), 34–51.

Boswell, A. A., & Spade, J. A. (1996). Fraternities and collegiate rape culture: Why are some fraternities more dangerous places for women? *Gender and Society, 10,* 133–147.

Bourdieu, P. (1977). Cultural reproduction and social reproduction. In J. Karabel & A. H. Halsey (Eds.), *Power and ideology in education* (pp. 487–511). New York: Oxford University Press.

Breton, R. (1964). Institutional completeness of ethnic communities and the personal relations of immigrants. *American Journal of Sociology, 70,* 193–205.

Breton, R. (1979). Ethnic stratification viewed from three different theoretical perspectives. In J. E. Curtis & W. G. Scott, *Social stratification: Canada* (pp. 270–295). Scarborough, ON: Prentice-Hall Canada Inc.

Brines, J. (1994). Economic dependency, gender and the division of labor at home. *American Journal of Sociology, 100,* 652–688.

Brizendine, L. (2006). *The female brain.* New York: Broadway Press.

Broverman, I. K., Vogel, S. R., Broverman, D. M., Clarkson, F. E., & Rosenkrantz, P. S. (1972). Sex-role stereotypes: A current appraisal. *Journal of Social Issues, 28*(2), 59–78.

Brownmiller, S. (1975). *Against our will.* New York: Simon and Schuster.

Brubaker, R. (1985). Rethinking classical theory: The sociological vision of Pierre Bourdieu. *Theory and Society, 14,* 723–744.

Carlson, N. R. (1977). *Physiology of behavior.* Boston: Allyn & Bacon.

Carroll, M. P. (2005). Who owns democracy? Explaining the long-running debates over Canadian/American value differences. *Canadian Review of Sociology and Anthropology, 42*(3), 267–282.

Chambliss, W. (1969). *Crime and the legal process.* New York: McGraw-Hill.

Chambliss, W. (1975). Toward a political economy of crime. *Theory and Society, 2*(2), 151.

Cheal, D. (1990). Authority and incredulity: Sociology between modernism and post-modernism. *Canadian Journal of Sociology, 15*(2), 129–147.

Cherney, I. D. (2008). Mom, let me play more computer games: They improve my mental rotation skills. *Sex Roles, 59,* 776–786.

Chodorow, N. (1978). *The reproduction of mothering.* Berkeley: University of California Press.

Clement, W. (1975). *The Canadian corporate elite: An analysis of economic power.* Toronto: McClelland and Stewart.

Cloward, R., & Ohlin, L. (1960). *Delinquency and opportunity.* New York: The Free Press.

Collins, P. H. (1990). *Black feminist thought: Knowledge, consciousness, and the politics of empowerment.* Boston: Unwin, Hayman,

Connell, R. W. (2002). *Gender.* Oxford: Polity Press.

Connell, R. W. (2005). Change among the gatekeepers: Men, masculinities, and gender equality in the global arena. *Signs: Journal of Women in Culture and Society, 30*(3), 1801–1825.

Cooley, C. H. (1930). *Sociological theory and social research.* New York: Holt, Rinehart and Winston.

Cooley, C. H. (1964). *Human nature and the social order.* New York: Schocken.

CRIC. (June 2003). CRIC–*Globe and Mail* survey on "the new Canada." Centre for Research and Information on Canada, book no. 11.

Curtiss, S. (1977). Genie: A Psycholinguistic study of a modern-day "wild child." Boston: Academic Press.

Dahl, R. A. (1957). The concept of power. *Behavioural Science, 2*(3), 201–215.

Dahl R. A. (1958). A critique of the ruling elite model. *American Journal of Political Science, 52*(2), 463–469.

Dalgard, O. S., & Kringler, E. (1976). A Norwegian twin study of criminality. *British Journal of Criminology, 16,* 213–232.

Davis, K. (1947). Final note on a case of extreme isolation. *American Journal of Sociology, 52,* 432–447.

Davis, K. (1953). A reply. *American Sociological Review, 18,* 394–397.

Davis, K., & Moore, W. (1945). Some principles of stratification. *American Sociological Review, 10,* 242–49.

Delaney, T. (2005). *Contemporary social theory: Introduction and application.* Upper Saddle River, NJ: Prentice-Hall.

Denno, D. W. (1988). Human biology and criminal responsibility: Free will or free ride? *University of Pennsylvania Law Review, 137*(2), 659–671.

Derrida, J. (1967). *On grammatalogy.* Baltimore: John Hopkins University Press.

Diamond, J. (1999). *Guns, germs, and steel: The fates of human societies.* New York: W.W. Norton & Company.

Diamond, M., & Sigmundson, H. K. (1997). Sex reassignment at birth: A long term review and clinical implications. *Archives of Pediatrics and Adolescent Medicine, 151,* 298–304.

DiMaggio, P. (1982). Cultural capital and school success: The impact of status culture participation on the grades of U.S. high school students. *American Sociological Review, 47,* 189–201.

Dobash, R. E., & Dobash, R. (1978). Wives: The "appropriate" victims of marital violence. *Victimology: An International Journal, 2*(3–), 426–442.

Dobash, R. P., Dobash, R. E., Wilson, M., & Daly, M. (1992). The myth of sexual symmetry in marital violence. *Social Problems, 39*(1), 71–91.

Dobb, A. (1997). The new role of parliament in Canadian sentencing. *Federal Sentencing Reporter, 9,* 239–244.

Dooley, P. A. (1984). Class management during teaching practice. In E. C. Wragg (Ed.), *Classroom teaching skills* (pp. 21–46). London, UK: Croom Helm.

Durkheim, E. (1951) [1938]. *Suicide: A study in sociology.* Glencoe, IL: Free Press.

Durkheim, E. (1964) [1933]. *The division of labour in society.* London, UK: The Free Press.

Durkheim, E. (1982). *Rules of sociological methods.* New York: Free Press.

Eagly, A. H., & Steffen, V.J. (1986). Gender and aggressive behavior: A meta-analytic review of the social psychological literature. *Psychological Bulletin, 100,* 309–330.

Eichler, M. (1985). And the work never ends: Feminist contributions. *Canadian Review of Sociology, 22*(5), 619–644.

England, D. E., Descartes, L., & Collier-Meek, M.A. (2011). Gender role portrayal and Disney princesses. *Sex Roles, 64,* 555–567.

Engles, F. (1972). *The origin of the family, private property and the state.* New York: International Publishers.

Entman, R. M. (1991). Framing U.S. coverage of international news: Contrasts in narratives of the KAL and Iran air incidents. *Journal of Communication, 41*(4), 6–27.

Erickson, B. H. (1991). What is good taste good for? *Canadian Review of Sociology and Anthropology, 28*(2), 255–278.

Erikson, R., & Goldthrope, J.H. (1992). *The constant flux: A study of class mobility in industrial societies.* Oxford, UK: Clarendon Press.

Estes, S. B., Noonan, M. C., & Maume, D. J. (2007). Is work family policy use related to the gendered division of housework? *Journal of Family and Economic Issues, 28*(4), 527–545.

Farnworth, M., Thornberry, T., Krohn, M., &. Lizotte, A. (1994). Measurement in the study of class and delinquency: Integrating theory and research. *Journal of Research in Crime and Delinquency, 31,* 32–61.

Feirstein, B. (1982). Real men don't eat quiche. In J. E. Faulkner, *Sociology through humor* (pp. 47–50). New York: West Publishing Company.

Feng, J., Spence, I., & Pratt, J. (2007). Playing an action video game reduces gender differences in the brain. *Current Directions in Psychological Science, 19,* 280–283.

Fennema, E., Peterson, P. L., Carpenter, T. P., & Lubinski, C. A. (1990). Teachers' attribution and beliefs about girls, boys, and mathematics. *Educational Studies in Mathematics, 21*, 55–69.

Ferraro, G. L. (1972) [1911]. *Criminal man.* Montclair, NJ: Patterson Smith.

Firestone, S. (1970). *The dialectic of sex.* New York: William Morrow and Company.

Fox, B. (1990). Comment on "authority and incredulity." *Canadian Journal of Sociology, 15*(3), 336–340.

Freud, S. (1964). *New introductory lectures on psychoanalysis* (J. Strachey, Trans. & Ed.). London, UK: Penguin Books.

Frideres, J. S. (1988). *Native peoples in Canada: Contemporary conflicts.* Scarborough, ON: Prentice-Hall Canada Inc.

Frideres, J. S. (1996). Racism and health: The case of native people. In S. Bolaria & D. Dickinson (Eds.), *Health, illness, and health care in Canada* (pp. 202–220). Toronto: Harcourt Brace.

Friedan, B. (1963). *The feminine mystique.* New York: Dell Publishing.

Furnham, A., & Thomas, P. (1984). Pocket money: A study of economic education. *Journal of Social Psychology, 2*, 205–212.

Furth, H.G. (1980). *The world of grown-ups: Children's conception of society.* New York: Elsevier.

Giddens, A. (1971). *Capitalism and modern social theory: An analysis of the writings of Marx, Durkheim and Max Weber.* Cambridge: Cambridge University Press.

Giddens, A. (1987). *Sociology: A brief but critical introduction.* San Diego: Harcourt Brace Jovanovich.

Goffman, E. (1963). *Stigma: Notes on the management of spoiled identity.* Englewood Cliffs, NJ: Prentice-Hall.

Goring, C. (1919). *The English convict* (rev ed.). London, UK: His Majesty's Stationary Office.

Gottfredson, M. R., & Hirschi, T. (1990). *A general theory of crime.* Stanford, CA: Stanford University Press.

Grabb, E. (1990). *Theories of social inequality: Classical and contemporary perspectives.* Toronto: Holt, Rinehart, and Winston of Canada.

Grabb, E., & Curtis, J. (2005). *Regions apart: The four societies of Canada and the United States.* Don Mills, ON: Oxford University Press.

Grasmick, H. G., Tittle, C. R., Bursik, R. J., Jr., & Arneklev, B. (1993). Testing the core empirical implications of Gottfredson and Hirsch's general theory of crime. *Journal of Research in Crime and Delinquency, 30*(1), 5–29.

Greaves, L. (1996). *Smoke screen: Women's smoking and social control.* Halifax: Fernwood Publishing.

Greenberg, D. (1985). Age, crime, and social explanation. *American Journal of Sociology, 91*(1), 1–21.

Griffin, T., & Wooldridge, J. (2006). Sex based disparities in felony dispositions before versus after sentencing reform in Ohio. *Criminology, 44*, 893–923.

Guimond, S., Palmer, D., & Begin, G. (1989). Education, academic program and intergroup attitudes. *Canadian Review of Sociology and Anthropology, 26*(2), 193–216.

Gunderson, E. A., Ramirez, G., Levine, S. C., & Bellock, S. L. (2012). The role of parents and teachers in the development of gender-related math attitudes. *Sex Roles, 66*, 153–166.

Hackett, R. (1991). *News and dissent: The press and the politics of peace in Canada.* Norwood, NJ: Ablex.

Hagan, J. (1977). *The disreputable pleasure: Crime and deviance in Canada.* Toronto: McGraw-Hill Ryerson.

Hagan, J. (1984). *Disreputable pleasures.* Toronto: McGraw-Hill Ryerson.

Hagan, J. (1994). *Crime and disrepute.* Thousand Oaks, CA: Pine Forge Press.

Hagan, J., Simpson, J., & Gillis, R. (1987). Class in the household: A power-control theory of gender and delinquency. *American Journal of Sociology, 92*(4), 788–816.

Harlow, H. (1971). *Learning to love.* New York: Ballantine.

Harlow, H., & Harlow, M. (1962). Social deprivation in monkeys. *Scientific American, 207*(5), 136–146.

Harpster, P., & Monk-Turner, E. (1998). Why men do housework: A test of gender production and relative resources model. *Sociological Focus, 6*(3), 366–394.

Harris, M. (1977, November 13). Why men dominate women. *The New York Times Magazine.*

Hart, B., & Risley, T. (1995). *Meaningful differences in everyday experience of young children.* Baltimore, MD: Paul Brookes Publishing Company.

Hartmann, H. (1980). The historical roots of occupational segregation: Capitalism, patriarchy, and job segregation by sex. *Signs, 1,* 137–169.

Hartmann, H. (1981). Summary and response: Continuing the discussion. In L. Sargent (Ed.), *Women and revolution* (pp. 363–373). Boston: South End Press.

Henry, F., & Ginzberg, E. (1985). *Who gets the work? A test of racial discrimination in employment.* Toronto: The Urban Alliance on Race Relations and the Social Planning Council of Metropolitan Toronto.

Henry, F., Tator, C., Mattis, W., & Rees, T. (2000). *The colour of Democracy: Racism in Canadian Society* (2nd ed). Toronto: Harcourt Brace.

Herrnstein, R. J. (1990). Still an American dilemma. *The Public Interest, 98,* 3–17.

Hiderbrandt Karraker, K., Vogel, D. A., & Lake, M. A. (1995). Parents' gender-stereotyped perceptions of newborns: The Eye of beholder revisited. *Sex Roles, 33,* 687–701.

Hiller, H. (1991). *Canadian society: A macro analysis.* Scarborough, ON: Prentice-Hall Canada Inc.

Hird, M. J. (2000). Gender's nature: Intersexuality, transsexuality and the "sex/Gender." *Feminist Theory, 1*(3), 347–64.

Hirschi, T. (1969). *Causes of delinquency.* Berkeley: University of California Press.

Hirschi, T., & Gottfredson, M. (1983). Age and the explanation of crime. *American Journal of Sociology, 89,* 552–584.

Hochschild, A. (1989). *The second shift: Working parents and the revolution at home.* New York: Viking.

Hooks, b. (1984). *Feminist theory: From margin to center.* Boston: South End Press.

Jahoda, G. (1979). The construction of economic reality by some Glaswegian children. *European Journal of Social Psychology, 9,* 115–127.

Jahoda, G. (1983). European "lag" in the development of an economic concept: A study in Zimbabwe. *British Journal of Developmental Psychology, 1,* 113–120.

Jencks, C., & Phillips, M. (1998). *The black-white test score gap.* Washington: Brookings Institution Press.

Kamo, Y. (1988). Determinants of household division of labour: Resources, power and ideology. *Journal of Family Issues, 9*(2), 177–201.

Keane, C., Maxim, P., & Teevan, J. J. (1993). Drinking and driving, self-control, and gender: Testing a general theory of crime. *Journal of Research in Crime and Delinquency, 30*(1), 30–46.

Kimura, D. (2002, May 13). Sex differences in the brain. *Scientific American.*

Kirk, R., Drake, W., & Drake, S. (1980). Social structure and criminalization: An empirical examination of the conflict perspective. *The Sociological Quarterly, 21*(4), 563–575.

Kiuru, N., Burk, W., Laursen, B., Salmela-Aro, K., & Nurmi, J. (2010). Pressure to drink but not to smoke: Disentangling selection and socialization in adolescent peer networks and peer groups. *Journal of Adolescence, 33*, 801–812.

Kohlberg, L., & Gilligan, C. (1971). The adolescence as philosopher: The discovery of self in post conventional world. *Daedalus, 100,* 1051–1086.

Lacan J. (1968). *The language of the self.* New York: Delta Books.

Li, P. (2000). Earning disparities between immigrants and native-born Canadians. *Canadian Review of Sociology and Anthropology, 37*(3), 289–312.

Lian, J.Z., & Matthews, D.R. (1998). Does the vertical mosaic still exist? Ethnicity and income in Canada, 1991. *Canadian Review of Sociology and Anthropology, 35*(4), 461–482.

Lipset, S. M. (1963). The value patterns of democracy: A case study in comparative analysis. *American Sociological Review, 28*(4), 515–31.

Lipset, S. M. (1965). Revolution and counter-revolution: The United States and Canada. In T. R. Ford (Ed.), *The revolutionary theme in contemporary America* (pp. 21–64). Leamington, KY: University of Kentucky Press.

Lipset, S. M. (1986). Historical traditions and national characteristics: A comparative analysis of Canada and the United States. *Canadian Journal of Sociology, 11,* 113–55.

Lipset, S. M. (1990). *Continental divide.* New York: Routledge.

Lipset, S. M. (2001). Defining moments and recurring myths: A reply. *Canadian Review of Sociology and Anthropology, 38,* 97–100.

Lombroso, C. (1918) [1899]. *Crime: Its causes and remedies* (rev ed.). Boston: Little, Brown.

Maccoby, E. E., & Jacklin, C. N. (1974). *The psychology of sex differences.* Stanford, CA: Stanford University Press.

Mager, J., & Helgeson, G. (2011). Fifty years of advertising images: Some changing perspectives along with enduring consistencies. *Sex Roles: A Journal of Research, 64,* 238–252.

Marcuse, H. (1961). *Eros and civilization.* Boston: Beacon.

Marx, K. (1976). *The German ideology.* Moscow: Progress Publishers, Moscow.

Marx, K., & Engels, F. (1977). Manifesto of the communist party. In D. McLellan (Ed.), *Karl Marx: Selected writings.* London, UK: Oxford University Press.

Matza, D. (1964). *Delinquency and drift.* New York: Wiley.

McGloin S. (2008). The trustworthiness of case study methodology. *Nurse Researcher, 16*(1), 45–55.

McGue, M., & Buchard, T., Jr. (1998). Genetic and environmental influences on human behavioral differences. *Annual Review of Neurosciences, 21,* 1–24.

Mead, G. H. (1962) [1934]. *Mind, self and society: From the standpoint of a social behaviorist* (C. W. Morris, Ed.). Chicago: University of Chicago.

Merton, R. K. (1938). Social structure and anomie. *American Sociological Review. 3*(5), 681.

Merton, R.K. (1949). Discrimination and the American creed. In R.H. MacIvor (ed.) *Discrimination and National Welfare.* New York: Harper and Row.

Merton, R. K. (1967). *On theoretical sociology.* New York: Free Press.

Millard, G., Riegel, S., & Wright, J. (2002). Here's where we get Canadian: English-Canadian nationalism and popular culture. *American Review of Canadian Studies, 32*(1),

Mills, C. W. (1974). *The sociological imagination.* New York: Oxford University Press.

Mitchell, J. (1971). *Women estate.* Harmondsworth, UK: Penguin Books.

Mitchell, J. (1974). *Psychoanalysis and feminism.* New York: Pantheon Books.

Money, J., & Ehrhardt, A. A. (1972). *Men and women, boys and girls: The differentiation of dimorphism of gender identity from conception to maturity.* Baltimore: John Hopkins University Press.

Muuss, R. E. (1996). *Theories of adolescence* (6th ed.). New York: McGraw-Hill.

Nagler, M. R. (1975). *Natives without a home.* Don Mills, ON: Longman.

Nakhaie, M. R. (1993). Knowledge of profit and interest among children in Canada. *Journal of Economic Psychology, 14,* 147–160.

Nakhaie, M. R. (1995). Housework in Canada: The national picture. *Journal of Comparative Family Studies, 26*(3), 409–426.

Nakhaie, M. R. (1996). The reproduction of class relations by gender in Canada. *Canadian Journal of Sociology, 21*(4), 523–558.

Nakhaie, M. R. (1997). Vertical mosaic among the elites: The new imagery revisited. *Canadian Review of Sociology and Anthropology, 1*(34), 1–24;

Nakhaie, M. R. (1998). Asymmetry and symmetry of conjugal violence. *Journal of Comparative Family Studies, 29*(3), 549–567.

Nakhaie, M. R. (2000). Social origins and educational attainment in Canada, 1985–1994. *Review of Radical Political Economics, 32*(4), 577–609.

Nakhaie, M. R. (2002). Class, breadwinner ideology, and housework among Canadian husbands. *Review of Radical Political Economics, 34,* 137–157.

Nakhaie, M. R. (2004). Who controls Canadian universities? Ethnoracial origins of Canadian university administrators and faculty's perception of mistreatment. *Canadian Ethnic Studies, 36,* 92–110.

Nakhaie, M. R. (2006). A comparison of the earnings of the Canadian native-born and immigrants, 2001. *Canadian Ethnic Studies, 38*(2), 19–47.

Nakhaie, M. R. (2009). Professors, ideology and housework. *Journal of Family and Economic Issues, 30,* 399–411.

Nakhaie, M. R., & Pike, R. (1995). Victim, offender and bystander: Crime in the sky? *Canadian Journal of Sociology, 20*(3), 309–331.

Nakhaie, M. R., & Arnold, R. (1996). Class position, class ideology and class voting: Mobilization of support for the New Democratic Party. *Canadian Review of Sociology and Anthropology, 33*(2), 181–212.

Nakhaie, M. R., & Curtis, J. (1998). Effects of class positions of parents on educational attainment of daughters and sons. *Canadian Review of Sociology, 35*(4), 483–515.

Nakhaie, M. R., Silverman, R., & LaGrange, T. (2000). Self-control and social control: An examination of gender, ethnicity, class and delinquency. *Canadian Journal of Sociology, 25*(1), 35–59.

Neapolitan, J. (1998). Cross-national variation in homicides: Is race a factor? *Criminology, 36,* 139–155.

Ng, S. H. (1983). Children's ideas about the bank and shop profit: Developmental stages and the influence of cognitive contrasts and conflict. *Journal of Economic Psychology, 4,* 209–221.

Ng, S. H. (1985). Children's idea about the bank: A New Zealand replication. *European Journal of Social Psychology, 15,* 121–123.

Ogmundson, R., & McLaughlin, J. (1992). Trends in the ethnic origins of Canadian elites: The decline of the BRITS? *Canadian Review of Sociology and Anthropology, 29*(2), 227–242.

Oreopoulos, P. (2009). Why do skilled immigrants struggle in the labor market? A field experiment with six thousand résumés. *Metropolis BC Working Paper No. 2009-3.*

Oreopoulos, P., & Dechief, D. (2011). Why do some employers prefer to interview Matthew, but not Samir? New evidence from Toronto, Montreal, and Vancouver. *Metropolis BC Working Paper No. 2011-13.*

Parker, R. N. 1989. Poverty, subculture of violence, and type of homicide. *Social Forces, 67,* 983–1007.

Parr, J. (1990). *The Gender of breadwinners.* Toronto: University of Toronto Press.

Pasterski, V. L., Geffner, M. E., Brain, C., Hindmarsh, P., Brook, C., & Hines, M. (2005). Parental hormones and postnatal socialization by parents as determinants of male-typical toy play in girls with congenial adrenal hyperplasia. *Child Development, 76,* 264–278.

Pavlov, I. P. (1927). *Conditioned reflexes* (G. V. Anrep, Trans.). London, UK: Oxford University Press.

Pearce, F. (1976). *Crimes of the powerful.* London, UK: Pluto Press.

Piaget, J. (1962). Three lectures. *Bulletin of the Menninger Clinic, 26,* 120–145.

Plomin, R., Foch, T., & Rowe, D. (1981). Bobo clown aggression in childhood: Environment, not genes. *Journal of Research in Personality, 15,* 331–342.

Plomin, R., Nitz, K., & Rowe, D. (1990). Behavioral genetics and aggressive behavior in childhood. In M. Lewis and S. M. Miller (Eds.), *Handbook of developmental psychopathology.* New York: Plenum.

Pollack, F. (1976). Empirical research into public opinion. In P. Connerton (Ed.), *Critical sociology* (pp. 225–236). New York: Penguin Books.

Porter, J. (1965). *The vertical mosaic: An analysis of social class and power in Canada.* Toronto: University of Toronto Press.

Posavac, H., Posavac, S., & Posavac, E (1998). Exposure to media images of female attractiveness and concern with body weight among young women. *Sex Roles, 38*(314), 187–201.

Potvin, M. (2000). Some racist slips about Quebec in English Canada between 1995 and 1998. *Canadian Ethnic Studies, 32,* 1–26.

Quinney, R. (1977). *Class, state, and crime: On the theory and practice of criminal justice.* New York: D. McKay Co.

Rachlin, A. (1988). *News as hegemonic ideology.* New York: Praeger.

Ransby, B. (1992). Columbus and the making of the historical myth. *Race & Class, 33,* 79–86.

Red Deer College. (2012). What can I do with a bachelor of arts degree in sociology? Retrieved from http://www.rdc.ab.ca/current_students/campus_services/counselling_career_learning_centre/Documents/BA-Sociology%20Updated%20August%202012.pdf

Richer, S. (1982). Equality to benefit from schooling: The issue of educational opportunity. In D. Forcese & S. Richer (Eds.), *Social issues: Sociological views of Canada* (pp. 336–374). Scarborough, ON: Prentice-Hall Canada Inc.

Ritzer, G. (1992). *Contemporary sociological theory.* New York: McGraw-Hill.

Ritzer, G. (1996). *Sociological theories.* New York: McGraw-Hill.

Roberts, J., & Dobb, A. (1997). Race, ethnicity and criminal justice in Canada. In M. Tonry (Ed.), *Ethnicity, crime and immigration: Comparative and cross-national perspectives.* Chicago: University of Chicago Press.

Robinson, R. V. (1984). Reproducing class relations in industrial capitalism. *American Sociological Review, 49,* 182–196.

Robinson, R. V., & Garnier, M. A. (1985). Class reproduction among men and women in France: Reproduction theory on its own home ground. *American Journal of Sociology, 91*(2), 250–280.

Roland-Levy, C. (1990). Economic socialization: Basis for international comparison. *Journal of Economic Psychology, 11,* 469–482.

Ross, J., Roeltgen, D., & Zin, A. (2006). Cognition and the sex chromosomes: Studies in Turner Syndrome. *Hormone Research, 65,* 47–56.

Rowbotham, S. (1973). *Women's consciousness, man's world.* Baltimore: Penguin Books.

Rowe, A., & Tittle, C. (1977). Life cycle changes and criminal propensity. *Sociological Quarterly, 18,* 223–236.

Rowe, D. C. (1986). Genetic and environmental components of antisocial behavior: A study of 265 twin pairs. *Criminology, 24*(3), 513–532.

Rowe, D. C., &. Osgood, D. W. (1984). Heredity and sociological theories of delinquency: A reconsideration. *American Sociological Review. 49,* 526–540.

Rubin, G. (1975). The traffic in women: Notes on the "Political economy of sex." In R. Reiter (Ed.), *Toward an anthropology of women.* New York: Monthly Review Press.

Rubin, J. Z., Provenzano, F. J., & Luria, Z. (1974). The Eye of beholder: Parents' views on sex of newborns. *American Journal of Orthopsychiatry, 44,* 512–519.

Rushton, J. (1995). Race and crime: International data for 1989-90. *Psychological Reports, 76,* 307–312.

Sampson, R., & Laub, J. (1993). *Crime in making: Pathways and turning points through life.* Cambridge: Harvard University Press.

Schwendinger, J., & Schwendinger, H. (1983). *Rape and inequality.* Beverly Hills, CA: Sage.

Scully, D., & Marolla, J. (1985). Riding the bull at Gilley's: Convicted rapists describe the rewards of rape. *Social Problems, 32*(3), 251–263.

Sheldon, W. H. (1949). *Varieties of delinquent youth.* New York: Harper & Row.

Sherif, M. (1936). *The psychology of social norms.* New York: Harper.

Sherif, M. (1937). The psychology of slogans. *Journal of Abnormal and Social Psychology, 32,* 450–461.

Skinner, B. F. (1953). *Science and human behavior.* New York: Macmillan.

Smart, C. (1976). *Women, crime and criminology: A feminist critique.* London, UK: Routledge and Kegan Paul.

Smiler, A. P. (2011). Sexual strategies theory: Built for the short term or the long term. *Sex Roles, 64,* 603–612.

Stasiulis, D. (1999). Feminist: Intersectional theorizing. In P. S. Li (Ed.), *Race and ethnic relations in Canada* (pp. 347–398). Don Mills, ON: Oxford University Press.

Statistics Canada. (1986). *General social survey.* Public use microdata files.

Statistics Canada. (1995). *General social survey.* Public use microdata files.

Statistics Canada. (1998). *General social survey.* Public use microdata files.

Statistics Canada. (2001, December 18). Catalogue no. 85-002-XIE Vol. 21 no. 11. *The Daily.* Retrieved from http://www.statcan.gc.ca/daily-quotidien/011218/dq011218b-eng.htm.

Statistics Canada. (1971). *1971 Census.* Public use microdata files.

Statistics Canada. (1981). 1981 *Census.* Public use microdata files.

Statistics Canada. (1986). 1986 *Census.* Public use microdata files.

Statistics Canada. (1991). 1991 *Census.* Public use microdata files.

Statistics Canada. (2001). *2001 Census.* Public use microdata files.

Statistics Canada. (2006). *2006 Census.* Public use microdata files.

Statistics Canada. (2002). Table 358-0002: Household Internet use survey, household internet use by location of use, annual (percentage of households. CANSIM (database).

Statistics Canada. (2006). Tables 4 and 5: The evolution of wealth inequality in Canada, 1984–1999, No. 11F009 and No. 187.

Statistics Canada. (2008). Canadian Centre for Justice Statistics. Data Liberation Initiative, 2008. Retrieved from http://equinox2.uwo.ca/dbtw-wpd/exec/dbtwpub.dll?TN=Equinox&RF=User DisplayCrepuqEN&AC=QBE_QUERY&QF0=Uniqueid&QB0=and&QI0=IVT-CCJS2008

Statistics Canada. (2011). Table 202-0102: Average female and male earnings, and female-to-male earnings ratio, by work activity. CANSIM (database).

Steffensmeier, D., & Demuth, S. (2006). Does gender modify the effect of race-ethnicity on criminal sanctioning? Sentence for male and female white, black and Hispanic defendants, *Journal of Quantitative Criminology, 22*, 241–261.

Straus, M. A. (1979). Measuring intrafamily conflict and violence: The conflict tactics (CT) scales. *Journal of Marriage and Family, 41*, 75–86.

Straus, M. A., & Gelles, R. J. (1990). *Physical violence in American families: Risk factors and adaptations to violence in 8,145 families.* New Brunswick, NJ: Transaction.

Sutherland, E. (1947). *Principles of criminology.* Washington: Lippincott.

Sykes, G. M., & Matza, D. (1957). Techniques of neutralization: A theory of delinquency, *American Sociological Review, 22,* 664–670.

Taylor, I., Walton, P., & Young, J. (1973). *The new criminology.* London, UK: Routledge and Kegan Paul.

Taylor, I., Walton, P., & Young, J. (1975). *Critical criminology.* London, UK: Routledge and Kegan Paul.

Tellegen, A., Alterman, A., & Edwards, K. (1988). Personality similarity in twins reared apart and together. *Journal of Personality and Social Psychology, 54*(6), 1031–1039.

Thompson, L. (1991). Family work: Women's sense of fairness. *Journal of Family Issues, 12,* 181–196.

Thompson, T. L., & Zerbinos, E. (1995). Gender roles in animated cartoons: Has the picture changed in 20 years? *Sex Roles, 32,* 651–673.

Thorndike, E. (1913). *The psychology of learning.* New York: McGraw-Hill.

Tiedemann, J. (2002). Teachers' gender stereotypes as determinants of teachers' perception in elementary school mathematics. *Educational Studies in Mathematics, 50,* 49–62.

Tieger, T. (1980). On the biological basis of sex differences in aggression. *Child Development, 51*(4), 943–963.

Trivers, R. L. (1972). Parental investment and sexual selection. In B. Campbell (Ed.), *Sexual selection and the descent of man* (pp. 136–179). Chicago: Aldine Publishing Company.

Tuckett, A. G. (2005). Applying thematic analysis theory to practice: A researcher's experience. *Contemporary Nurse, 19*(1–2), 75–87.

Turiel, E. (1978). The development of concepts of social structure: Social convention. In J. Glick & K. A. Clarke-Stewart, *The development of social understanding.* New York: Gardner Press.

Turk, A. (1969). *Criminology and legal order.* Chicago: Rand McNally

Tumin, M. (1953). Some principles of stratification: A critical analysis. *American Sociological Review, 18,* 387–393.

Tumin, M. (1953). A rejoinder. *American Sociological Review, 18.*

Turner, J. H, Turner, P. R., Maryanski, A., Allen, K., Colony, P., Powers, C., Fuchs, S., Li, R., & Wagner, D. (1998). *The structure of sociological theory.* New York: Wadsworth Publishing Company.

Udry, J. R. (1988). Biological predisposition and social control in adolescent sexual behavior. *American Sociological Review. 53,* 709–722.

Weiss, L. (1994). Timing is everything. *The Atlantic Monthly Review 273*(1), 32–45.

Weiss, R. (2005, December 17). Scientists find a DNA change that accounts for white skin. *Washington Post.*

Westhues, K. (1982). *First sociology.* Toronto: McGraw-Hill Ryerson.

White, R., & Haines, F. (1996). *Crime and criminology: An introduction.* South Melbourne, Australia: Oxford University Press.

Whyte, W. F. (1943). *Street corner society.* Chicago: The University of Chicago Press.

Wister, A., & Avison, W. (1982). "Friendly persuasion": A social network analysis of sex differences in marijuana use. *The International Journal of the Addiction, 17*(3), 523–541.

Wollstoncraft, M. (1971). *A vindication of the right of women.* New York: Source Book Press.

World Values Survey. (2009). Official Aggregate v.20090901, 2009. World Values Survey Association: http://www.worldvaluessurvey.org. Aggregate File Producer: ASEP/JDS, Madrid.

Wortley. S. (1999). A northern taboo: Research on race, crime, and criminal justice in Canada. *Canadian Journal of Criminology, 41*(2), 261–274.

Wortley, S. (2002, November 25). Profiling one source of alienation: Both sides of debate get support in recent survey. *Toronto Star.*

Wortley, S., & Tanner, J. (2003). Data, denials and confusion: The racial profiling debate in Toronto. *Canadian Journal of Criminology and Criminal Justice, 45,* 367–389.

Wright, E. O. (1985). *Classes.* London, UK: New Left Books.

Zeitlin, I. M. (2001). *Ideology and the development of sociological theory* (7th ed.). Scarborough, ON: Prentice-Hall Canada Inc.

Zimring, F. (1981). Kids, groups and crime: Some implications of a well-known secret. *Journal of Criminal Law and Criminology, 72,* 867–885.

CREDITS

Chapter 4

Pages 76–85

Item Description: Sociological Example: Three Views of the Downing of Flight 655

Source: Based on M. Reza Nakhaie and Robert Pike. (1995). "Victim, offender and bystander: Crime in the sky?" *Canadian Journal of Sociology,* 20(3), 309–331. [Original article is abbreviated.]

Page 81

Item Description: Table 4.1.1 Value Identification of Downing Flight 655

Source: M. Reza Nakhaie and Robert Pike. (1995). "Victim, offender and bystander: Crime in the sky?" *Canadian Journal of Sociology,* 20(3), 309–331.

Page 82

Item Description: Table 4.1.2 Neutralization of Downing Flight 655

Source: M. Reza Nakhaie and Robert Pike. (1995). "Victim, offender and bystander: Crime in the sky?" *Canadian Journal of Sociology,* 20(3), 309–331.

Page 82

Item Description: Table 4.1.3 Criminalization of Downing Flight 655

Source: M. Reza Nakhaie and Robert Pike. (1995). "Victim, offender and bystander: Crime in the sky?" *Canadian Journal of Sociology,* 20(3), 309–331.

Chapter 5

Pages 112–119

Item Description: Sociological Example: Cognitive Maturity of Children's Economic Knowledge

Source: Reprinted from the *Journal of Economic Psychology,* 14, M. Reza Nakhaie, "Knowledge of profit and interest among children in Canada," 147–160 (1993), with permission from Elsevier. [Original article is abbreviated.]

Page 116

Item Description: Table 5.1.1 Children's Understanding of Profit and Interest

Source: Reprinted from the *Journal of Economic Psychology,* 14, M. Reza Nakhaie, "Knowledge of profit and interest among children in Canada," 147–160 (1993), with permission from Elsevier.

Chapter 6

Pages 148–155

Item Description: Sociological Example: Role of Self and Social Control for Crime

Source: Based on M. Reza Nakhaie, Robert A. Silverman, and Teresa C. LaGrange. (2000). "Self-control and social-control: An examination of gender, ethnicity, class and delinquency." *Canadian Journal of Sociology,* 25(1): 35–59. [Original article is abbreviated.]

Page 152

Item Description: Table 6.1.1 Means for Self and Social Control and Delinquency Measures by Predictors

Source: M. Reza Nakhaie, Robert A. Silverman, and Teresa C. LaGrange. (2000). "Self-control and social-control: An examination of gender, ethnicity, class and delinquency." *Canadian Journal of Sociology,* 25(1): 35–59.

Chapter 7

Pages 176–183

Item Description: Sociological Example: Housework Contribution of Professors

Source: With kind permission from Springer Science+Business Media: *Journal of Family and Economic Issues,* "Professors, ideology and housework," 30, 2009, 399–411, M. Reza Nakhaie. [Original article is abbreviated.]

Page 181

Item Description: Figure 7.1.1 Canadian University Professor's Average Share of Housework by Predictors

Source: With kind permission from Springer Science+Business Media: *Journal of Family and Economic Issues,* "Professors, ideology and housework," 30, 2009, 399–411, M. Reza Nakhaie.

Chapter 8

Pages 202–212

Item Description: Sociological Example: Class Background and Educational Attainment

Source: Based on M. Reza Nakhaie and James Curtis. (1998). "Effects of class positions of parents on educational attainment of daughters and sons." *The Canadian Review of Sociology and Anthropology,* 35(4), 483–515; and M. Reza Nakhaie. (2000). "Social origins and educational attainment in Canada, 1985–1994." *Review of Radical Political Economics,* 32(4), 577–609. [Original article is abbreviated.]

Chapter 9

Pages 236-243

Item Description: Sociological Example: Race and Ethnic Inequality

Source: Based on M. Reza Nakhaie. (2006). "A Comparison of the earnings of the Canadian native-born and immigrants." *Canadian Ethnic Studies,* 38(2), 19–46; and M. Reza Nakhaie. (1997). "Vertical mosaic among the elites: The new imagery revisited." *Canadian Review of Sociology and Anthropology*, 1(34), 1–24; and M. Reza Nakhaie. (2004). "Who controls Canadian universities? Ethnoracial origins of Canadian university administrators and faculty's perception of mistreatment." *Canadian Ethnic Studies,* 36, 92–110. [Original article is abbreviated.]

Page 240

Item Description: Table 9.1.1 Index of British Elite Representation

Source: M. Reza Nakhaie. (1997). "Vertical mosaic among the elites: The new imagery revisited." *Canadian Review of Sociology and Anthropology,* 1(34), 1–24.

Page 241

Item Description: Table 9.1.2 Educational, Occupational, and Income Attainment of Ethno-racial Groups, Full-time, Ages 25–65, 2001

Source: Statistics Canada, (2001). *2001 Census.* Public use microdata files.